Reclaiming Universit
a Runaway World

SRHE and Open University Press Imprint
General Editor: Heather Eggins

Current titles include:

Catherine Bargh et al.: *University Leadership*
Ronald Barnett: *Beyond all Reason*
Ronald Barnett: *The Limits of Competence*
Ronald Barnett: *Higher Education*
Ronald Barnett: *Realizing the University in an Age of Supercomplexity*
Tony Becher and Paul R. Trowler: *Academic Tribes and Territories (2nd edn)*
Neville Bennett et al.: *Skills Development in Higher Education and Employment*
John Biggs: *Teaching for Quality Learning at University (2nd edn)*
Richard Blackwell and Paul Blackmore (eds): *Towards Strategic Staff Development in Higher Education*
David Boud et al. (eds): *Using Experience for Learning*
David Boud and Nicky Solomon (eds): *Work-based Learning*
Tom Bourner et al. (eds): *New Directions in Professional Higher Education*
John Brennan et al. (eds): *What Kind of University?*
Anne Brockbank and Ian McGill: *Facilitating Reflective Learning in Higher Education*
Stephen D. Brookfield and Stephen Preskill: *Discussion as a Way of Teaching*
Ann Brooks and Alison Mackinnon (eds): *Gender and the Restructured University*
Sally Brown and Angela Glasner (eds): *Assessment Matters in Higher Education*
James Cornford and Neil Pollock: *Putting the University Online*
John Cowan: *On Becoming an Innovative University Teacher*
Sarah Delamont, Paul Atkinson and Odette Parry: *Supervising the Doctorate*
Sarah Delamont and Paul Atkinson: *Successful Research Careers*
Gerard Delanty: *Challenging Knowledge*
Chris Duke: *Managing the Learning University*
Heather Eggins (ed.): *Globalization and Reform in Higher Education*
Heather Eggins and Ranald Macdonald (eds): *The Scholarship of Academic Development*
Gillian Evans: *Academics and the Real World*
Andrew Hannan and Harold Silver: *Innovating in Higher Education*
Lee Harvey and Associates: *The Student Satisfaction Manual*
David Istance, Hans Schuetze and Tom Schuller (eds): *International Perspectives on Lifelong Learning*
Norman Jackson and Helen Lund (eds): *Benchmarking for Higher Education*
Merle Jacob and Tomas Hellström (eds): *The Future of Knowledge Production in the Academy*
Peter Knight: *Being a Teacher in Higher Education*
Peter Knight and Paul Trowler: *Departmental Leadership in Higher Education*
Peter Knight and Mantz Yorke: *Assessment, Learning and Employability*
Mary Lea and Barry Stierer (eds): *Student Writing in Higher Education*
Ian McNay (ed.): *Higher Education and its Communities*
Elaine Martin: *Changing Academic Work*
Louise Morley: *Quality and Power in Higher Education*
Moira Peelo and Terry Wareham (eds): *Failing Students in Higher Education*
Craig Prichard: *Making Managers in Universities and Colleges*
Michael Prosser and Keith Trigwell: *Understanding Learning and Teaching*
John Richardson: *Researching Student Learning*
Stephen Rowland: *The Enquiring University Teacher*
Maggi Savin-Baden: *Problem-based Learning in Higher Education*
Maggi Savin-Baden: *Facilitating Problem-based Learning*
Peter Scott (ed.): *The Globalization of Higher Education*
Peter Scott: *The Meanings of Mass Higher Education*
Michael L. Shattock: *Managing Successful Universities*
Maria Slowey and David Watson: *Higher Education and the Lifecourse*
Anthony Smith and Frank Webster (eds): *The Postmodern University?*
Colin Symes and John McIntyre (eds): *Working Knowledge*
Peter G. Taylor: *Making Sense of Academic Life*
Richard Taylor, Jean Barr and Tom Steele: *For a Radical Higher Education*
Malcolm Tight: *Researching Higher Education*
Penny Tinkler and Carolyn Jackson: *The Doctoral Examination Process*
Susan Toohey: *Designing Courses for Higher Education*
Paul R. Trowler (ed.): *Higher Education Policy and Institutional Change*
Melanie Walker (ed.): *Reconstructing Professionalism in University Teaching*
David Warner and David Palfreyman (eds): *Higher Education Management of UK Higher Education*
Gareth Williams (ed.): *The Enterprising University*
Diana Woodward and Karen Ross: *Managing Equal Opportunities in Higher Education*

Reclaiming Universities from a Runaway World

Edited by Melanie Walker and Jon Nixon

The Society for Research into Higher Education
& Open University Press

Open University Press
McGraw-Hill Education
McGraw-Hill House
Shoppenhangers Road
Maidenhead
Berkshire
England
SL6 2QL

email: enquiries@openup.co.uk
world wide web: www.openup.co.uk

and Two Penn Plaza, New York, NY 10121-2289, USA

First published 2004

Copyright © Melanie Walker and Jon Nixon

All rights reserved. Except for the quotation of short passages for the purposes of criticism and review, no part of this publication may be reproduced, stored in a retrieval system, or transmitted, in any for, or by any means, electronic, mechanical, photocopying, recording or otherwise, without the prior permission of the publisher or a licence from the Copyright Licensing Agency Limited. Details of such licences (for reprographic reproduction) may be obtained from the Copyright Licensing Agency Ltd of 90 Tottenham Court Road, London, W1T 4LP.

A catalogue record of this book is available from the British Library

ISBN 0335212913 (pb)   0335213871 (hb)

Library of Congress Cataloging-in-Publication Data
CIP data applied for

Typeset by YHT Ltd
Printed in the UK by Bell & Bain Ltd., Glasgow

Contents

Notes on Contributors   vii

Preface   x

Introduction   1
Melanie Walker and Jon Nixon

Part 1: Dark Times   13
1. Managerial Governmentality and the Suppression of Ethics   15
   Lew Zipin and Marie Brennan
2. Reclaiming Academic Research Work from Regulation and Relegation   35
   Lisa Lucas
3. The Neo-Conservative Assault on the Undergraduate Curriculum   51
   Steven Selden
4. Higher Education, Globalization and the Knowledge Economy   67
   Michael Peters

Part 2: Languages of Reconstruction   83
5. Training the Imagination to go Visiting   85
   Jean Barr and Morwenna Griffiths
6. Sitting Uneasily at the Table   100
   Judyth Sachs
7. Learning the Language of Deliberative Democracy   114
   Jon Nixon

Part 3: Pointing to Hope   129
8. Pedagogies of Beginning   131
   Melanie Walker

9 The New Media in an Old Institution: Implementing Change/
   Containing the Potential for Transformation   147
   Rob Walker
10 Under New Management? A Critical History of Managerialism in
   British Universities   160
   Colin Bundy
11 Beyond the Impossibly Good Place: Research and Scholarship   178
   Melanie Walker

Epilogue
Reclaiming Universities from a Runaway World   195
Ronald Barnett

Index   209

Notes on Contributors

Ronald Barnett is Professor of Higher Education at the Institute of Education, University of London, where he was also Dean of Professional Development from 1995–2002. He has written extensively on the theory of higher education and the idea of the university, his many books including the prizewinners, *The Idea of Higher Education* and *The Limits of Competence: Knowledge, Higher Education and Society*. His most recent book is *Beyond All Reason: Living with Ideology in the University* (2003). He is Vice-Chair of the Society for Research into Higher Education.

Jean Barr is Professor of Adult and Continuing Education at the University of Glasgow. She has previously worked at the Universities of Stirling and Warwick. Her research interests include feminist knowledge and praxis and higher education policy. She is the author of *Liberating Knowledge, Research, Feminism and Adult Education* (1999) and a co-author with Richard Taylor and Tom Steele of *For a Radical Higher Education* (2002).

Marie Brennan is Professor of Education and Dean of Education at the University of South Australia. Her research interests include school and public sector reform; policy activism; action research and the use of critical social theory in education.

Colin Bundy trained as an historian, and is best known in this capacity for his *The Rise and Fall of a South African Peasantry*. His academic career saw him teach in the UK, the USA and South Africa. He held executive office at two South African universities before taking up his current post as Director and Principal of SOAS. He is also Deputy Vice-Chancellor of the University of London.

Morwenna Griffiths is Professor of Educational Research at Nottingham Trent University. She is currently working on action research with teachers in Creative Partnerships Nottingham, an Arts Council funded project. Her books include: *Action for Social Justice in Education: Fairly Different* (2003); *Educational Research for Social Justice: Getting Off the Fence* (1998*)*; and *Feminisms and the Self: The Web of Identity* (1995).

Lisa Lucas is a Lecturer in Education in the Graduate School of Education at the University of Bristol. Her main research interests are in the organization, funding and development of higher education in a global context. She is the author of *The Research Game in Academic Life* (forthcoming).

Jon Nixon is Professor of Educational Studies and Head of the School of Education at the University of Sheffield. He previously held Chairs at the University of Stirling and at Canterbury Christ Church University College. He is currently completing a book on 'the moral bases of academic practice'.

Michael Peters is Professor of Education at the University of Glasgow (UK) and the University of Auckland (NZ), and Adjunct Professor of Communication Studies at the Auckland University of Technology. He has research interests in educational theory and policy, and in contemporary philosophy. His recent books include: *Poststructuralism, Marxism and Neoliberalism* (2001); *Wittgenstein: Philosophy, Postmodernism, Pedagogy* (1999) with James Marshall; and *Poststructuralism, Politics and Education* (1996).

Judyth Sachs is Professor in the Faculty of Education, University of Sydney, co-director of the Centre for Practitioner Research, and currently Chair of the Academic Board of the University. She has recently published *The Activist Teaching Profession* and is currently working on a book on women and leadership to be published by State University of New York Press. She is also editor of the journal *CHANGE: Transformations in Education*. Much of her research has an activist intent and is aimed at improving the status of the teaching profession.

Steven Selden is Professor in the Curriculum Theory and Development Programme in the EDPL Department in the College of Education, at the University of Maryland College Park, USA. He received the Education Press Association of America's Distinguished Achievement Award for Excellence in Educational Journalism and has written extensively on the history of the American Eugenics Movement. His book, *Inheriting Shame: The Story of Eugenics and Racism in America* (Teachers College Press, 1999) received the Gustavus Meyer Award for books contributing to anti-racist thought.

Melanie Walker is Reader in the Department of Educational Studies at the University of Sheffield. She was previously Research Professor at the University of the West of England. She is currently working with colleagues in South Africa on a research project on pedagogy, identity and social justice.

Her most recent book is *Reconstructing Professionalism in University Teaching* (2001).

Rob Walker is Professor and Director of CARE (Centre for Applied Research in Education) at the University of East Anglia and also a member of the Centre for Academic and Staff Development. He was previously a Professor of Education at Deakin University in Australia, where he spent 15 years learning to be a distance educator.

Lew Zipin lectures in sociology/policy of education at the University of South Australia. His research interests include critical theories of power in education; issues of policy, governance, work and ethics in schools and higher education; and education for social justice.

Preface

This book has emerged, in the first instance, from conversations between Melanie Walker and Jon Nixon. However, the process of putting the book together involved the chapter authors from an early stage. Once the contract with the SRHE/Open University Press had been agreed, authors circulated an early outline of their proposed chapter. In late March 2003, most of the chapter authors were able to meet for a one-day seminar at the University of Sheffield where we discussed and commented on each others' draft chapters. The idea was that the book should be more than a loose collection, and that the sum of the book should be more than its constituent parts, although we also recognize that with an edited collection readers may well pick and choose from the chapters and not read the book as whole.

We would also like to acknowledge the support for our project from John Skelton, then commissioning editor for higher education at Open University Press. We are grateful for his willingness to take risks with books in higher education (not just our own) and so create a valuable intellectual space in a publishing market increasingly dominated by what will sell large numbers of copies. Certainly without his support our project would in all likelihood not have seen the light of day, or at least not in the form we wanted.

Melanie Walker and Jon Nixon
University of Sheffield
September 2003

Introduction

Melanie Walker and Jon Nixon

> It is because ethical concern is directed to *connected others* that those who reject injury must reject activities, institutions and practices that gratuitously or systematically deceive, thereby destroying or fragmenting trust and social bonds and so indirectly injuring the connections between lives.
>
> (Onora O'Neill 1996: 180, author's emphasis)

Why we wanted to do this book

When we first discussed the idea for this book, our conversation turned on our concerns with the increasingly instrumental direction of higher education, the growing idolatory of market forces, and higher education's seeming dislocation from a contribution to sustaining deliberative democracy in the broader society. While the 'bottom-line' accounting and audit discourse that has taken hold seems most apparent in England, nevertheless there was and is evidence of a similar trajectory in higher education across the world as public institutions are increasingly being asked to do more with less public money (see, for example, Coady 2000 and Giroux 2002). And all this at a time when generous funds for military exploits and war are made available. Moreover, as Blake et al. (1998) argue, the dominant cognitive, performative and economic genres currently work very effectively to drive out or silence other ways of understanding and acting and speaking in society, including the moral or ethical basis of our professionalism.

The philosopher Martha Nussbaum, in her account of liberal higher education, captures the difficulty and the threat to university education when she cites the story of Jacob Marley's ghost in Charles Dickens's *Christmas Carol* as an image of 'bad citizenship' and a 'blunted imagination'. This is how we encounter Marley, the 'good man of business', who appears to Scrooge as a frightening apparition, fettered by heavy chains, bemoaning his fate to wander the earth after death, witnessing the human interaction and care he cannot now share but which he might have shared on earth:

> Again the spectre raised a cry, and shook its chain and wrung its shadowy hands. 'You are fettered', said Scrooge trembling. 'Tell me why'. 'I wear the chain I forged in life', replied the Ghost. 'I made it link by link, and yard by yard; I girded it on of my own free will, and of my own free will I wore it. Is its pattern strange to you? ... I cannot rest, I cannot linger anywhere. My spirit never walked beyond our counting house – mark me!' – in life my spirit never roved beyond the narrow limits of our money-changing hole; and weary journeys lie before me!' ... 'But you were always a good man of business, Jacob,' faltered Scrooge ... 'Business', cried the Ghost, wringing its hands again. 'Mankind was my business. The common welfare was my business; charity, mercy, forbearance, and benevolence were all my business. The dealings of my trade were but a drop in the comprehensive ocean of my business'.
>
> (Dickens 1843; 1988: 20–21)

Nussbaum comments that higher education risks producing all too many individuals – managers, lecturers and students – who are like Marley's ghost. All this sounds worryingly familiar to us working in the UK, where an ethical imperative not amenable to measurement has been eclipsed by accounting, and higher education is increasingly regarded as a private asset rather than a public good. The 'good life' is then seen as the accumulation of material goods, highly individualized notions of what it means to be a 'citizen', and 'democracy' as synonymous with capitalism, consumerism and the unrestrained pursuit of profit.

Furthermore contemporary conditions, current modes of regulation and accountability fabricate new professional subjectivities, requiring us to add certain kinds of value to our professional selves, for example the entrepreneurial subject, and work to erase others, for example the collaborative academic. Nor are we able simply to shrug off the effects of this performativity on academic life. As Ball (2000: 1) explains, 'Performativity is a technology, a culture, a mode of regulation, or a system of "terror" in Lyotard's words, that employs judgements, comparisons and displays as a means of control, attrition and change'. The point is, Ball emphasizes, that performativity does not simply get in the way, 'it fundamentally changes what academic life is'. In this climate we can, it seems, never be good enough, as we constantly remake and reinvent our biographies in response to institutional requirements that we perform as all of these, all the time: teachers, managers, researchers and fund-raisers.

A 'runaway world'

We chose the metaphor of a 'runaway world' from Ulrich Beck's and Elizabeth Beck-Gernsheim's (2002) analysis of what they call 'institutionalized individualism'. The world is experienced as 'runaway', they argue, because of the 'decline of narratives of given sociability' in the face of 'a non-linear, open-ended, highly ambivalent, ongoing process of individualization' (xxii). Within such a world the social form of one's own life 'becomes filled with incompatibilities, the ruins of traditions, the junk of side-effects' (p.23). It also becomes restless and migrant: 'a travelling life, both literally and metaphorically, a nomadic life, a life spent in cars, aeroplanes and trains, on the telephone or the internet, supported by the mass media, a transnational life stretching across frontiers' (p.25). Individualization, detraditionalization and globalization must, therefore, be analysed together as the conditions which determine emergent modes of institutional formation and association.

Some decry what they see as the decline of cultural values implicit in these new conditions. They point to the breakdown of relationships and connectivity, the erosion of civic purposefulness and engagement, and the loss of boundary and identity, as inevitable consequences of the 'runaway world' within which we find ourselves. Others are more likely to highlight the new freedoms – of identity, lifestyle, choice, orientation – that such a world would seem to open up: a world of infinite possibility within which any notion of 'limit' is rendered off-limits. Yet others remind us of the dark side of this 'runaway world': its emergent underclass, its deep inequalities, its concentrations of multiple disadvantage. Each of these perspectives provides a very different value orientation to the processes of 'detraditionalization' and 'globalization' which is captured in the phrase 'runaway world'.

These different perspectives do, however, have in common two shared assumptions: that this 'runaway world' is characterized by a rapid acceleration in the pace of individualization and that this accelerating process highlights the importance of institutions while posing a severe threat to their continuity and integrity. Traditionally, our sense of institutional 'membership' and 'belongingness' has been structured around notions of commonality and sameness. The 'runaway world' of accelerating individualization renders those notions less secure and at the very least forces us at the level of practice and organizational structure to confront the ever-increasing intrusions of cultural and ideological difference. Institutions that were founded on the assumption of homogeneity are having to come to terms with the heterogeneity that now characterizes our 'runaway world'. In a world of increasing individualization, detraditionalization and globalization, institutions gain renewed significance within the emergent order.

Contesting educational purposes

How do we, then, as professionals in higher education, speak back to the globalizing forces of neo-liberalism and the associated economizing of education, the hollowed-out language of the market, the commodification of knowledge and consumer gratification, all exemplified in the notion of the 'McUniversity' (Parker and Jary 1995)? Out of such shared concerns this edited book has emerged. Importantly we wanted to sketch current conditions of higher education so that we might understand the context of a corporate consumerist higher education in which we find ourselves positioned, but more than this we wanted to generate languages which would enable us to think about alternative ways of being and working in higher education. Even more than this we wanted to 'point to' hope, to show at least some instances where different practices in higher education were working to sustain critical stories about democratic life, critical learning and ethical deliberation, however delicate and fragmented. As Kenway (1995) has pointed out, there is always more than one way to tell a story about (higher) education. She notes that social institutions are made up of many different, often competing, discourses and discursive fields. Universities are then 'fragile settlements' between and within competing discourses, 'subordinate, dominant, co-existing and competing but always open to challenge and change, to reworking meaning and "truth"' (Kenway 1995: 141).

At issue is how we might contribute to better, more just higher education institutions and to democratic public life. 'Just institutions and practices', O'Neill (1996: 182) argues, 'provide the specifications for judging the justice of particular acts or decisions'. But even apparently limited individual actions, notwithstanding Beck and Beck-Gernsheim's (2002) emphasis on the significance of institutions, should not be lightly dismissed for their possible failure to generate immediately observable systemic change. Onora O'Neill reminds us when our institutions [of higher education] may not be just or not just enough, embodying justice in individuals ('capabilities', 'virtues') might mean that individual good might survive when broader justice does not. In this case, the 'dispersed acts of solidarity' by individuals might still have 'cumulative public effects: this is the power of the powerless even in hard times' (O'Neill 1996: 201). Our individual actions help to make our institutions more just, our just institutions enable us to act with greater justice. At issue is that for all the fragility of the 'reclaiming universities' project, higher education in its institutions and its individual acts continues to be a site for keeping alive the tensions between market values and higher learning values.

We know also that higher education, as much as other aspects of education, plays a key role in promoting and reproducing what we take to be desirable forms of social life. The process of educational change and social change are then mutually constitutive and dialectically related. Thus the system of education we have now, have had in the past, and might build for the future reflects but also reconstructs the understanding of democracy that a society holds to be legitimate at any one time. But education is also a contested concept, so that what it is to be an 'educated person' is always a matter for political and social dispute. An example is to be found in the shifts in educational discourse in the UK, in the 1980s, from an educational emphasis on the 'whole person' (or child) to a concern with education for a particular world of work, for employability, 'entrepreneurship' and economic growth. The issue here is less about whether the citizen of the twenty-first century needs *either* cultural knowledge for public life *or* knowledge for economic participation, but rather what particular view of the world of work and the economic organization of society is held to be dominant. Thus contemporary educational debates in England, in particular, are also debates, albeit somewhat opaque, 'about which existing patterns of political, economic and cultural life ought to be reproduced and which ought to be modified or transformed' (Carr and Hartnett 1996: 24).

Moreover different visions of the good life (and hence the good society), will have effects for how higher education is organized and governed – whether institutional or individual dissent is allowed or removed, and whether local (department) structures as places of countervailing power and dialogue are fostered or reduced. If the good life is to be pursued only in a 'free' market society in which economic roles (our lives as producers, consumers and workers) are held to be all important, we can expect higher education to take one trajectory. If, however, our version of the good life is one which can best be realized in a deliberative democracy (see Dryzek 2000; Young 2000), which we take to involve inclusion across differences, political equality, and collective decision-making processes that promote social justice, then our identities as citizens are held to be as important as our economic roles. In this case we might expect education in universities to be organized along a different trajectory so as to develop and foster the social knowledge and capabilities (see Nussbaum 1997; 2000) needed for active participation and deliberation.

The point is that disputes about education 'always reveal the ideological tensions occurring in a society as it struggles to come to terms with changing cultural circumstances and new economic conditions' (Carr and Hartnett 1996: 25). We argue, therefore, not only for education of a particular form and practice, but also for the vision of the good life that underpins our views on education. Michael Apple (2001) usefully points to the particular kinds of morality which underpin competing versions of (higher) education. On the one hand a 'thick morality' is grounded in notions of the common good as the ethical basis for policy and practice; while a 'thin morality' is grounded in competitive individualism and hierarchical divisions. Put another way would be to ask whether the purpose of higher education holds ethical values to be central, as much as the development of knowledge and skills? These competing views will in turn shape our approaches to academic practices, the construction and sanctioning of professional and learner identities that flow from these practices, and the way in which we describe our practices. In contesting education and its purposes and values, we contest interpretations of social life.

We therefore think that matters of social justice should take priority in our reflections on society and its higher education arrangements (and in the books we write). Speaking about justice is emphatically not, we assert, 'what you mention when you have nothing else to say' (Nussbaum 2000: 33). It is to assert that we still believe in higher education as/for democratic life, and in the value of critical inquiry which maps the relations of power and the operations of knowledge that inflect towards or away from democratic versions of the good life. Richard Hofstadter reminds us that the best reason for supporting higher education institutions 'lies not in the services they can perform ... but in the values they represent' (quoted in Aronowitz and Giroux 2000: 332). Civic agency, citizenship and democratic participation are then integral to the purposes of higher education and educating students for democratic public life. Education, Seddon (1997) concurs, is a social practice 'where we learn to be as well as how to labour', realized through curriculum and pedagogy in university classrooms and constructed through the interactions of lecturer, students, knowledge and interpersonal processes.

Against current trends and patterns in which money alone is becoming the literal and metaphorical currency of higher education and the measure of our individual and collective worth, we set out in this book both to generate disciplined readings which expose the workings and effects of power, and to produce imaginative possibilities and alternative readings that take us beyond the current situation in which higher education finds itself. We speak for and turn towards renewal and change in which the relationship between higher education and democratic life is reinstated as a matter of urgent debate and action. In short, we attempt in this book to learn how to 'speak for hope', as Raymond Williams (1989) said, 'while not suppressing the nature of danger'. At stake, then, is the repositioning of higher education towards democracy and civic life, and away from marketization, commodification and performativity.

Sections and chapters

We have divided the book into three parts, although in practice we have found that the descriptive and analytical borders between each section are more or less permeable. In different ways each of the chapter authors sketches the dark times, develops a language of critique and gestures to hope. There is a kind of iterative revisiting of these three themes in each chapter and throughout the book, but the different chapters and parts seek to do different work. The degree of emphasis on each of these does therefore vary across each section of the book. Thus the chapters in Part 1, *Dark Times*, map compellingly the apparent triumph of the economy over education and the increasingly strident emphasis that higher education 'skill' graduates for their economic roles. This has been accompanied by a rhetoric and practices of managerial regulation and control over everyday academic life and teaching (Zipin and Brennan, Chapter 1), the tight regulation of research through the UK's Research Assessment Exercise (Lucas, Chapter 2), and to curriculum contestation (Selden, Chapter 3). In these first three chapters we hear eloquent accounts of the effects for everyday academic life and the impact on our academic identities. Both Zipin and Brennan, and Lucas examine how academic life is experienced at an inter-subjective level: what Bourdieu calls 'habitus'. It is argued that new 'rules of the [academic] game' are creating severe conflict within the dispositional constitution of professional identities, especially in the suppression of the dispositions to be ethical agents in the everyday life of our field of work. Selden elaborates on the 'neo-conservative assault' by 'capital and culture' on the undergraduate curriculum in the USA by foundations using their financial leverage to control curriculum content. Michael Peters' Chapter 4 then opens out into a broader focus on what might be driving these everyday cases and effects, showing how the modern concept of the university is in crisis in face of globalization, neoliberal policies and the knowledge economy.

In Part 2, *Languages for Reconstruction*, we shift the emphasis on to constructing new ways and recovering older ways to talk about and to reclaim the space of higher education for critical dialogue and debate about the goods of learning. In Chapter 5 Barr and Griffiths explore the nature of a public space that can accommodate and re-construct public knowledge. Drawing on feminist philosophy and postmodern ideas they propose a model of rationality which is true to Hannah Arendt's injunction to 'train the imagination to go visiting'. Judyth Sachs follows with her chapter, in which she recounts her experiences over the past few years in quality assurance and the impact of audit cultures, which have seen a paradoxical alignment between collegial and managerial processes. 'Sitting uneasily at the [management] table', she works to develop a language and practice of activist academic professionalism which is negotiated, collaborative, socially critical, future oriented, strategic and transparent. In the third chapter in this section, Jon Nixon introduces some of the resources necessary for developing a language of reconstruction based on the principles and precepts of deliberative democracy in which individual flourishing and organizational structure are included within the framework of understanding.

In Part 3, *Pointing to Hope*, we shift the emphasis to making hope 'practical' by pointing more firmly to how we might speak back to market values. In Chapter 8 Melanie Walker outlines a language and practice for pedagogies of beginning. Drawing on a number of empirical cases, she describes teaching and learning processes which foster critical dialogue and critical knowledge-making and 'democratic' learner and professional identities. Rob Walker takes up the issue of new technologies in higher education in the next chapter. He acknowledges the 'dark side' of the 'digital diploma mills', but also considers institutional and individual responses which suggest the democratic promise and possibilities of virtual learning environments. Colin Bundy bravely takes up the case of the governance and management of universities, tracing the historical shifts in British higher education from 'donnish domination' to the emergence of the contemporary managerial university. Drawing on his own experiences, he proposes a critical alternative to managerialism in its narrow form – university management practice which is self-critical, reflexive and open-ended. In the final chapter in this section Melanie Walker turns to the all important matter of research and scholarship to construct her argument for ethical 'thoughtfulness' in research practice so that our research and scholarship contribute both to social knowledge and to public debate and deliberation about the production and dissemination of knowledge and its benefits.

Finally, in an *Epilogue* Ronald Barnett offers his commentary on all the preceding chapters and engages with our notion of 'reclamation' by developing his ideas around three dimensions: of the university's self-story, of its practices and of spaces in which the university can be itself. He argues for the 'authentic' university and suggests that the contributions to the book suggest that there is still space to win back this authenticity.

Concluding remarks

In many ways, working together on this book has underlined for us the fragile nature of our project. Yet we are not willing to abandon hope, even if higher education often appears depressingly beleaguered on all fronts. David Halpin (2001) argues persuasively that hope is fundamental to the educational process. Out of hopefulness, he reminds us, 'grows surprising novelty and success' (2001: 312). To this we might add, what Freire (1998) describes as 'opportunities for hope', which aid our thinking about how to realize an 'improved' way of educational life. Moreover, Iris Marion Young shows us that our struggles for a more expansive and inclusive higher education, like all democratic struggles, cannot wait for perfect conditions of dialogue and debate because subordinated discourses, groups and individuals cannot wait for the process to become fair. There are often so many contending interests and issues, she says, that 'oppressed and disadvantaged groups have no alternative but to struggle for greater justice under conditions of inequality' (2000: 50), including conditions of inequality in higher education. Above all we need to understand the shape of the 'dark times', produce new ways of talking and thinking about our work in higher education, and begin 'pointing' to the doing of critical pedagogies, the fostering of enabling learner identities, and the forging of activist professionalism.

There is arguably not yet a mainstream consensus on higher education or its restructuring, even as the naturalized language of market forces works to manufacture the object (corporate higher education) of which it speaks. David Bridges (2001) offers a further resource to examine our own work and professional lives in higher education where the overall purpose remains that of defending universities as social and educational zones of critique, disputation, innovation and reconsideration, as much as places for producing, conserving and applying knowledge. He suggests that universities are (or should be) places where scholarship is cultivated, where evidence and argument are practised, places of sustained enquiry and higher level analysis, of freedom to create and invent, of openness to peer and public criticism, and where academic virtues of honesty, courage and self-knowledge, among others, are cultivated.

The point is surely that even in these hard times for higher education, then, we can still choose forms of professional agreement-making which are collaborative, reflexive and deliberative regarding the ends and purposes of our own and our students' learning. A 'better' higher education, we think, recognizes the potential of our students, but also involves acting to enable them to realize their capacities – *both* reflection *and* action. 'Better', we think, means producing storylines 'against the grain', which foreground ethical lecturer and student identities and values of equity and social justice for individuals and social groups. 'Better' acknowledges and celebrates the complexity of professional judgements and uncertainty as part of the job, not a troublesome process to be expunged through performance indicators.

What kind of society should education, then, foster? What kind of social, educational and political arrangements will best enable all members of a society to lead collective and individually fulfilling and worthwhile lives? What narratives and stories (curriculum content) are thinkable and allowable? How are knowledge, skills and forms of consciousness reproduced (or transformed)? Is education to be a public good or a private concern? What conceptualization of the good life are our educational proposals and policy frameworks promoting and making possible? In the end, we do not, in this book, claim or even set out to resolve the difficulties we face working in higher education. Our intentions are both more modest and yet more ambitious as we seek to gesture towards conditions of trust and connection and social practices of communication, tolerance, recognition and participation which sustain and 'breathe life' into individual capabilities and reformed institutions. We point hopefully 'in dark times' (Arendt 1995) to a revitalized human agency against current trends, to the possibility of a higher education which inflects towards deliberative democracy, and to transforming both individual practices and public institutions.

Raimond Gaita (2000: 42) reminds us that sometimes universities 'must resist their times if they are not to betray their students'. In his essay on *Truth and the University*, he draws our attention to a potentially alternative language for speaking about higher education practices. Turning to Arendt's (1977) essay on *The Crisis in Education*, he directs us to her explication of the complex relation to past, present and future that is required of students and teachers:

> Education is the point at which we decide whether we love the world enough to assume responsibility for it and by the same token save it from that ruin which, except for renewal, except for the coming of the new and the young, would be inevitable. And education, too, is where we decide whether we love our children enough not to expel them from our world and leave them to their own devices, not to strike from their hands their chance of undertaking something new, something foreseen by no-one, but to prepare them in advance for the task of renewing the common world.
>
> (Arendt 1977: 196)

Arendt (1977: 34) insists that we have to 'think again and again about ... what it means to raise this question today'.

References

Apple, M. (2001) Comparing neo-liberal projects and inequality in education, *Comparative Education*, 37(4):409–23.
Arendt, H. (1959) *The Human Condition*. Chicago: University of Chicago Press.
Arendt, H. (1977) *Between Past and Future*. Harmondsworth: Penguin Books.
Arendt, A. (1995) *Men in Dark Times*. New York: Harcourt Brace.
Aronowitz, S. and Giroux, H. (2000) The corporate university and the politics of education, *The Educational Forum*, 64:332–9.
Ball, S. (2000) Performativities and fabrications in the education economy: Towards the performative society?, *The Australian Educational Researcher*, 27(2):1–24.
Beck, U. and Beck-Gernsheim, E. (2002) *Individualization*. London: Sage.
Blake, N., Smith, R. and Standish, P. (1998) *The Universities We Need*. London: Kogan Page.
Bridges, D. (2001) A response to Stephen Rowland, *The Psychology of Education Review*, 25(2):7–8.
Carr, W. and Hartnett, A. (1996) *Education and the Struggle for Democracy: The Politics of Educational Ideas*. Buckingham: Open University Press.
Coady, T. (ed.) (2000) *Why Universities Matter*. St Leonards: Allen and Unwin.
Dickens, C. (1998) *A Christmas Carol*. Oxford: Oxford University Press (first published 1843).
Dryzek, J. S. (2000) *Deliberative Democracy and Beyond. Liberals, Critics, Contestations*. Oxford: Oxford University Press.
Freire, P. (1998) *A Pedagogy of the Heart*. New York: Continuum Publishing Company.
Gaita, R. (2000) Truth and the university, in T. Coady (ed.) *Why Universities Matter*. St Leonards: Allen and Unwin.
Giroux, H. (2002) Neoliberalism, corporate culture and the promise of higher education: The university as public sphere, *Harvard Educational Review*, 72(4):425–63.
Halpin, D. (2001) Utopianism and education: The legacy of Thomas More, *British Journal of Educational Studies*, (49)3:299–315.
Kenway, J. (1995) Having a postmodernist turn or postmodernist angst: a disorder experienced by an author who is not yet dead or even close to it, in R. Smith

and P. Wexler (eds) *After Postmodernism: Education, Politics and Identity*. London: Falmer Press.

Nussbaum, M. (1997) *Cultivating Humanity*. Cambridge, Mass.: Harvard University Press.

Nussbaum, M. (2000) *Women and Human Development. The Capabilities Approach*. Cambridge, Mass.: Cambridge University Press.

O' Neill, O. (1996) *Towards Justice and Virtue*. Cambridge: Cambridge University Press.

Parker, M. and Jary, D. (1995) The McUniversity: organization, management and academic subjectivity, *Organization*, 2(2):319–38.

Seddon, T. (1997) Restructuring Australian education. Paper presented to the European Educational Research Association annual conference, Lahti, Finland.

Young, I. (2000) *Inclusion and Democracy*. Oxford: Oxford University Press.

Williams, R. (1989) *Resources of Hope*. London: Verso.

Part 1
Dark Times

Part 1

1
Managerial Governmentality and the Suppression of Ethics

Lew Zipin and Marie Brennan

Introduction

The university sector in Australia is particularly vulnerable to shifts in federal government policy and funding mechanisms. It is a largely public system and federally funded, requiring annual reports provided each year to the government on a range of measures such as student numbers, attrition rates, student satisfaction, management, research output and financial expenditure, covering all aspects of university activity. Industrial relations are likewise circumscribed by federal legislation, dictating approaches to salary bargaining and conditions. Since 1996, operating budgets for universities have been cut across the board by 40 per cent, with concomitant expectations of income diversification from other sources, which are very difficult to achieve in a country of small population where philanthropic activity and foundations are almost non-existent. This fiscal shift has occurred at a particularly difficult time for the university system in Australia, as the 1990s were a period of significant tertiary massification, with a 30 per cent expansion in student numbers, while at the same time teaching-only staff were reduced by 8 per cent, and teaching/research staff by 1 per cent (Nelson 2002; University of South Australia 2002).

We discuss in this chapter how, under such conditions, a certain kind of 'managerialism' has emerged, altering the functions and nature of leadership positions, and the practical relations between staff and management. Indeed, an oppositional culture between 'workers' and 'management' has become entrenched with the introduction of local bargaining within a national framework. Such changes – including the very normalization of the use of the word 'management' within the university – have been discussed quite widely in Australian circles, although we note that the form of institution which Marginson and Considine (2000) have called 'the enterprise university' is, with variations, not only a feature of Australia but also operates in the UK, the US (Slaughter and Leslie 1997) and elsewhere.

In this chapter we wish to evoke the level of lived experience of 'managerialism' in universities, and to analyse it through a lens of concepts from the work of Bourdieu. To introduce our discussion of the 'managerialized' structural realignment of lived practices, social relations and inter-subjective dispositions (especially ethical dispositions) in university work, we begin with a fictionalized critical incident – a 'morality tale' – which we consider to have illustrative and heuristic value. While this is not a 'true' tale in the sense that all the situations and events 'really' occurred in a given time and place, we consider it a 'realistic' tale – a 'verisimilitude' – as it draws upon events and situations we have experienced, observed or received testimony about from across a range of university sites. Jumping off from this 'morality' tale, we discuss Bourdieu's concept of 'reflexive sociology', and then further elaborate his conceptual framework, focusing on the production of 'habitus' within a professional 'field'. We then link these concepts to a discussion of broader shifts and restructurings of governance in Australian universities. Finally, we interpret the new 'governmentality' and its suppression of ethical dispositions, which we suggest is indicative of a 'crisis of habitus' in the university sector.

An illustrative morality tale

The start of the new academic year at University X (UX) held the promise of workload relief for academic staff. The University had recently signed off on a trial workload policy that had been agreed upon between the local Union branch and University management. It had come into being after a jointly sponsored research project into academic workloads, based on interviews with all University Heads of Schools (HoSs) and Divisional Pro Vice-Chancellors (PVCs), and focus groups with 'non-managerial' academic staff. The report found an endemic condition of indecent work overload for many staff, with serious consequences to health, morale and research prospects. A joint Union-Management Working Party endorsed these findings. A second report, presenting a workload policy formula and rationale, was substantially adopted in a draft Trial Workload Policy which had been distributed to all academic staff. The UX Vice-Chancellor (VC), his Deputy and the President of the local Union branch had together met with HoSs on two occasions, stating that Union and Management had 'shaken hands' on this trial policy, and wanted it implemented to the degree possible. As the start of the academic year approached, the VC sent an email to all staff saying:

> It is understood that immediate and full implementation of all aspects of the draft policy may not be possible. This is not a reason for inaction, or for giving up the attempt to improve workloads. I want to emphasise that the University has a responsibility to audit and address the problem of unhealthy and unsustainable workload patterns. Deci-

sions as to how to address such problems have to be made consultatively and equitably, and Heads of Schools have had several discussions about the whole process. Please play your part. It will help me estimate the extent to which the University is understaffed. I will not be able to do everything that people would wish, but without some modelling and trialling everything will remain vague and wishful.

However, it did not prove easy for Heads of Schools to 'play their part'. Just two working days before the start of Semester 1, the HoS of Teacher Education at UX called an 'emergency meeting' to discuss a reconsideration of workloads previously allocated and approved for the semester. The 'emergency' was that the PVC of the Division had, the day before, told each HoS that the Division had suffered a 'budget clawback'. To cover the loss, the PVC had instructed all six HoSs immediately to cut casual staff by 15 per cent. Since programmes could not be cut on such short notice, reducing casual staff meant that the HoS had to get more work from permanent and contract staff. She thus sought to assign to most staff either more class groups (called 'tutorials' in Australia) and/or practicum supervision than had earlier been approved.

Programme heads and other staff in attendance grumbled but started working out ways to accommodate the cuts. However, one young staff member, just a year into his first full-time academic job as a Lecturer A (equivalent to 'Assistant Professor' in the US), actively argued against compliance. The HoS replied that she didn't expect staff to wear the full 15 per cent cut; however, before asking the PVC to look elsewhere for funds, she needed to make sure 'we are all squeaky clean'. This implied that many staff workloads – which she had already approved, and had in past moments acknowledged as exceeding what is desirable for staff health or quality teaching – could now somehow be interpreted as less than what past custom and rules allowed her to expect. Indeed, she told the objecting staff member that his previously approved workload had 'some gaps' and so she was assigning him a further tutorial in a course he was coordinating (as a first-time coordinator). Although not said by the HoS, the staff member quickly realized he was thus expected to withdraw a work offer to one of his casually employed tutors. Yet all his tutors had relinquished options to do other work, which it was too late now to reclaim; and they all needed the money for the work he'd offered them, with the HoS's approval to do so. Moreover, they were Indigenous- and Asian-Australian women, whereas he was a white male, in a course titled 'Diversity in Educational Settings'.

The HoS's expectation that he retract his offer on such short notice was thus painfully felt as an ethical burden, emboldening the early-career Lecturer to talk back in explicitly ethical language. He asked: 'Do you think it's ethically decent for our School in this way to deprive a tutor, on such short notice, of promised livelihood? Do you think it's fair to ask me to break this promise when it was made after you approved it?' The HoS's terse answer was: 'We haven't signed a contract with her yet.' The staff member replied that, on ethical grounds, he would not dismiss his tutor, and would refuse to teach the tutorial if the School did so.

The Lecturer was nonplussed at the HoS's legalistic answer to a question of ethical import; yet the HoS was discernibly nonplussed at being called into question on ethical grounds. The Lecturer sensed that he was violating unwritten norms of conduct in asking her to be ethically accountable – which was generally not done even one-on-one, let alone in front of others. He sensed also that others in the room were inured to the 'necessity' of conforming to unwritten rules which expected them to absorb extra work – even in violation of Enterprise Agreements – if their immediate, collegially located manager exports onto them budget pressures that the PVC, presiding aloofly above all Schools in the Division, applies to her through the power of a 'line-management' structure that makes her accountable to him first and foremost. Colleagues in the room also appeared uncomfortable at his challenge, and remained silent. The Lecturer sensed that, if their newly increased workloads required that they dismiss tutors to whom they had promised work, they would share his terrible feeling about it, but they would wear it silently rather than force the HoS to address it, let alone expect her to bear the direct shame, and pain, of delivering the blow to the tutor.

In response to the Lecturer's refusal, the HoS asked him to reconsider and reply in writing. The next day he sent an email stating his reasons why he would not reconsider, including both unethical treatment of the tutor, and that extra work assigned to him and colleagues violated previous workload practice and was especially indecent at a time when trial of a policy for reducing workloads was scheduled to begin. On the first day of the new semester, he found a revised workload sheet under his door in which the HoS assigned him the extra tutorial. An attached note said that this was within the powers of her position as HoS, and that he should see the PVC if he was still dissatisfied. When he did so, the PVC said the HoS had informed him of the situation, and that 'I have to back my manager'. The staff member re-stated his objections and his reasons, posing to the PVC the same questions about whether it was ethical thus to take away work promised to a tutor. The PVC replied: 'I can see how you might think it's not' (thus ducking the ethical import in a more suave way than the HoS). The staff member reiterated his refusal to do the tutorial, come what may. The PVC responded that, 'on pragmatic grounds', he would allow the tutor to stay 'this time' but the staff member would be expected to accept any such work assignments from the HoS in future.

Why is it that a new staff member might raise the issue when others under less risk might not? What is it about conditions in Australian universities that make this 'fictive' tale 'ring true' (as it has among 'critically disposed' academic audiences at a couple of national conferences where we have presented it as a heuristic narrative)? What can we learn about the ways in which immersion in a set of practices tends to position and socialize staff to make dispositional adaptations in compliance with conditions that are debilitative for quality university teaching as well as disturbing of ethical integrity? What 'morals of the story' can we learn about educational leadership and governance from the analysis of such a tale? In particular, what can we learn about the processes of lived ethics in such conditions within an educational organization?

Our methodological warrant for 'telling tales': the importance of reflexive sociology

In constructing this fictionalized story, we draw from sites and incidents in our working lives at a few universities, as well as stories academics tell one another: at conferences, dinner tables and in the corridors of their working life spaces. Unfortunately there are only too many such incidents, but rarely are they the focus of sustained research and analysis. We suggest there is need for educators to treat such 'tales of our fields' – intimately personal, yet illustrative of current conditions of our professional practice – as a telling kind of 'data' for what Bourdieu (1992) calls 'reflexive sociology'.

Bourdieu argues the need for 'reflexive vigilance' in which professionally situated agents critically analyse how power operates in career spaces 'of direct interest ... in which they are deeply invested ... no matter how painful it may be' (1992: 88–9). Such scrutiny of the contexts of our own professional lives can indeed be painful socio-therapy, rupturing defense mechanisms by which we deny what we don't believe we can change and thus may rather not face. Bourdieu further notes the risk that colleagues could take revealing representations of our/their lived contexts personally, and 'denounce as gratuitous cruelty what is in fact ... a socioanalysis' (1992: 63). Adds Bourdieu: 'I have in mind here several passages [in my work] which separated me from some of my best friends' (1992: 63). Still, Bourdieu affirms the importance of taking such socio-analytical risks, since reflexive exploration of the contexts of our own career-invested work/life spaces can give us:

> a small chance of knowing what game we play and of minimizing the ways in which we are manipulated by the forces of the field in which we evolve, as well as by the embodied social forces that operate from within us ... Therefore I think that there is indeed a philosophical or an ethical usage of reflexive sociology... When you apply reflexive sociology to yourself, you open up the possibility of identifying true sites of freedom, and thus of building small-scale, modest, practical morals.
>
> (1992: 198–9)

In the interest of enabling healthier expression of repressed dispositions to be honest, self-critical and otherwise 'practically moral', we pursue in this chapter a 'reflexive sociology' of the games of manipulative and embodied social forces in university spaces where our lives have been deeply invested. If this appears 'dangerous', we argue that the greater danger for academics, as Bourdieu compellingly notes (1984, 1990), is in coming to think it appropriate to turn their critical analytic gaze on every other institutional field of practice but the one in which they themselves engage.

We need to make clear that our intention, in telling and (later) analysing the above 'morality tale', is not to 'tell tales out of school'. In constructing our characterizations of the HoS, PVC or colleagues, we do not seek to shame anyone; nor do we see any of these characters as 'ethically deficient' personalities who easily could have acted differently. Rather, we render 'ideal types', or what Bourdieu (1990) calls 'epistemic individuals'; that is they perform the constraints and inducements of positions in a governance structure which compel suppression of their own dispositions towards more ethical conduct. How, then, are such dispositions effectively suppressed? And, what counter-dispositions are inculcated through positioning within 'managerial' modes of governance?

Our concern, in raising such questions through the device of a 'realistic' story, is to explore the effects of dispositional suppression using a heuristic methodology that can disclose shameful codes and effects of a structure of governance relations that can put people in positions to endure painful ethical dilemmas and at the same time suppress their ability even to talk about these dilemmas. We present the Lecturer's ethical contestation, in our 'morality tale', as unusual. It is more typical that the 'line-managerial' mode which characterizes 'restructurings' of governance relations in Australian universities – as well as in other nations and across schooling sectors, spreading like an international pandemic (Levin 1998) – socializes staff to acquiesce in silent self-suppression of dispositions toward ethical contestation. How do people's practical participations in changed organizational forms become thus 'normalized'?

As an analytic lens to interpret our morality tale, we find that Bourdieu's conceptual framework allows us to address this question at the level of everyday life, yet not be limited to a personal or phenomenological perspective, in being able to link the 'life world' to broader social practices, relations and structures of the field. Using Bourdieu's socio-analytic toolkit, we will suggest that a new kind of 'governmentality' (Foucault 1991) has, in a couple of decades, infused Australian university and other educational fields with such dissonant norms and rules, relative to the dispositions that have drawn many to become educators, as to verge on a psycho-emotive identity crisis.

Habitus and field in Bourdieu's methodology

Working from the passage by Bourdieu quoted in the previous section, we can look again at our 'morality tale' to understand the emergency School meeting as representing a space and moment in a certain 'game we play'. The metaphor of a 'game' is not meant to trivialize the ethical stakes, which matter greatly. Moreover, as we will discuss, there are not only ethical stakes in terms of what values are central to the 'game' of our careers – as its rules, or norms (a more ethically-tinged word) – but also stakes in terms of powers of position and career possibilities; and these value and power dimensions are significantly linked.

In such 'games', says Bourdieu, players' gambits are motivated by 'forces of the field in which we evolve, as well as by the embodied social forces that operate from within us'. On the one hand there is a field: a professional sector – in our case, a 'university sector' – that can be distinguished from other significant sectors in social space. On the other hand, there are embodied social forces: internalized dispositions for strategizing how to play in the 'games' we inhabit.

Bourdieu uses the term habitus to define the embodiment of dispositions that come to 'inhabit' us – as internalized, more-or-less subconscious patterns in our psychic makeup – through practical immersion in the lived cultural conditions of positions we inhabit in social space (for example, positions in class, gender and race/ethnic structural relations, as well as positions in occupational fields). The dispositions of a given habitus constitute a person as a social agent at once 'individual', in embodying a somewhat unique complex of multiple dispositions; and at the same time linked to broad-based 'group' identifications. That is, certain people are latently perceived as 'like myself' (in manifesting similar dispositional markers), as distinct from 'others' (whose interactional styles and responses signify dispositions 'different from mine').

The inner dispositions of habitus thus derive from the differentiated social positions that given agents inhabit over time and across social spaces, partly in fields of career work, but more primarily in lived conditions that precede and lead to career fields. Bourdieu gives the term 'primary habitus' to dispositions acquired in very early stages of childhood maturation, in contexts of family and neighborhood. As such, the primary habitus embodies very deeply underlying dispositions – written into the body at a pre-verbal, motor level (what Bourdieu calls a 'bodily hexis') – and which continue to operate across one's life trajectory, as more or less subconscious patterns for perceiving, interacting and identifying in new social settings from early schooling through to adult career fields (Bourdieu 1977). Indeed, career 'choices' of professional field (often accessed according to how one is sorted and selected across levels of schooling) are fundamentally 'made' through an underlying resonant sense, in the subconscious depths of habitus, that, as compared to other spaces of career possibility, the 'chosen' field more likely values the deep-seated primary dispositions one embodies.

The players in our 'morality tale' of the School meeting are thus drawn to a field where they latently expect certain normative rules of the game to operate – norms in which they might hope to share an investment of deep-seated values. This does not mean they each equivalently share dispositions to abide by rules as encountered. In our tale, different dispositions are at work, depending in part on position within the field (PVC, HoS, Program Head, Lecturer A), and particularly for a young staff member not yet acculturated to the daily workings of local norms in School workspaces, including the unstated protocols for such meetings. Moreover, dramatic changes in conditions, such as rapid student massification and at the same time budget cuts, can lead to substantial shifts in the norms of the field – for example a shift to 'managerial' governance practices and relations – which unsettle the habitus of many 'players' in 'the game'.

If rules of the game thus change radically, there may be dispositional dissonances in which it is difficult for many to make the sort of internalized accommodations that Bourdieu calls 'secondary habitus'. Such accommodations develop across a life trajectory, as a person moves through a sequence of new institutional settings beyond childhood, which never resonate in full synchrony with the dispositional composite of primary habitus. However, the human organism continues to integrate the normative codes of new and diverse practical settings, accommodating to them by scaffolding the primary habitus with secondary interweavings and overlays (Bourdieu 1990). This is provided, however, that these secondary inculcations are not overly dissonant with the dispositional patterns deeply embodied in early life habitats. If so, habitus tends to shun the practices that inculcate such secondary dispositions, perceiving them as alien and 'other' to any comfortable coherence of 'oneself'. Habitus thus has a self-conserving tendency; it tends to maintain identity around a deeply underlying sense of what is normatively to be 'valued' – both an egoic and an ethical sense of 'integrity'.

Indeed, for many people – those whose early-life acculturation is in the conditions of relatively less powerful social-cultural positions – dissonant rather than accommodative habitus characterizes later experiences in various 'mainstream' institutional settings. Even when a person finds an adult career field that seems to value the species of capital s/he embodies, there will still be tensions between primary dispositions, and normative forces of the field that exert pulls for secondary adaptations. However, this will be more the case for some than others. To explain, we must further elaborate the social-historical complexity of professional fields.

'In highly differentiated societies,' says Bourdieu (1992: 97), 'the social cosmos is made up of a number of ... relatively autonomous social microcosms', that is 'fields', each with a 'logic and necessity that is specific and irreducible to those that regulate other fields.' Like the 'differentiated society' they comprise, field 'microcosms' as sizeable as, say, a national 'university sector' are of course not homogenous entities. Such a field is far-flung and complex in the diversity of its institutions, processes and projects. However, this complex diversity is held cohesive by what might be thought of as the central gravity of the field – what Bourdieu calls its 'specific logic', irreducible to that which regulates other fields. This has to do with charismas of the field by which those outside the field, and especially those who have power in other significant fields in social space, see certain activities as 'core' to the field, as better done there than in other fields, and as important to the society as a whole. Nonetheless, different fields encroach upon each other. 'The more autonomous the field,' that is the more powerful it is relative to others, says Bourdieu, 'the more it is capable of imposing its specific logic, the cumulative product of its particular history' (1992: 105), in relation to other fields. Many pressures that currently besiege universities, and that express in the tensions across players in our 'morality tale', have to do with the relatively lesser and declining autonomy of 'academic' fields in relation especially to the powers of political and economic sectors of the broader social space.

It is important to understand that the special logics of a given field are historical products, continually renewed and changed by those who inhabit it, in interaction with surrounding conditions and events. A field is socially populated by players diverse enough to contest what should be the values of the field, but who also share some 'core' dispositional sense of the value this field holds for them, as compared to other fields in social space. As Bourdieu says, the field comprises situations in which 'players ... oppose one another, sometimes with ferocity, only to the extent that they concur, by the mere fact of playing, ... that the game is worth playing ... This collusion is the very basis of their competition' (1992: 98). However, the game gets more ferocious if changing conditions create acute unsettlement and discord among players about the deep-seated core values of the field. This can happen especially if a field undergoes radical 'restructurings' that, with scope and power, intrude new normative rules of the game into micro-spaces and processes of the field – indeed, into the very governance structures, thus instituting radically changed norms as new core 'governmentalities' of the field. The force of such normative shifts may derive from encroachments of other more powerful sectors in social space, imposing agendas and designs ill-suited to the dispositions of many within the sector on which they impinge. When this is the case – as with the government and business-driven 'new managerialism' that has entered universities – there can be clashes in which players who embodied comfortable fits to prior norms lock horns with others who enter the field as embodiments of new norms, perhaps in authoritative governance positions. The 'game', suggests Bourdieu, may then take on volatile dimensions as players make gambits to 'transform, partially or completely, the immanent rules of the game ... through strategies aimed at discrediting the form of capital [that is embodied dispositions which reflect value investments] upon which the force of their opponents rests ... and to valorize the species of capital they preferentially possess' (1992: 99).

In the 'morality tale' we have constructed, the unusually direct and tense contestation over ethical values can be read to reflect unsettling conditions – workload intensification and much more – that provoke value shifts and clashes which, we believe, are getting more ferocious. The emergency meeting of the School can be seen as a micro-political space and moment of play in the broader 'main game' of the field (Zipin 1999), in which the various players' dispositional values and powers are simultaneously (1) organized and constrained within certain 'rules of the game'; and (2) in active high-stakes contestation over the very rules of the game. From conference responses we have had to this heuristic narrative, we believe that our tale evokes how new 'managerial' norms are troubling the hearts and spirits of many academics in the university field who sense that the very dispositions which led them into the field are in jeopardy. (Although in this chapter we highlight increasingly suppressed dispositions to be reflexively critical and ethical agents, there are other serious frustrations – for example, of dispositions to be researchful when workloads allow increasingly less time for research.)

To argue this compellingly, we need to explain more amply the context of 'managerial' governance restructurings in the Australian university field. After this, we will further interpret how our 'morality tale' illustrates a crisis of academic dispositions, in dissonance with recent shifts in the 'governmentalities' of the field.

Restructuring of governance in the Australian university sector

To give our tale more resonance across nations and educational sectors, we need to explain the (re)structural context for shifting logics of the Australian university field. We suggest that shifts in structure, affecting practice, have been similar in closely related fields such as public service sectors. However, the wider fiscal, ideological and other contexts for such restructurings are taken up differently in different fields and, within fields, at different times and sites.

In the past 15 years or so, many governments have sought to redefine the roles of public institutions in 'economic rationalist' terms. As part and parcel of this, they have sought to restructure the governance of public institutions along 'corporate-managerial' lines (Pusey 1992; Taylor et al. 1997). In the Australian university sector, these broad policy commitments have been forcefully mobilized, thus significantly altering the normative logics of the field.

It needs again to be emphasized that the Australian university sector, like the UK, has nowhere near the degree of relative autonomy of, say, the US sector, as it is funded by federal government and directed by federal policy to a much greater degree. Moreover, none of the 38 Australian public universities (there are only four small privates), including the elite 'sandstones', have the alternative revenue sources – alumni and philanthropic donations, stock portfolios, small business enterprises, sports teams, and so on – of many US universities. Consequently, and perversely, the federal government can cut funding provisions and thereby even more successfully compel universities – made more desperate for whatever pittance they can get – to accept policy criteria attached to funding. The power of the field's relative autonomy has as a consequence eroded, to the point where VCs and other high-level leaders within the field manifest increasing tendencies not to criticize central policy criteria that they might, in the past, have challenged as wrong-headed.

The earlier noted funding cuts combined with student massification and staff reductions have impacted differentially on given universities within the field. Newer universities (a significant portion of the field, created since 1988 from amalgams of non-university tertiary institutions) struggle especially for student numbers, allotted by government to each institution through negotiation, as well as for research funds, won through competition based on government criteria. Australian universities have in general found little success with 'entrepreneurial' solutions beyond the international student 'market', wherein competition is intense. Still, federal government – intent to sustain its budget surplus by spending less on public institutions – continues to insist that university fiscal problems are solvable by 'more efficiency' and 'better management'.

Over a short number of years this push for 'efficient management' has evolved into a runaway trend to 'rationalize' governance practices so as to privilege fiscal and other 'accountabilities'. This entails greater standardization in measures, categories and other report requirements within and across universities; nor do criteria stay the same from year to year. There has been a voluminous increase in number and kinds of reporting on all dimensions of work, initially imposed by government criteria and now institutionalized among management as 'best practice'.

Stipulated 'quality performance' criteria are often unclear, and difficult to meet given the limited resources provided; and yet institutions must appear to meet them in order to receive funding. Thus, promotion of images of 'quality performance' can take precedence over reporting of actually achieved quality. That is, PVCs, HoSs, Human Resource personnel and others learn to respond to impossible criteria for their own and the institution's 'performance' by producing what are, in effect, command performances of virtual rather than substantive 'quality achievements'. In being inscribed repetitively in such practices – which encode what Ball (2000), following Lyotard (1984), calls a 'post-modern performativity principle' – agents of university management acquire newly internalized 'performativity' habits (or secondary habitus) as part of their dispositional repertoire.

Significant realignments of the university field have ensued in all this, including an intensified top-down restructuring of the management of academic programmes. There has been a weakening of the relative autonomy of traditional disciplinary faculties through bundling multiple faculties into Schools within Divisions. If we imagine a UX restructure of governance positions that is typical of the field, it might have a Vice-Chancellor atop the line-management chain, with a Deputy VC and a layer of Pro Vice-Chancellors, some within the Chancellory (for example PVC-Academic, PVC-Research), others presiding over Divisions, under whom Heads of School serve, with weak powers, as 'middle-managers'.

Growth of managerialism has also altered customary relations of academic governance, shifting the 'balance of powers' between executive (management) and legislative (academic) domains. Increasingly, line-management controls the agenda of debates. At UX, the President of the Academic Board might be nominated by the Vice-Chancellor, with membership consisting of middle-managers (that is HoSs) plus Professors. However (as compared to the US) there are few Professors without management portfolios; most are in fact HoSs. It therefore becomes difficult to distinguish between managerial and legislative concerns and processes.

Thus, for most members, Academic Board is not an exercise of collegial decision-making or a venue to raise concerns but merely a formality to ensure proposals are passed through correct procedural avenues. Procedures are there to be suffered through, to ensure appeals or litigation won't occur. And yet, inclinations to resist or challenge such 'proceduralism' – while sometimes expressed in talk among middle-managers – tend to be overridden, in actual behaviour, by the effectiveness with which such regulatory practices inculcate 'proceduralist' dispositions in the habitus of middle-managers.

Such proceduralism enables the Board to meet its terms of reference, yet avoid ethical exploration of the impacts of shifting conditions and pressures within the University. Ethical issues can become swallowed and obscured within institutionalized procedures, and the boundaries of what counts as permissible discussion are inter-subjectively policed (at a habitus level) by other members. Struggles to re-position oneself within this space can occur: depending on many factors, someone who raises ethical concerns might be seen (negatively) as a 'troublemaker', or (positively) as someone who alerts the group to 'risk management' issues. To be positioned as troublemaker of course makes it difficult to be taken seriously. However, to be treated as alerting the collective to 'risk' co-opts the person within a discourse of 'managing risks'. One is thus positioned as a licensed exception to 'managerial' norms, rather than as an agent with power to shift normative discourse toward recognized needs for ethical dialogue. Over time, one is likely to abandon ethical questions in thus being treated as a lone exception to the norm.

This syndrome of governance realignment makes central policy decisions more easily implemented, but creates an upward-looking management structure, responding to top-down requirements for initiatives, planning, monitoring and accountability. Such restructuring has implications in terms of the dispositions of people who inhabit different structural positions within the field. Among those in PVC and HoS positions, there has been erosion of the sense, often held by erstwhile Deans of faculties, that one's prime role was 'leadership' of programmes, that is in sustaining academic quality and integrity, and in mentoring staff in terms of teaching and research capacities. As a 'managerial' mentality displaces such 'leadership' mentalities, there can be retreat from, or avoidance of, management positions by academics with 'leadership' dispositions. The vacuum is filled by those with dispositions more suited to the govern-mentalities of a managerial restructuring. Increasingly, those at the highest levels of university governance steer hiring panels convened to fill 'middle-management' positions, such that panels will select for properly 'performative' and 'procedural' dispositions.

The 'foot-soldier' academics, who mostly teach (and, if workload allows, do some research), have workaday access to this management chain only at the 'middle-level' of the HoS. However, governance pressures of 'upward' responsibility along the line-management chain mean that increasingly the HoS, although dwelling among academics as a 'colleague', feels compelled to suppress dispositions toward substantive 'collegial' consultation. As documented by Marginson and Considine (2000), line-management restructuring, with its 'one man band' mode of power and authority, is marked by a forceful ascendance of 'managerial' over 'collegial' relations, practices and discourses.

As we will now discuss further in terms of our earlier 'morality tale', such radical shifts in the structure of governance positions within the university field are a context for shifting imposition of 'the forces of the field in which we evolve' (Bourdieu 1992). Dispositions constituting primary habits of perception, communication and professional identity are imposed upon to realign within forceful overlays of new managerial govern-mentality (or dispositionality). The interplay between primary habitus, and unsettling secondary overlays of often contradictory mentalities – infused in powerful discourses, relations and practices of the field – can play out variously, ranging from conformity to contestation, depending partly on one's position within work and governance structures of institution and field.

Our 'morality tale' revisited: new governmentality and the suppression of ethics

In the context of restructurings discussed above, the complicity of staff in their own workload intensification at the emergency School meeting, and in breaking work promises to tutors, can be understood not as an aberrational instance, but as involving secondary dispositional 'resignations', recently yet effectively inculcated. A powerful inculcating force has been the new managerial centring of 'budget responsibility' as a supreme criterion – to the point of a 'higher value' – for survival of the institution and jobs within it. Valorization of 'budget' has come to infuse daily discourses and practices around academic work. It is here important to appreciate how the Divisional PVC is positioned between VC and HoSs in a managerial chain that polices compliance through – among other mechanisms – annual performance reviews conducted hierarchically, that is by the PVC for the HoS; and by the VC for the PVC. While the PVC presumably has 'duties of care' for staff health and safety, research development, and so on, the accountability criteria to which he must answer 'up' to the VC are so greatly defined in budget-balancing terms as to render him a budget policeman *über alles*.

For 'middle-level' managerial players to stand against such performative pressures would take dispositions for rare gumption, with so many institutional levers working to inculcate and discipline more conformist dispositions. It is thus understandable that, at the habitus level, the HoS in our morality tale would seek strategies for avoiding sanctions from above, as well as avoiding painful ethical self-questioning in fulfilling dictates from above. In this case, the HoS had made it a protocol not to have formal contracts signed by casual tutors until the very first day of a semester. Thus, when challenged over the ethical legitimacy of expecting School staff to rescind approved promises of work to casual tutors, her strategic impulse was to shift the discursive register from ethical to legalistic legitimacy: 'We haven't signed a contract yet.'

Our interpretation of the inter-subjective level of this exchange is that the HoS took refuge in 'forces of the field' which she had internalized as secondary dispositions of her managerial position, and which she deployed in defensive desperation, overriding more primary dispositions whereby, 'deep down', she herself would feel the ethical indecency of procedures she defended. In this way, procedural dispositions can override ethical ones, but not without affective costs: that is a habitus crisis of contradictory professional identities. Dispositionally, the HoS in our story is thus caught between (1) avoiding vertical sanctions that can descend powerfully to enforce line-managerial obligations; and (2) responding to tugs of horizontal responsibility to colleagues who surround her both in the meeting space and in the everyday settings of her working life.

Nor are the colleagues around her immune from self-disciplinary suppression in response to forces which they, too, internalize as part of a shift in governmental norms. They sit as uncomfortable players at a 'game' where the dispositional norms they had bargained for (in the career 'choice' of their habitus) are rapidly changing, seemingly from outside their locus of control. As new 'rules of the game' gain secondary influence on their dispositional make-ups, in conflict with certain primary dispositions, their reactions may range from conformist self-suppression to risky resistance. In the meeting, only one staff member took that risk. However, it is quite possible – likely, we'd argue – that others in the room shared silent impulses to take it, and may later have broached concerns to the HoS in private. After all, they realized they were being asked to submit to workload intensification in a semester when the beginning of relief from chronic overloads had been promised; and they realized that, in gambits played by managers under conditions of tightly constrained budget, a 'temporary' add-on might later be invoked as precedent.

We suggest, then, that the silence of colleagues at the meeting was not simply a matter of having primary ethical dispositions 'beaten out of them'. Nor was it simply a matter of being exhausted by struggles with what might seem an unbeatable power of managerial coercion. Staff silence was not out of agreement with actions and justifications presented by the HoS; nor out of fundamental acceptance of compromised ethics encoded in the relational structure of UX governance positions. Rather, there was sympathy for the person put in a position that might seem to force her to extract extra work from them, as well as to finesse that fact and, indeed, to impose on them – without acknowledging it – ethically compromised acts of breaking promises to casual staff. They understood that, in holding her stance as if with conviction, she, too, felt ethically compromised at a 'deep down' level of self-integrity, and paid prices with cuts to her heart.

In other words, collegial/ethical dispositions – impulses not to make a troubling positional dilemma even harder for their HoS 'colleague' – were alive and well among staff. Perversely, this ethical decency restrained their proactive agency to speak and act against indecent effects of budget-centred restructurings that the HoS performed from her position. They latently understood that she was caught in a middle-management squeeze between vertical and horizontal 'responsibilities', as a saliently unethical effect of structural alignments they all suffered. Acting from virtuous dispositions, they were thus co-opted, and self-divided, by institutionally coded governmental suppressions of other virtuous dispositions, for example critical capacities to 'talk truth (about power) to power'.

At a habitus level (that is not with articulate thought, but more-or-less subconsciously), the oppositional Lecturer also sensed the unethical squeeze on the HoS; and he sensed his colleagues' sympathy for her plight. He found himself alone in venting his impulse toward overt resistance, and in the uncomfortable position – early in his first academic job – of sensing that his colleagues might find him 'too confrontational'. His impulse to 'talk truth to power' – which we suggest is an eminently academic disposition; a 'special logic' of the field (which does not mean that all academics share it in degree or quality) – was alive but not faring well. With our colleagues in many Australian universities (Coady 2000), we find such dispositions recently more constrained within discursive practices that, while not directly prohibiting conversation in ethical terms, do effectively suppress ethical language within performative and procedural regimes that leave increasingly less safe room for ethical articulation.

We argue that line-managerial realignment has the extremely unethical effect of devolving to the HoS – the lowest rung of managerial response-ability – the 'dirty work' of forcing suppression of ethical dispositions (her own as well as others') through procedural neutralization of ethical discourse in everyday settings of academic practice. We therefore urge colleagues to seek strategic and sensitive ways to overcome their understandable reluctance to add further stress to the strains on middle-managers. If middle-managers do not find themselves ready to join in resisting suppression of collegial/ethical dispositions, then staff cannot afford to be sentimental about putting pressure on the position – despite the fact that a 'colleague' inhabits it – in order to compel better hearing of their proactive voices up the line-management chain.

Our [im]morality tale shows how, in the structure of University governance relations, the HoS is in the worst position to suffer squeeze plays of dispositional crisis, in having to perform 'dirty work' upon those amongst whom she works. We also see how the Divisional PVC sits at a remove from this 'dirty work'. While not in the room where his budgetary pressure was enacted, his was a powerfully 'present' absence. It took an atypical act of resistance to force him into presence as a speaking character in our tale. Even so, he held a hierarchically aloof power to instruct the HoS to send the new staff member 'up' for a private meeting, unwatched by other staff. From this remove, he also had time to prepare more slippery responses to ethical questions.

Again, we are not indicting people, but rather a structure of positions wherein ethically suppressive governmentalities are acquired and enacted. And there is a further 'absent presence' from the scene of the meeting: where is the Vice-Chancellor, who, in ethical terms, has responsibility to 'make good' on his e-mail promise to oversee a policy trial that delivers at least some workload relief? The answer is that the VC is not about to relinquish his structural remove from the 'dirty' scenes of everyday life in Schools. It behooves him to perform the same devolutionary handwashing, in relation to the PVC, that the latter enacts on the HoS.

The VC thus does not intervene when the PVC, acting on budget-balancing mandates, fails to 'do his part', and so nips the incipient workload policy trial in the bud. The VC does not keep his ear close to a ground where he can know how overburdened workloads really are. This might force him to acknowledge, consciously, what he suppresses 'deep down' (in his habitus): that is his own complicity in enforcing performance criteria for PVCs that require them to balance budgets 'at all costs'. The PVC position is the VC's means for 'stopping the buck' in budget-balancing priorities – but 'outside' the domain of his office, such that he remains detached from how this compromises his ethical hortatory about the University's 'responsibility to audit and address the problem of unhealthy and unsustainable workload patterns'.

Given the pressures that have induced all VCs to adopt governance restructurings of the sort we have discussed, they typically come to affirm the necessity of such governance realignments. Many then come, over time, to rationalize these necessities as somehow desirable. Thus, the VC position induces dispositions for 'making a virtue of necessity'. In embodying such denial mechanisms, it helps to remain distant from the daily grinds of staff. Such dispositional denials may extend to a loss of capacity for honest appraisal of the conditions of work in one's own institution – and thus an abdication of responsibility to see the substantive complexity of problems and remedies. Many VCs, when compelled to address workload issues during Enterprise Bargaining periods, resort to mantric suggestions that staff can 'work smarter' (that is Schools don't really need further resources); or that Schools can earn needed resources through greater 'entrepreneurial' efforts. However well intended, we argue that such are ultimately performative investments in magical thinking rather than substantive solutions.

Conclusion: a habitus crisis?

We are hardly the first to claim a 'crisis' in the Australian university sector. There is much testimony to this condition, including the publication of a Senate Inquiry (whose report, 2001, is entitled *Universities in Crisis*). Indeed, the strongest testimony to that inquiry came from the head of the Australian Vice-Chancellors Committee, Ian Chubb. Government Ministers replied, with force, that the only problem universities have is their own bad management. Not surprisingly, given the dispositional denial mechanisms we discussed above, other VCs have declined to join Chubb, at least not aloud; and some have publicly countered that there is no crisis. We suggest that both the aggression and the hush that deny crisis are themselves symptoms of crisis.

In this chapter, we have considered how ethical crisis is emerging among academics at a deeply dispositional level of 'self'-integrity. The 'evidence' of our morality tale, and many others we could have told, is that, while many staff are not yet ready to articulate their crises in ways that compel universities to sit up and take notice, this bespeaks powerful suppressive 'forces of the field', beneath which professional identities are nonetheless agitated. We suggest that dispositions to be reflexive, ethical, and collegial are too primary in the habitus of too many academics to be kept 'down' much longer. A crisis of occupational health and safety proportions, and of teaching-and-learning quality, is increasingly declared in conferences and other sites of 'more protected' dialogue, along with testimonies of 'personal' suffering in terms of job satisfaction, professional identity and much more. We argue that it is not just foot-soldier staff who suffer such crises, but also 'leaders', who increasingly sense the damage to their dispositions to lead – to take ethical responsibility – and not merely to 'manage' (in the sense of 'cope').

Perhaps political events within the field will bolster our interpretation of 'crisis'. From our viewpoint as 'sociologists', we recognize that our analysis of a single fictive 'critical incident' is not sufficient 'evidence'. We encourage further telling of illustrative stories from a ground of experience within the field. At the same time, we aim to pursue further study of the more systematic sort that Bourdieu might have undertaken: for example broadbased interviews, statistical data analysis and policy document analysis.

Methodologically, this chapter has been a heuristic foray, exploring the usefulness of Bourdieuian analytical tools for reflexive socio-analysis that probes the levels wherein any crisis 'of the field' is a crisis that 'we' inter-subjectively live. We encourage our colleagues in other educational sectors, such as schooling, early childhood, and youth affairs, to reflect on their experiences and to undertake research that explores the utility of Bourdieuian concepts in their own settings, linking 'lived experience' to broader managerial shifts in governance, and evaluating the impacts on staff identities and relations. To care about our field not only as researchers, but also as pro-active agents who value the 'social good of the field', is to remember that we have agency to shift even the most seemingly intractable 'necessities'. Moreover, it is in critical times that surprising moments for agentic action arise. Although some have read Bourdieu's concept of habitus as 'deterministic,' we consider this a serious misreading. Says Bourdieu:

> The tendency toward self-reproduction of the structure is realized only when it enrolls the collaboration of agents who are ... nonetheless *active producers* ... Having internalized the immanent law of the structure in the form of habitus, they realize its [apparent] necessity in the very spontaneous movements of their existence. But what is necessary to reproduce the structure is still a historical action, accomplished by true *agents* ... [who] are the products of this structure and dialectically make and remake this structure, which they may even radically transform under definite structural conditions.
>
> (1992: 140, original italics)

'Definite conditions' for radically transformative agency exist, we believe, when forceful 'secondary dispositions' of the field create too much dissonant clash with the primary dispositions of too many players who – in ethical registers – care too much about the 'game' to let normative suppressions of their ethics come to rule the field irreversibly. Such a situation creates conditions for rare proaction. Says Bourdieu:

> The lines of action suggested by habitus may very well be accompanied by a strategic calculation of costs and benefits, which tends to carry out at a conscious level the operations that habitus carries out in its own way. Times of crises, in which the routine adjustment of subjective and objective structures is brutally disrupted, constitute a class of circumstances when indeed 'rational choice' may take over, at least among those agents who are in a position to be rational.
>
> (1992: 131)

This chapter has been written in the spirit of such reflexive search for critical mindfulness – our own, and that of colleagues. We seek to arouse a sense of the ethical necessity of raising our consciousness to take more reflexively articulate looks at the usually subconscious layers of dispositional tendency within our field. In a time of brutal disruption within the very constitutions of our professional identities, we cannot afford to let our dispositions for pronounced and proactive ethical agency lie too low.

Acknowledgements

Another version of this chapter appears in the *International Journal of Leadership in Education* 6(4). The authors thank the *IJLE* for permission to adapt it for this chapter.

References

Ball, S. (2000) Performativities and fabrications in the education economy: Towards the performative society?, *Australian Educational Researcher*, 27(sb2):1–23.
Bourdieu, P. (1977) *Outline of a Theory of Practice*, translated by Richard Nice. Cambridge: Cambridge University Press.
Bourdieu, P. (1984) *Homo Academicus*, translated by Peter Collier. Stanford: Stanford University Press.
Bourdieu, P. (1992) The purpose of reflexive sociology, in P. Bourdieu and L. Wacquant, *An Invitation to Reflexive Sociology*. Chicago: University of Chicago Press.
Bourdieu, P. and Wacquant, L. (1992) *An Invitation to Reflexive Sociology*. Chicago: University of Chicago Press
Coady, T. (ed.) (2000) *Why Universities Matter: A Conversation about Values, Means and Directions*. St Leonards, NSW: Allen and Unwin.
Foucault, M. (1991) Governmentality, in G. Burchell, C. Gordon and P. Miller (eds) *The Foucault Effect: Studies in Governmentality*. Chicago: University of Chicago Press.
Levin, B. (1998) An epidemic of education policy: (What) can we learn from each other?, *Comparative Education*, 34(2):131–42.
Lyotard, J.F. (1984) *The Postmodern Condition: A Report on Knowledge*. Minneapolis: University of Minnesota Press.
Marginson, S. and Considine, M. (2000) *The Enterprise University: Power, Governance and Reinvention in Australia*. Cambridge: Cambridge University Press.
Nelson, B. (2002) *Higher Education at the Crossroads: An overview paper*. Canberra: Department of Science and Training.
Pusey, M. (1992) *Economic Rationalism in Canberra: A Nation-building State Changes its Mind*. Cambridge, NY: Cambridge University Press.
Senate Employment, Workplace Relations, Small Business and Education References Committee (2001) *Universities in Crisis: Report of the inquiry into the capacity of public universities to meet Australia's higher education needs*. Canberra: Commonwealth of Australia.
Slaughter, S. and Leslie, L. (1997) *Academic Capitalism: Politics, Policies, and the Entrepreneurial University*. Baltimore: Johns Hopkins University Press.
Taylor, S., Rizvi, F., Lingard, R. and Henry, M. (1997) *Education Policy and the Politics of Change*. London: Routledge.
University of South Australia (2002) *Submission to the 'Higher Education at the Crossroads' Ministerial Discussion Paper*

http://www.dest.gov.au/crossroads/submissions/pdf/109_2.pdf

Zipin, L. (1999) Simplistic fictions in Australian higher education policy debates: A Bourdieuian analysis of complex power struggles, *Discourse: Studies in the Cultural Politics of Education*, 20(1):21–39.

2
Reclaiming Academic Research Work from Regulation and Relegation[1]

Lisa Lucas

Introduction

> Demoralisation was not therefore confined to those who found themselves on the wrong side of the research active-inactive divide, nor to low-rated departments. It was general to a substantial number of academics in... universities who were conscious of the material and symbolic violence done to the profession, their discipline and themselves but who lacked the opportunity or the will to resist.
> On the contrary, the RAE is such an effective mechanism of management control precisely because it does not need to replace one type of discourse with another. In co-opting peer review for managerial ends, the RAE offers individuals the possibility of securing material and symbolic rewards without ostensible violence to the traditional value systems which constitute academic identity.
>
> (Harley and Lowe 1998: 22)

> but also, and above all, the melancholy consequences of disapprobation.
>
> (Halsey 1995: 268)

Much of the current literature on the academic profession within the UK is embedded in the discourse of 'change' and 'crisis' (Parker and Jary 1994; Halsey 1995; Miller 1995; Trowler 1998). Successive government policies, including severe budget cuts to universities, rapid growth in student numbers, the ending of the binary divide, and the imposition of 'quality' assurance measures and, significantly for this chapter, the introduction of the Research Assessment Exercise (RAE), have been analysed in relation to the impact on life and work within higher education institutions (Jenkins 1995; Cuthbert 1996; McNay 1997a, 1997b; Henkel 2000).

Within all of this literature is a lament for a past that has been lost and the changed 'structure of feeling' of academia (Sidaway 1997). Managerialism, it is argued by some, has eroded the collegial community, weakened professional control structures and changed the working conditions of academics at the same time as fundamentally altering the subjective experience of their work and the meanings attached to it (Parker and Jary 1994).

The RAE is a mechanism that is used to evaluate research work in all university departments in the UK and to fund university research activity on the basis of the 'quality' of the work as measured by the RAE. Evaluation is done by a process of peer review whereby research outputs are judged for their standing of national and international 'quality' and awarded corresponding grades from 1 to 5*. After its introduction in 1986, the RAE has been modified during each of its five yearly cycles and is currently undergoing further change in light of the Roberts Report (2003),[2] which suggests how the 2007 one may be conducted. The process of research assessment and evaluation is not unique to the UK but can be found in other national contexts. Hong Kong has a similar RAE to that of the UK, and Australia has a similar process of assessment, although it is based on the analysis of quantitative outputs. New Zealand is just in the process of introducing new means of funding and evaluating research. The funding of research is linked directly to the evaluation of research in Hong Kong and Australia; however, in other systems such as Holland there is no direct link between the processes of evaluation and the processes of funding.[3] Debates occurring in the UK, therefore, over the working of the RAE have relevance for many other national systems of higher education.

This chapter is concerned with exploring the material and symbolic value within academic life, as referred to in the opening quotes. The analysis seeks to understand the impact of the RAE on specific forms of material and symbolic *capital* (Bourdieu 1988) relevant to academics. The chapter uses data from a study of academics in two different UK universities. Their experiences of the 1996 RAE are used to illustrate the theoretical argument being made. There is an examination of the ways in which these forms of capital shape the means by which academic research work is managed and regulated. The issues of how these forms of symbolic capital serve to differentiate academic research work and academic staff is also considered. In terms of providing a comprehensive sociological study of higher education institutions, *Homo Academicus* (Bourdieu 1988) is a key text and the collective works of Bourdieu provide a useful framework and set of 'thinking tools' to help analyse the current system of higher education and the importance of the RAE within the UK context.

Understanding Bourdieu's sociology of higher education

Bourdieu has developed a number of 'thinking tools' to enable an analysis of particular social situations. These include the notions of 'field' and 'habitus' and the concepts of *symbolic* capital, namely *material, cultural* and *social* capital. He also uses the idea of the 'game' in particular social fields and the importance of the concept of 'illusio' in ensuring individual involvement in these social games. All of these central concepts will be briefly illustrated and discussed.

Bourdieu's development of the concepts of 'field' and 'habitus' stem from his argument that agents and the social world (structure and agency) are 'two dimensions of the social' (Calhoun et al. 1993), they are simultaneously constructed. 'Social agents are incorporated bodies who possess, indeed, are possessed by structural, generative schemes which operate by orientating social practice' (Grenfell and James 1998: 12).

'Habitus' is understood as the incorporation or internalization of social structures as lived experience. These structures determine the conditions of possibility of social action, but these processes are intertwined such that 'agents are socially determined to the extent that they determine themselves' (Bourdieu 1989). The knowing subject is a precondition to the structuring of social action. Agents are not automatons responding to the laws of social structure but neither do they exist in a state of voluntarism or rationally calculated choices and decisions according to rational action theory (RAT). They are instead following a social logic, which propels them towards possible social destinies already inscribed in their historical and cultural background and into which they insert themselves (Bourdieu 1998).

Bourdieu is concerned to ensure that this process is not interpreted as subjects following social rules or their action being determined by a fixed social mechanism. The process is more dynamic and there are multiple configurations of possible social action. The social background of an individual implies a particular social trajectory of possible futures. However, these are in no way inscribed. *There is everything to play for.*

The structural features of the social world are organized by 'fields' (Bourdieu 1993). A central feature of the understanding of a field is that it must be analysed 'relationally'. For Bourdieu, therefore, the 'real is relational' but this does not refer to relations between agents, as in intersubjectivity, but as 'objective relations' between positions in a field (Bourdieu and Wacquant 1992: 97).

The key to the functioning of a particular field, or the main 'invariant' feature, is that it is a site of struggle. The struggle is over the boundaries and who is legitimated to enter. The precise terms of the struggle, however, must be determined by an empirical study of each particular field. The invariants can be summarized as struggles and strategies to be used and interests and profits which are yielded. Bourdieu wishes to distance his form of analysis of fields and interests from the traditional, neo-classical interpretation of interest as economic interest and investment and profit as monetary or material profit. Bourdieu uses these terms to signify the particular 'social' profits obtained by engaging in the struggles within particular fields. He argues that 'the specifically social magic of institution can constitute almost anything as an interest' (Bourdieu 1993). Bourdieu summarizes the interrelationship between field and habitus as follows:

> Investment is the disposition to act that is generated in the relationship between a space defined by a game offering certain prizes or stakes (what I call a field) and a system of dispositions attuned to that game (what I call a habitus) – the 'feel' for the game and the stakes, which implies both the inclination and the capacity to play that game, to take an interest in the game, to be taken up, taken in by the game.
> (Bourdieu 1993: 18)

The relationship between habitus and field is not one of a 'cynical calculation' to gain the maximum social profit from any field but more of an unconscious following of the 'natural bent' of the habitus. The process, or game, is not one of conscious rationalization but more one of unconscious involvement and psychological and emotional investment of energy or 'libido'. Misunderstanding of the terminology used by Bourdieu has caused the idea of investment and interest to be interpreted as a 'conscious project' or rational calculation. He argues, however, that it 'is not true to say that everything that people do or say is aimed at maximising their social profit; but one may say that they do it to perpetuate or to augment their social being' (Bourdieu 1995).

The struggle to augment one's social being, for Bourdieu, is a struggle for *symbolic* life and death. In each social field, agents struggle to accumulate forms of 'symbolic capital'. The maximizing of social profit, therefore, is a maximizing of the symbolic capital, which is operable within any given social field. Symbolic capital is the social product of the field. The different forms of capital are 'social', 'cultural' and 'economic'. A crude distinction of each would be that 'social' capital refers primarily to the network of social relations one has, or of 'more or less institutionalised relationships of mutual acquaintance and recognition' (Bourdieu 1986). 'Economic' capital refers to the material wealth. 'Cultural' capital is identified as a complex array of educational qualifications and forms of cultural differentiation in terms of language and general proximity to and knowledge of cultural institutions. However, cultural capital cannot simply be thought of as cultural 'objects' to be acquired or possessed.

Agents are positioned within a social field by virtue of their total accumulation of symbolic capital, which can be gained from any combination of economic, cultural and social capital. Power within a field is ultimately gained by the possession of symbolic capital. The site of struggle within fields, however, is not just over possession of capital but over the very definition of what capital is at stake and what is valued. In this sense, therefore, capital is arbitrary and the determination of what capital is valued is constantly being defined and redefined. The invariant of a field is that it is a site of struggle; the variants of a field are what need to be analysed in order to understand its operation. Thus, the variants of forms of capital are different across and within fields, at different times. Analysis of social fields is a process of understanding the different forms of capital and how they are valued within it. Fields are structured by the differential possession of forms of capital but individuals are also motivated to increase their possession of this capital. There is, therefore, a dynamic process of a reproduction of social fields but also a motivational force either to increase one's capital or struggle to re-determine the conditions of value placed on certain forms of capital. It is these processes which analysis of social fields seeks to understand. Forms of capital are also interchangeable with, for example, economic capital enabling accumulation of cultural capital and vice versa.

In his book *Homo Academicus*, Bourdieu (1988) identifies two main forms of hierarchical structure within the academic field, namely *academic* and *scientific* (or research) capital, academic capital being the primary involvement of reproduction within the system and scientific capital relating to research activities and the production of knowledge. There is a hierarchical ordering of these activities, according to Bourdieu, with academic power as less valued than the research activities of scientists:

> It is understandable that academic power is so often independent of specifically scientific capital and the recognition it attracts. As a temporal power in a world which is neither actually nor statutorily destined for that sort of power, it always tends to appear, perhaps even in the eyes of its most confident possessors, as a substitute, or a consolation prize. We can understand too the profound ambivalence of the academics who devote themselves to administration towards those who devote themselves, successfully to research – especially in a system where institutional loyalty is weak and largely unrewarded.
> (Bourdieu 1988: 99)

The key to the positioning of academics within these hierarchical divisions of academic labour is the amount of time invested in the particular activities and means of production which afford an accumulation of the specific capital operative within each division (Bourdieu 1998).

The academic field is highly differentiated according to type of institution or faculty, discipline and sub-specialism, age, gender and the status of academic staff. Academics can be located according to their position within the different hierarchies and their possession of the different types of capital. All of these criteria determine their value or the extent to which their symbolic capital has power or is recognized within the academic field. The struggle to determine the classifications within the hierarchies, the construction of 'value' by which judgement is made, is the struggle for 'symbolic life and death' (Bourdieu 1988) of agents in the academic field.

The trajectory of agents within the academic field is principally determined by what could be termed the 'academic habitus', the 'feel for the game' which they have. This refers to their 'practical sense' of the principle of hierarchization discussed above and their attempts to maximize their *symbolic profits* by accumulating the necessary capital. It must be re-emphasized that these strategies are intended to maximize the specific symbolic or social profits within the academic field and cannot be equated with an economic reductionism. Furthermore, Bourdieu is concerned to emphasize that these strategies or practices should not be interpreted as a cynical calculation of ends and means. The strategies are more an unconscious attempt to realize one's potential in the academic field than a form of rational choice or conscious decision-making.

Critical to the correspondence between habitus and practice is the concept of 'illusio'. The idea is that agents involved in the 'game' within a social field do not perceive it as a game; they believe in it, they take it seriously. The strategies and systems of values within a field may appear illusory to anyone outside of the field, for example the philosophy field and its concerns may seem alien to the economist. However, the participants of the field have an intense involvement with the rules of the game. It is an investment in a social field that Bourdieu argues could equally be described as a form of 'libido'. It exists as a means of social expression and form of legitimization for the players involved, indeed, it is their struggle to 'augment their social being' in an expression through this game which is both socially instituted (objective/field) and is incorporated in their bodily self (subjective/habitus). Bourdieu describes it thus:

> What is experienced as obvious in *illusio* appears as an illusion to those who do not participate in the obviousness because they do not participate in the game ... Agents well-adjusted to the game are possessed by the game and doubtless all the more so the better they master it. For example, one of the privileges associated with the fact of being born in the game is that one can avoid cynicism since one has a feel for the game; like a good tennis player, one positions oneself not where the ball is but where it will be; one invests oneself not where the profit is, but where it will be.
>
> (Bourdieu 1998: 79)

For Bourdieu's theory of practice, therefore, agents have strategic intentions but these are rarely experienced as conscious intentions. Agents have a 'practical sense' of the game, they do not consciously manoeuvre and calculate their aims. When they are involved in a social field or game, they are 'possessed by the ends' of that field and 'they may be ready to die for those ends' (Bourdieu 1998).

This chapter is concerned with the operation of 'symbolic' capital, particularly 'research' capital in academic life and the influence that the RAE has had on the symbolic significance of this form of capital. It could be argued, that the 'game' of the *discipline* or of *academia* has been overshadowed or interpenetrated by the 'game' of the RAE and particularly the 'game' of *research submission*. The variety of ways in which the RAE has served as a tool to manage and regulate academic research work and also the means by which academic staff are relegated depending on the degree of their conformity to the 'rules' of research submission will be analysed.

The 'game' of RAE submission: 'regulating' research work

> We play the game. We try and maximize the benefit to the department by the rules set on us. At least I do. And there are people in the department who say that it is absolutely silly. And I am afraid I think, as head of department the job is to maximize the resource in the department and to try and get it running well. You know, so you make decisions based upon these things. You learn the rules and you work to them, I am afraid. I am a shamed player of that game. If the government is going to play games with us and say this is the right work, I respond, and eh whether I approve or not is irrelevant.
>
> (Professor Meggitt, ex-Head of Department, Science, GCU)

The departments under discussion in this chapter are a science department in a pre-1992 university, which I have called Golden County University (GCU) and a science department in a post-1992 university, which I have called Royal County University (RCU).[4] These universities were chosen because they provide a number of contrasts in terms of organization and structure of the university, research and teaching missions and composition of students and staff.

Taking the example of the formation of research policy and specifically the submission of the RAE gives an insight into one aspect of the authority structures and decision-making processes within these departments. At GCU, Professor Meggitt took a leading role in the RAE submission and policy formation and was described by one member of staff as being 'obsessed' with getting a high rating for the department in the RAE. Professor Meggitt himself maintains that he had made a 'personal declaration' to increase the research rating of the department after becoming head.

He relates the events of the RAE submission and the decisions surrounding it almost as a personal crusade with him steering a steady course of decision making, faced with disagreements both from the university research committee and the science department research committee. He took the final decision on the RAE submission, believing that 'it was my responsibility to present it and I was going to take the flack and so I did it the way I thought I should'. He had calculated that the income for the department would be six times greater if the department increased their rating in the 1996 RAE. For this reason, Professor Meggitt felt justified in taking what he believed to be the best decisions for the department in order to maximize this income. This could only be done at the cost of submitting a smaller number of staff, thereby achieving a lower rating on the number of staff submitted but a higher overall rating on the 'quality' of the research work in terms of 'international' excellence. He believed that having a smaller number of staff submitted was of lesser significance than the overall rating, which was considered to be the most important goal. Professor Meggitt explains the disagreements over this decision in the following way:

Professor Meggitt: And so we ended up missing a total of seven people off the submission out of 70 so we submitted 63 instead of 70 because in our judgement that gave us the best overall return ... we viewed it as a game where a) it was essential to become a higher rating and b) it was essential within that to maximize income. And we viewed it as exactly that and the strategy was to achieve those aims and we viewed that as more important than the university or the Vice-Chancellor's desire to have it as a full department representation. Keep asking ...

Interviewer: So you just went ahead in terms of the ... ?

Professor Meggitt: Well we said we were going to. I sent a letter to the university research committee saying that we were intending to do that and they said you shouldn't and we said we should. And another department ended up following our example. And I think the result shows that we were quite right because we will be known as a (highly) rated department ... (and income was increased). So for all reasons it was the right strategy. But that was one that was made basically by me as head of department, I would have done that, eh I didn't have total support in the department. A lot of people felt that is was really bad news for the seven missed off and we had to deal with that but it seemed to me that that was the right strategy.

(Professor Meggitt, HoD, Science, GCU)

As Professor Meggitt acknowledged, however, not all staff were in agreement with the decisions that had been taken. Those members of staff who had not been put forward in the RAE were unhappy with the outcome and there were others who supported their objections. Dr Dray expressed his dismay at the decisions taken and of one particular colleague being excluded from the submission:

There was some general consultation with the department in so far as the head of the department produced a paper about the RAE with the Chair of the research committee and they tried to explain some of the decisions that they were taking em and why they were taken and in particular why some members of staff were not going to be in the RAE. They weren't named of course but I think it finished that six members of staff were not on the RAE. I was not involved in the decisions. When I heard who one of the members of staff was I was frankly outraged because this person is a good member of staff who was producing good publications and so on and who got good grant income and he was left off. And it turned out that he was left off because it just so happened in that particular four year period of the exercise he had not spoken at an international conference and the strategic decision had been taken that the only people to go on the RAE would be those who had spoken at an international conference. The decision was basically we will show that everybody at GCU can be represented as being international and whether the committee bought that or not is another matter. Em but certainly nobody was going to go into the RAE unless they could be represented as being of international standard, good national wasn't considered enough. So I wrote to the head of department to say that I thought this was quite outrageous and actually went to see the head of department and did my best to get that decision reversed but was unsuccessful.

(Dr Dray, Scientist, GCU)

All the evidence from the accounts of members of staff interviewed in the department indicates that the head of department took a 'strong' managerial role in the preparation and submission of the RAE. In terms of the general research policies and direction of research funds within the department, the research committee carries this out. Unlike the subject committee, which admits all members of staff, the research committee is made up of only seven members of staff, the 'research stars' of the department as they were referred to by one member of staff. The seven members of staff are mainly senior members of staff and are all successful researchers. Members include the head of department, five professors and one lecturer. This form of decision-making involves only a minority of staff is referred to as 'restricted collegiality' (Bush 1998).

In terms of the organization of research activities, there is some support for the idea that managerialism has increased within university departments (Parker and Jary 1994; Harley and Lowe 1998). But managerial practices and the effects of this are not uniformly felt but vary across administrative and committee structures and practices within departments and across different departments and disciplines as well as across institutions. This is evident in the way that different forms of organizational features predominate in different ways within this science department such that, for example, greater 'collegiality' is evident in decision-making over teaching than over research.

The organizational and ideational structures within university departments are not primarily to be understood in relation to the battle between collegiality and managerialism but within the wider principles of differentiation within academic and research work and the means by which symbolic *capital* (value) is generated. This is evidenced by Professor Meggitt's perception of what would be valued most by the RAE panel. The extent of 'international' reputations of staff in the department is an important form of differentiation. The area of research is another important principle of differentiation. An example of this was given by the head of department of science at RCU.

> But this (research area) is not looked upon very highly in terms of the high academic biological scientists who were sitting on the (RAE) panel ... And in general we thought that if you were a really top rate molecular scientist, for example, which a lot of the panel members were, they would not look particularly favourably on this (research area). So although I take that particular person who was slightly upset

at not being included (in the RAE submission), I think we probably made the right decision given the nature of the panel.

(Professor Laing, HoD, Science, RCU)

The object of the game therefore is to maximize the research grading of the department. But the ability to score highly in this game is dependent on the 'feel for the game' based on long-established principles of differentiation and evaluation within the discipline (and sub-specialisms) and within the academic system more generally. This works through the system at all levels from the activities and decisions of each individual academic to the strategies of institutional leaders. Struggles to define and classify what is valued within academic life in terms of research work are made by all, with success being dependent on one's positioning within the academic field.

There was much evidence to suggest that the members of this science department perceived that their research work was becoming more regulated in terms of conforming to the areas of research that were judged more highly than others, with some members of staff saying that they had moved into new research areas in order to bolster the prestige of their research. The situation was much less extreme than that presented by Slaughter and Leslie (1999) at one university in the US where 'the university went so far as to specify the journals in which faculty should publish and the areas of research in which they should concentrate' (1999: 225).

There have been many pro-RAE voices that have pointed to the better management of research activity in UK universities and there is plenty of evidence to support this, including the ever-increasing RAE scores with more departments achieving a 5 score (although increasing scores may signify only the increased ability to 'play the game'). But these managerial practices also serve to substantially regulate academic research work – demanding conformity to the rules afforded greater success in RAE submissions. Regulation of academic research work was achieved in a number of ways by setting down expectations in terms of quality of research outcomes, including highly regarded areas of research, 'types' of publications and award of research funding. These expectations were implicitly and also explicitly stated. Failure to conform to the expectations set by the rules of research submission could result in the relegation and possible exclusion of academic staff and their loss of being awarded the new forms of research 'capital', namely the title of being considered 'research active' or of engaging in research of 'national' or 'international' importance.

Principles of differentiation: 'relegating' academic staff

The metaphor of football divisions is often used by commentators on the RAE (Tight 2000) to compare with divisions within higher education and so the language of 'relegation' would seem appropriate here. Relegation can mean a threat to demote someone to a lower order or position of less importance and it can refer to a total exclusion of the person, their banishment or order into exile.[5] In terms of the classification of academic staff, the RAE has served to 'relegate' members of staff within university departments in each of these forms.

The policy of GCU is to have all staff involved in research and this means that they should be research active in a way that meets the criteria set by the RAE. Similarly, all staff except those deemed 'research only' are involved in teaching and administration. The consensus around the department and an approximation given by the head of department is that those staff employed to do teaching and research should spend 40 per cent of their time on teaching, 40 per cent on research and 20 per cent on administration. Other members of staff are expected to do 100 per cent research.

Two things are important here: first, the *economy of time* spent by those staff in the department who are employed to teach and particularly those members of staff occupying key positions within the department in the organization of teaching activities; and second, the forms of specific *academic* capital and *research* capital which members of staff possess.

Some of the members of staff interviewed expressed a concern that a lot of their time was taken up by teaching and administrative duties. This was especially apparent for members of staff who have a central administrative role within the department. For example, Dr Merrygold held an important administrative position, which is very time-consuming and as he claims would take up substantially more than the stated 20 per cent administration time. Other members of staff like Dr Sinclair, who also holds an important administrative role within the department, illustrate how the time spent on administrative tasks is not only extensive but also difficult to control.

The overwhelming perception of both of these members of staff is that the teaching and administration work that they carry out is undervalued when compared to the value and prestige attached to research work (Hannan and Silver 2000). Bourdieu (1988) argues that the roles associated with the reproduction of the academic system – teaching and administration associated with teaching – produces important forms of *academic* capital such as the examples given here of positions of importance in executive committee meetings for teaching across the university. However, these forms of academic power are seen as secondary to that of research. As Dr Sinclair argues:

> ... within a department it actually causes a lot of alienation of people who spend a lot of time, to take a case in point, as (an important role in) administrative work and have a heavy teaching load. They feel they are being squeezed out of the system when they are actually contributing to the department probably more than a number of people who are doing their own thing. And that did actually cause a lot of ill feeling and I am not just speaking for myself (but) other people.
> (Dr Sinclair, Scientist, GCU)

Those members of staff, therefore, who believe that they have extra teaching and administrative responsibilities have correspondingly less time to spend on research activities.

Members of staff such as Dr Martin, Dr Sinclair, Dr Eccles and Dr Merrygold are active researchers although they spend much less time on research than they do on teaching and administration. For the purposes of the RAE, however, they were not put forward in the submission and thus were labelled as being 'research inactive'. To this end they are not classified as researchers within the department. The extent to which the teaching and administrative duties carried out by these staff is perceived to be undervalued goes alongside the lack of value placed on their research activities, which are not judged adequate for RAE purposes. This classification of members of staff as research inactive is deeply felt:

> People who are about to be declared research inactive find this, well most of them, some of them cope with it very well, but some of them find it exceedingly stressful because they regarded it as a recognition or been assigned as being inadequate in some way. And academics are used to having their esteem partly built on their achievements doing research and to be suddenly told that you are not valued is extremely damaging to them.
>
> (Dr Martin, Scientist, GCU)

Being put forward for submission in the RAE, therefore, becomes a critical form of 'symbolic' capital in academic life and not to be submitted can be experienced as 'relegation' to an inferior academic role. Non-submission can occur with an academic who has more 'academic' capital and less 'research' capital but can also occur if the 'research' capital that an individual has is deemed not suitable for RAE purposes as the following case study shows.

Case study: Dr Merrygold (GCU)

During the period of the RAE Dr Merrygold held an important administrative role in the department and he managed to maintain his teaching and research activity. However, despite his successful research record, which included funding from a multitude of sources and a list of publications, he was not included in the RAE submission. Dr Merrygold was unhappy about this decision and he is uncertain about how his work is being judged or whether he will merit future inclusion in the RAE. He was informed that his profile was not perceived to be *international*.

Dr Merrygold has accumulated similar forms of research capital to the other members of staff in the department. He is involved both in the laboratory work (although this is only possible in vacation time) and the presentation and development of his research work, including applying for research funding. The differences between him and staff classified as 'research active' were that Dr Merrygold held an administrative post, a role which took up more than the nominated 20 per cent of his time. For this reason, he had less time to spend on research. Furthermore, this responsibility meant a close involvement with departmental and institutional matters. During the period prior to the 1996 RAE, therefore, he did not have research links with universities from other nations nor had he travelled to international conferences. He does not believe that the possibility of international links is necessarily a constant in research work since it depends on what is appropriate for the development of research in a particular area:

> There are certainly some research projects where there are particular groups and there are examples in this department, I think people you have probably talked to, where there are particular people related to them in different countries and it is very sensible. But there is no point in doing it just for the sake of being able to say you are doing it, it is pointless.
>
> (Dr Merrygold, Scientist, GCU)

The reason for the non-inclusion of Dr Merrygold was that he did not appear to have an *international* reputation in research. The strategy of the department was to achieve a high rating in the RAE and therefore had to have a majority of staff of international acclaim. However, the precise meaning of what 'international reputation' means is arbitrary and struggles over the definition of this important term remain. Dr Merrygold resists the possibility of re-orienting his practices to include more overseas research work but for this he is excluded from the classification of being 'research active'; something which he feels undermines the value of his work.

The evidence presented from the scientists at GCU is that time spent on administrative and teaching activities ensures that less time can be devoted to research. Furthermore, the undertaking of teaching and administrative roles within the department is perceived to be of lesser value than participation in research activities. The issues at stake, therefore, are first, the struggle for classification as a research active member of staff, which these academics are attempting to achieve. Second, the time spent on the different activities of research, administration and teaching and the extent to which time spent accumulating academic capital necessitates correspondingly less time accumulating research capital. Third, whether forms of academic capital constitute a form of power and a principle of positive evaluation.

It can be argued, therefore, that academic capital is no longer a 'rival principle of hierarchization' because the symbolic value of these forms of capital are being diminished in the face of the symbolic (and material) value of research capital. Some academics, however, struggle to retain the value of work, which serves to reproduce the academic system. Alongside this is the struggle for inclusion and recognition for research work that is also becoming increasingly more regulated by more narrow classification of what research work 'counts' in the RAE.

Conclusions: reclaiming research work?

In is not intended for this chapter to be placed alongside the chorus of nostalgic commentators who lament the 'golden age' of university life, although there can be no denying the material differences in the current higher education system from that of 30 years ago and the extent to which the drive for more (external) funding now dominates much of the direction of academic energy and time (Slaughter and Leslie 1999; Harvie 2000) than was previously the case. The main focus of this chapter was to explore the idea that there has been a 'symbolic' as well as 'material' violence (Harley and Lowe 1998) done to academics and the work that they do. The main aim was to explore the 'symbolic' struggles for recognition in academic life engaged in by research and teaching staff in universities. This chapter has looked at one aspect of the RAE process in the UK, the decision about who to include or exclude in departmental submissions for that exercise, in order to explore the significance of this for the sense of status and self-worth felt by those members of staff labelled as 'research active' and those labelled as 'non-research active'.

The importance of research activity within departments at an institutional and department level is indisputably high. Organization of research activity and the amount of effort and forward planning given to the RAE submission give testimony to this. Institutions and departments are concerned to raise their symbolic capital in the form of a high RAE rating since significant financial and reputational rewards can be gained. A multitude of strategies and forward planning of research activity both at an institutional and departmental level has been instigated within universities.

Research has usually held predominance over teaching in terms of status within academic life. *Homo Academicus* (Bourdieu 1988), although published in the 1980s, was written about higher education in the 1960s in France, and Bourdieu clearly represented the hierarchy of research and teaching with research placed at the top. What is of interest in the current UK context is the extent to which the system of funding and evaluation of research in the form of the RAE has become the dominant 'game' within academic life, which directs the investment of energy and passion.

The general feel for the research 'game' in any discipline, however, is not regulated solely by the RAE. Many of the interviewees discussed the multiple audience (and therefore evaluators) for their work. Dr Lester, a Research Fellow who was funded by an external agency, was caught between the demands of the department and those of his funders. Other members of staff struggled to have their research recognized and valued, and expressed confusion over the principles governing that evaluation. This was particularly the case for Dr Merrygold. The 'practical sense' and 'feel for the game' of many of these scientists, therefore, is constantly in flux and the RAE has had a profound effect on the principles of evaluation of their research work.

One of the main issues raised in this paper is whether academics are becoming increasingly more polarized between those classified as research active and those classified as non-research active. And whether the struggle for classification of being research active (based on RAE criteria) is changing the practices of scientists and subsequently the 'practical sense' and 'feel for the game' of these members of staff. Evidence from the small sample of scientists at GCU presented here suggests that this is the case. What is defined as 'excellent' becomes increasingly more to depend on the rules of the 'game' of the RAE. As Michael Peters argues in Chapter 4, following Readings (1996), the 'universities have been reduced to a technical ideal of performance' within a contemporary discourse of 'excellence', and further that this idea of 'excellence' is meaningless. However, the meaning of these terms is 'arbitrary' (Bourdieu 1993) and rather then accept the logic of the RAE 'game', academics may yet struggle to constantly re-define the means by which their work is defined and evaluated.

Notes

[1] The research presented in this chapter provides selected examples from a larger research study, which will be published as Lucas, L. (forthcoming) *The Research Game in Academic Life,* Maidenhead: SRHE/Open University Press.

[2] Full details of the RAE and the proposals of the Roberts Report can be found at the website for the Higher Education Funding Council for England (HEFCE) at www.hefce.ac.uk and further detailed information can be accessed at the Higher Education and Research Opportunities in the UK (HERO website) at www.hero.ac.uk.

[3] International comparison of research funding and evaluation can be found in Millar, J. and Senker, J. (2000) International approaches to research policy and funding: university research policy in different national contexts, Final Report prepared for the Higher Education Funding Council for England (HEFCE).

[4] For reasons of confidentiality pseudonyms have been used in all instances referring to institutions and individual academics. Descriptions of departments and individuals have been kept to a minimum and in some cases information has been changed so as to protect the anonymity of departments and individuals involved.

[5] *Collins Concise Dictionary* (1995) 3rd edn. Glasgow: HarperCollins.

References

Bourdieu, P. (1986)The forms of capital, in J.G. Richardson (ed.) *Handbook of Theory and Research for the Sociology of Education.* New York: Greenwood Press.
Bourdieu, P. (1988) *Homo Academicus,* translated by P. Collier. Cambridge: Polity Press.

Bourdieu, P. (1989) For a socio-analysis of intellectuals: on *Homo Academicus*, *Berkeley Journal of Sociology*, 34:1–29.
Bourdieu, P. and Wacquant, L. (1992) *An Invitation to Reflexive Sociology*. Cambridge: Polity Press.
Bourdieu, P. (1993) *Sociology in Question*, translated by R. Nice. London: Sage.
Bourdieu, P. (1995) Concluding remarks: for a sociogenetic understanding of intellectual works, in C. Calhoun, E. Lipuma and M. Postone (eds) *Bourdieu: Critical Perspectives*. Cambridge: Polity Press.
Bourdieu, P. (1998) *The Weight of the World: Social Suffering in Contemporary Society*. Cambridge: Polity Press.
Bush, T. (1998) Collegial models, in A. Harris, N. Bennett and M. Preedy (eds) *Organizational Effectiveness and Improvement in Education*. Buckingham: Open University Press.
Calhoun, C., Lipuma, E. and Postone, M. (1993) *Bourdieu: Critical Perspectives*. Cambridge: Polity Press.
Cuthbert, R. (ed.) (1996) *Working in Higher Education*. Buckingham: Open University Press.
Grenfell, M. and James, D. (1998) *Bourdieu and Education: Acts of Practical Theory*. London: Falmer Press.
Halsey, A.H. (1995) *Decline of Donnish Dominion: The British Academic Professions in the Twentieth Century*. Oxford: Oxford University Press.
Hannan, A. and Silver, H. (2000) *Innovating in Higher Education*. Buckingham: Open University Press.
Harley, S. and Lowe, P. (1998) *Academics Divided: The Research Assessment Exercise and the academic labour process*, Occasional Paper 48. Leicester: Leicester Business School.
Harvie, D. (2000) Alienation, class and enclosure in UK universities, *Capital and Class*, 71 (Summer): 103–32.
Henkel, M. (2000) *Academic Identities and Policy Change in Higher Education*. London: Jessica Kingsley.
Jenkins, Alan (1995) The Research Assessment Exercise, funding and teaching quality, *Quality Assurance in Education*, 3(2):4–12.
McNay, I. (1997a) *The Impact of the 1992 RAE on Institutional and Individual Behaviour in English Higher Education: the evidence from a research project*. Bristol: HEFCE.
McNay, I. (1997b) *The Impact of the 1992 Research Assessment Exercise on Individual and Institutional Behaviour in English Higher Education*. Chelmsford: Anglia Polytechnic University.
Parker, M. and Jary, D. (1994) *Academic Subjectivity and the New Managerialism*. Labour Process Conference, University of Aston, 23–25 March.
Sidaway, J.D. (1997) The production of British geography, *Trans. Inst. British Geography*, 22: 488–504.
Readings, B. (1996) *The University in Ruins*. Cambridge, MA: Harvard University Press.
Slaughter, S. and Leslie, L. (1999) *Academic Capitalism: Politics, Policies and the Entrepreneurial University*. Baltimore: The John Hopkins University Press.
Tight, M. (2000) Do league tables contribute to the development of a quality culture? Football and higher education compared, *Higher Education Quarterly*, 54(1):22–42.
Trowler, Paul (1998) *Academics Responding to Change: Higher Education Frameworks and Academic Cultures*. Buckingham: SRHE/Open University Press.

3

The Neo-Conservative Assault on the Undergraduate Curriculum

Steven Selden

> The final piece of evidence that the lunatics are running the academic asylum is now firmly in place. It was put there a few days ago by the National Alumni Forum, which, in a devastating report titled, 'The Shakespeare File: What English Majors Are Really Studying,' provided compelling proof that at most institutions that claim to set the standard for academic excellence, instruction in English literature that meets such a standard is difficult, albeit not quite impossible, to find.
> (Jonathan Yardley, 'For English Departments, a Major Change', *Washington Post*, 30 December 1996)

The readers of the summer 2002 issue of *Daedalus* found themselves witness to a colloquy between the Brookings Institution historian of education, Diane Ravitch, and a score of colleagues from across the academic landscape. Ravitch's point, agreed to by some and resisted by others, is that the US, and by implication the West, suffered from a crisis of 'cultural amnesia'. In their desire to create a 'multicultural person', textbook publishers' ignored the Western tradition, and created a 'contentless curriculum' (Ravitch 2002: 23). As a noted participant in the ongoing culture wars, Ravitch queries whether civilized life itself will be at risk if, 'we allow our culture to be highjacked by a handful of self-righteous pedagogical censors?' (2002: 23). While the piece chastises critics both left and right, the author's censure seems most strongly directed towards progressive educators. Those university academics concerned for epistemological and racial multiplicity, the reader is warned, threaten the traditional canon. An assault on their position must be undertaken.

In many ways, this jeremiad exemplifies the posture taken by a half-century of neo-conservative intellectual activists regarding the undergraduate curriculum. It offers strong support for programmes based in texts drawn from the Western literary and historical canon, and a decisive rejection of what Schrag (1988) has called the post-modern turn of mind. Ravitch's arguments are those of a principled conservative, and as such are in competition with principled positions of varying political stripes in the intellectual marketplace. But they are something more. They are part of a discourse, sponsored by a network of conservative foundations and their funded activist centres and intellectuals. This chapter focuses on this sponsored assault on the undergraduate curriculum by unpacking the connections between a set of conservative funders, their sponsored centres, and the products they create for public consumption. It does not identify any conspiracy, vast or right wing. All the data for this analysis have been drawn from the public domain.

In his provocative discussions of modern political life the Italian social critic Antonio Gramsci distinguished between 'wars of manoeuvre' and 'wars of position'. These wars, 'of manoeuvre occu[r] as parties face off against each other in elections and other confrontations' (Stefanic and Delgado 1996: ix). However, they are preceded by more substantive, 'wars of position', where ideological stances are developed and consolidated. This chapter thus also concentrates on 50 years of neo-conservative assaults in what Gramsci and others might have called, 'wars of [cultural] position' (Mayo 1999).

The conservative restoration and the curriculum

In *Educating the 'Right' Way* (2001), Michael Apple describes the conservative political, social and education restoration that has taken place internationally during the past 30 years. The restoration rests on the common ground held by four interest groups. These include neo-liberals who reckon that an unregulated market is the most efficient way to achieve just economic development; neo-conservatives who, like Professor Ravitch, argue for high cultural standards and traditional knowledge in the undergraduate curriculum; authoritarian populists who strive to bring God into all aspects of public and private life; and the new middle class, a group whose technical skills allow the management of any social construction. To use Apple's fructuous term, these interest groups have been 'sutured together' into a reasonably unified and powerful political discourse (Apple 2001). Its constituents have focused their attention on education at a number of levels.

Neo-liberal discourse and the academy

In *Universities and the Marketplace* (2003), Derek Bok offers an analysis of the impact of neo-liberalism on higher education. He worries that universities, in their zeal to make money, may compromise their core academic values. The discourse of the market now vies with the norms of critical scholarship;

programmes of Total Quality Management (TQM) compete with that of faculty governance; and the nomenclature of 'consumer' now vies with 'student' in university planning. While neo-liberalism is indeed a discourse, it would be unwise to separate it from the world of physical reality and of capital. Since this is in many ways a sponsored way of describing the world, it would be unwise to disconnect it from the interests of particular fractions of capital. We need to be clear that while capital does not directly construct discourse, it is often deeply and dialectically connected to its interests.

The conservative restoration in higher education: capital, culture and curriculum

Table 1.1 Capital, culture and curriculum

Category	Data Level	Contested Terrain	
Capital	Unregulated Markets	Increasing Equality	Decreasing Equality
Culture	Representation at Universities	Affirmative Action Admissions	Race-blind Admissions
Curriculum	Undergraduate Curriculum	Epistemological and Racial Multiplicity	Western Literary and Literary Historical Canon

Table 1.1 presents a frame within which to articulate the interrelationships between capital, culture and a particular type of coded discourse, the undergraduate curriculum.

By focusing on the first category, capital, one can map the tension between increasing or decreasing economic equality in the context of neo-liberal support for unregulated markets. As data from international comparisons suggest these policies often lead to increased inequality (Collins and Yeskel 2000).

At the diagram's second level, culture, a fierce battle is underway concerning the access of students of colour to institutions of higher learning. It is in the debates undertaken by neo-conservatives that one finds the most direct examples of the assault on higher education. In a series of cases recently heard before the US Supreme Court, the University of Michigan's affirmative admissions policies were challenged by a variety of well-funded conservative organizations (Cokorinos 2003). While General Motors and the US military strongly supported Michigan, there were four leading conservative organizations challenging those policies. Included here were the Center for Individual Rights (CIR), the American Civil Rights Institute

(ACRI), the Center for Equal Opportunity (CEO), and the National Association of Scholars (NAS) (Cokorinos 2003: 131). These organizations have been working diligently to change the public's conception of the meaning of fairness.

It is equally important to note that these are not marginal organizations. Their combined annual budgets are in excess of $4.5 million and their links to capital point in fascinating directions (Schmidt 2003: 3). Their support does *not* come in the form of $20.00 contributions from individual citizens. On the contrary, as Schmidt (2003: 3) points out, 'all four groups have derived a significant share of their financial support from many of the same conservative foundations'. These include, 'the John M. Olin Foundation, the Lynde and Harry Bradley Foundation, the Smith-Richardson Foundation, and the Sarah Scaife Foundation. To varying degrees, all four have worked with a network of other organizations, both conservative and libertarian to support their cause', and support for the major institutions is even more substantial. For progressive research centres, the field is hardly level. As Egen reports, 'the major think tanks in Washington':

> American Enterprise Institute, American Legislative Exchange Council, Cato Institute – have combined budgets of $45.9 million, while the progressive think tanks – the Centre for Policy Alternatives, the Institute for Policy Studies, the Centre for Budget and policy Priorities, and the Economic Policy Institute – have a combined budget of $10.2 million.
>
> (1996: 8)

The neo-conservative assault on the undergraduate curriculum

The neo-conservative assault has also focused on the higher education curriculum through a three-step production model for instituting conservative social change grant-making. Analyses of annual foundation IRS 990PF reports reveals the first step to be the *development of raw materials* through funding and creating of activist centres. The second step is to *convert these intellectual raw materials into products*. Having transformed conservatively oriented intellectual raw material into policy assets, the third and remaining step is to *market and distribute* these policies and programmes (Covington 1997: 5).

The intercollegiate studies institute

It is possible to trace conservative activist influences on the undergraduate curriculum in the USA to the person of William F. Buckley and the creation of the Intercollegiate Studies Institute (ISI) in the early 1950s. Buckley, ISI's first president in 1953, wrote of his distress at secular humanism's destructive influence at his alma mater in *God and Man at Yale* (1951). While secular humanism has now been eclipsed by anxieties regarding multiculturalism and postmodernism, ISI remains committed to, 'limited government, individual liberty, personal responsibility, free enterprise, and Judeo-Christian moral standards' (Intercollegiate Studies Institute 2003).

It would be unwise to dismiss a commitment to these principles too lightly. One reason for the success of conservative initiatives over the past three decades may be the public's perception that intellectuals on the political left do not generally support these values. Equally important is the realization that terms such as, 'Judeo-Christian moral standards', are open to various interpretations. Consider, for example, ISI's list of the '50 Worst Books of the Twentieth Century' (Intercollegiate Studies Institute 2003). One finds that John Rawls' classic in moral philosophy, *A Theory of Justice* (1971), is included. Rawls argued that citizens should make social policy as if behind a 'veil of ignorance'. Such a veil denies one insight into one's own future social location, and Rawls suggests that citizens unable to guarantee themselves a secure future should therefore protect society's least advantaged. In the absence of guarantees, one might end up among that number and be in need of such a safety net. Since Rawls' 'do unto others' policy seems to be an expression of Judeo-Christian values, what is the reader to make of Rawls' presence on ISI's 50 Worst?

Evidently, ISI's definition of Judeo-Christian morality focuses on individuals not communities, and on limited government regardless of the demands of social justice. It is a Hobbesian world for the arbiters of ISI's list of worst books. Interestingly enough, like the anti-inclusion activist centres recently attacking affirmative action, the Bradley, Olin, Earhart and Scaife Foundations also support ISI. Between 1985 and 2002 ISI received 143 grants totalling $13,324,100 million to influence America's best and brightest (Covington 1997; Media Transparency).

ISI attempts to influence more than the nation's most able. It also works to influence the undergraduate curriculum. In the mid-1990s, for example, after a hurried visit from ISI President T. Kenneth Cribb, Texas billionaire Lee Bass withdrew a promised $20 million grant to Yale for a programme in Western Civilization. Bass was moved to make the gift after hearing a speech in which Yale's Donald Kagen lamented liberalism's negative impact on New Haven community's academic standards. Nevertheless, the withdrawal of the grant became a *cause célèbre* for the American Right. Newt Gingrich argued that the money had to be returned because no one was willing to teach Western Civilization at Yale (1995), and *US News & World Report* detailed the story of 'How the West was Lost at Yale' (Leo 1995: 19).

But one may ask still whether 'multiculturalists' did in fact deny Western Civilization a place at Yale's high table? Whether 'tenured radicals' limited intellectual conversations only to topics judged as 'politically correct'? The answer is no. As is often the case in universities, the delay in assigning academic teaching staff to the Western Civilization offerings had more to do with budget than with ideology. '[Professor] Kagen urged a small, highly coherent program in which all of the students would take the same classes' (Wilson 1999: 433), but administrators, concerned by the costs of the cohort-programme, baulked. Further, while Professor Kagen wanted to hire assistant professors for the programme, administrators wanted to reassign faculty from other programmes. As Wilson reports (1999: 454), it was in this context that ISI President Cribb flew to Texas, 'to convince Bass to withdraw the $20 million donation'.Although Yale quickly agreed to implement the programme as Bass originally conceived it, Cribb persuaded Bass to demand the right to veto any faculty hired for the programme. Faced with a threat to academic freedom, Yale chose to return the money. Ironically, it was a conservative that blocked the programme's incorporation into the Yale community of scholars.

The Institute for Educational Affairs

The Institute for Educational Affairs (IEA) was created in 1978 with a grant of $100,000 from the Olin, Scaife, J.M. and Smith-Richardson foundations (Egen 1996: 13). Its leadership included the editor of the conservative journal, *The Public Interest*, Irving Kristol, and ex-Nixon Secretary of the Treasury and Olin Foundation President, William Simon. IEA was to 'seek out promising Ph.D. candidates and undergraduate leaders, help them to establish themselves through grants and fellowships and then promote them for jobs with activist organizations, research projects, student publications, federal agencies, or leading periodicals' (Egen 1996: 14). One approach to finding these students was through the financing of undergraduate journalism. The success of that initiative can be seen in the creation of the *Collegiate Network*, a national web of conservative undergraduate newspapers. Initially comprising of some 30 papers at schools including Harvard, Yale, Princeton and William and Mary, the *Network* has now grown into a system including some 70 schools (Intercollegiate Studies Institute 2003). Between 1985 and 1992, IEA received 31 grants totalling $1,677,293 (Media Transparency), and between 1985 and 2001 the *Network* itself received 33 grants from Olin, Scaife, Bradley and others totalling $3.5 million.

The Madison Center

By the mid-1980s, R. Randolph Richardson of the Smith-Richardson Foundation had argued that conservative change in the academy could be achieved through, 'high ground articulation'. Conservative activists could undertake, 'efforts to develop a critique of left-wing trends articulating the need for academic standards and intellectual rigor through new networks, student journalism projects, and the like' (Covington 1997: 11). In 1988 the

Madison Center was created to take just this high ground approach. The Center was spearheaded by two powerful voices of American neo-conservatism. The first was Professor Allen Bloom from the University of Chicago, author of *The Closing of the American Mind: How Higher Education has Failed Democracy and Impoverished the Souls of Today's Students* (1987). The second was William J. Bennett, an ex-Reagan administration Secretary of Education, Olin Fellow at the Hudson Institute and Distinguished Fellow for the Study of Cultural Policy at the Heritage Foundation. Under their leadership, the Center offered summer courses on the major works of Western Civilization to selected undergraduates. Between its founding in 1988 and 1991, the Center received pledges in excess of $1.5 million dollars from conservative foundations (Egen 1996: 14).

Madison Center for Educational Affairs

In 1990, the Madison Center merged with the Institute for Educational Affairs, taking on new life as the Madison Center for Educational Affairs (MCEA). With Charles Horner, ex-Reagan Administration Associate Director of the US Information Agency, as President, the *Collegiate Network* was transferred to its new organizational home. If the *Network* was designed to effect undergraduates after matriculation, MCEA also planned to influence high school students prior to their entering university. With the assistance of Olin Fellow Chester Finn, and the presidents of the Hudson Institute and the National Association of Scholars, MCEA assailed the undergraduate curriculum on the pages of *The Common Sense Guide to American Colleges* (Pyott 1991).

The *Guide* offered its readers reviews of some 62 well-respected US colleges and universities. Replacing academic critique with patriotism, and presaging the position taken a decade later by Finn in *September 11: What Our Children Need to Know* (Finn 2002), the *Guide* described its point of view as 'traditional', proudly noting that quality, excellence and achievement, 'are words we like' (Pyott 1991: 2). Going beyond calls for high standards and the Western canon it demanded patriotic fealty from the university. 'We have a generally high opinion of our civilization, our culture, and our country', the *Guide* opined, '[and] we think that one important measure of any college or university – though surely not the only measure – is whether it values them too' (Pyott 1991: 2).

But the *Guide* did not find American academics sharing these important values. It warned its readers by first assailing the university faculty. A 'left-of-center politically correct outlook now infects almost every aspect of higher education,' it explained, 'from investment decisions to hiring practices to the selection – and reception – of guest speakers' (Pyott 1991: 3). The assault continued in the reviews themselves. Institutions agreeable to the *Guide*'s orientation received high marks. For example, students choosing the University of Chicago can receive, 'perhaps the best education available today' but they must be careful to avoid particular departments and faculty (Pyott 1991: 83). 'Segments of the English and the humanities,' the *Guide* warns, 'have been co-opted by "tenured radicals" ', but, 'with some effort [the knowledgeable student] can still receive an excellent education even in these departments' (Pyott 1991: 81). Despite such cautions, the *Guide* is silent as to the location of these segments and the names of said faculty radicals, leaving students on their own when selecting courses other than the College's substantial required core. Thankfully, the reader learns that this core has resisted the winds of academic change. 'While certain books of questionable educational value have crept into parts of the Chicago canon,' the *Guide* laments, 'the incidents are relatively few. In any case, the curriculum is too baked in the humanistic tradition to crumble easily' (Pyott 1991: 81).

Not surprisingly, the prescribed curriculum of St. John's College of Annapolis and Santa Fe receives approbation. 'While many so-called liberal arts colleges are turning away from the traditional canon and toward the academic relativism that assigns equal value to all cultures,' the *Guide* counsels, 'St. John's continues to resist the winds of change and to hold aloft the standard of Western civilization' (Pyott 1991: 312). The *Guide's* sponsorship becomes important here. The Olin Foundation, which would provide financial support for a series of principled attacks on affirmative action in 2003, had also supported the *Guide's* production. It is not surprising then, that its position on affirmative action was also less than supportive.

In 1991, when comparing a putative academic world typified by racial admissions set-asides with the admissions process at St. John's, the *Guide* noted that St. John's 'has no racial or ethnic quotas, nor any affirmative action "goals," and minority students are, accordingly, the minority among applicants' (Pyott 1991: 316). While some might suggest that the few applications from minority students reflect less a lack of goals and more a sense of a hostile campus climate, the *Guide* demurs, noting that St. John's has no, 'ethnic or women's studies, no militant minority caucuses, [and no] speech codes ... ' (Pyott 1991: 316). For some observers, this continuing antagonism to the non-Western, to the critical, and the 'other' have always been central themes of the conservative restoration. Since the 1950s, those interested in developing these themes appear not to have wanted for financial support.

Of course, there are also institutions of higher education that do not meet the *Guide's* standards. This list includes Brown University, whose individualized course of study is reported by the *Guide* to be popular among its applicant pool. But its popularity, unlike that of Chicago, and St. John's, is based on a putative absence of academic rigour. 'Without doubt,' the reader is warned, '[Brown's] popularity among prospective undergraduates derive[s] from its ... policy of having a non-curriculum' (Pyott 1991: 47).

Vassar College also suffers in the eyes of the *Guide* in having no core curriculum and a minimal distribution requirement. The outcome, one learns, is that the, 'lazy or undisciplined can graduate knowing little about the liberal arts or the Western from which they sprang' (Pyott 1991: 367). The authors of the *Guide* use a technique often adopted by conservative critics of the academy. Without providing a thorough analysis of their syllabi, they nonetheless suggest that novel course titles imply a lack of academic rigour. Included among the unanalysed are, 'trendy courses' such as 'Women and the New Technology', 'Confrontations with Diversity', and 'Sex, Gender, and Society' (Pyott 1991: 367). Interestingly enough, the course description for the first of these offerings is included in the *Guide*, and it suggests a course both substantive and rigorous. This, however, does not dissuade the authors from describing Vassar as, 'a prime example of that growing American paradox: a college of the liberal arts that often fails to teach them' (Pyott 1991: 367).

This is only a paradox if one assigns the meaning of the liberal arts to something akin to the 'great books' curriculum; in such cases, any college not teaching that curriculum would be 'paradoxical'. However, if the curriculum is a means through which one is educated rather than the end of education itself, the paradox disappears. What we have here is less a paradox than competing empirical claims. On the one side stands the Madison Center for Educational Affairs and the claim that reading Cicero makes one a good citizen. On the other stands Vassar, claiming that the contents of 'Women and the New Technology' will do the same. Without evidence that great books make great democrats, the *Guide*'s critique of Vassar and Brown seems more an assault on a political and pedagogical orientation than on issues of academic substance. Nevertheless, between 1991 and 1995, MCEA received more than $1.6 million from the Bradley, Olin, Castle Rock, and Earhart foundations in support of this offensive (Media Transparency).

In 1996, MCEA ceased to function. The *Collegiate Network* was transferred to the Intercollegiate Studies Institute whose editors and writers would assist in producing *Choosing the Right College: The Whole Truth About America's Top 100 Schools*, a twenty-first-century incarnation of MCEA's *Common Sense Guide*. Among those penning dust cover accolades for *Choosing*, one finds William Kristol, editor of the conservative *Weekly Standard*; Roger Kimball, author of *Tenured Radicals: How Politics Corrupted Our Higher Education* (1990); Martin Anderson of the Hoover Institution; and Madison Center co-founder, William Bennett. In trying to understand the links between conservative foundations and sponsored scholarship, it is interesting to note that Kimball, Anderson and Bennett have been recipients of Olin largesse over the years. Between 1990 and 2000, for example, Olin targeted funding directly to Bennett through his associations with the Heritage Foundation, the Hudson Institute, and Empower America, Inc. In total, Bennett received over $900,000 from Olin, half of which came from the Hudson Institute (Media Transparency), described by one critic as a 'hard-right activist think tank that advocates the abolition of government-backed Social Security and an end to corporate income taxes' (Egen 1996: 9).

In the introduction to *Choosing the Right College*, Bennett warns of the dire state of US higher education due to, 'the widespread abandonment of academic standards and moral discipline, the politicisation of all aspects of campus life, and the deconstruction of academic disciplines ... '. All of which have, 'devastated the traditional mission of the liberal arts curriculum' (Wolfe 2002: x). As with the 1991 MCEA *Guide*, *Choosing* holds St. John's College in high esteem for its rejection of 'politically correct' policies. The reader is informed that, 'St. John's doesn't have to deal with speech codes, hiring or student body quotas, and the desire of a misguided administration to teach the latest ideological trends in order to rank high on someone else's ill conceived list' (Wolfe 2002: 501). Given the US Supreme Court Bakke decision, which found that quotas in hiring and student admissions were quite illegal, *Choosing*'s hostility to quotas seems somehow misplaced. However, this seeming hostility may reflect a principled belief that affirmative action policies, unlike quotas, are constitutionally offensive. It may be that this latter position best describes *Choosing*'s orientation. However, if this is so, the reader should keep in mind that it is a position well sponsored by conservative antagonists to affirmative action, including the Scaife, Bradley and Olin foundations. These foundations and others have provided the Intercollegiate Studies Institute, the current publisher of *Choosing the Right College*, with more than $12.5 million between 1985 and 2001 (Media Transparency).

National Alumni Forum/American Council of Trustees and Alumni

A hallmark of conservative foundation funding programmes is the discipline and focus they receive from grant recipients. And when one considers *The Common Sense Guide* and *Choosing the Right College*, the grantees are quite clearly on-message. As noted in the earlier analysis of the workings of ISI, IEA, MC and MCEA, the recipients often share a common pedagogical commitment. It combines support for a traditional core curriculum on the one hand, and resistance to the putative threat of 'political correctness', on the other. As we have also seen, these foundations have searched out conservative academics to give organizational structure and legitimacy to this vision.

We turn now to the National Alumni Forum (NAF), its transformation into the American Council of Trustees and Alumni (ACTA), and to its Director, Lynne V. Cheney. While in government service during the Reagan administration, Dr Cheney used the 'bully pulpit' of the secretariat of the National Endowment for the Humanities (NEH) to launch a strongly ideological attack on those with whom she disagreed regarding the curriculum in higher education. In *Telling the Truth* (Cheney 1992), the last report before departing the NEH, Cheney charged that the humanities had been taken over by radical feminist Marxists who abhorred the traditional literary and historical canon. This cabal, according to Cheney, rejected objectivity and the notion of truth, and used the university as a platform for their political beliefs. Propaganda, she claimed, not education, was their goal and they threatened higher education from within. The only hope for conservative activists, it would appear, would be to bring external pressure on the university.

An organization was needed to undertake this task, and in 1994, with support from ISI, the National Alumni Forum (NAF) was created. It was to be a conservative education advocacy group focusing upon 'the mobiliz[ation] of alumni on behalf of academic freedom and excellence on college campuses' (http://www.goacta.org). By 1998, again with Dr Cheney serving as Director, NAF was transformed into a sixth and last organization considered in this chapter, the American Council of Trustees and Alumni (ACTA). While the name had been changed, the focus of this activist think tank remained; ACTA was committed to defending Western canonical literature and historical knowledge against the perceived threat of liberal higher education pedagogues and policies.

As with the first four activist organizations listed above, NAF and ACTA also received financial sponsorship from conservative foundations, including Olin, Bradley, Scaife, Castle Rock and Earhart. Using their tax records, Hohneke (2003) reports that between 1996 and 2001, NAF/ACTA received $3,458,156 to instruct trustees and alumni of their role in shaping the university curriculum to the NAF/ACTA vision. Under Dr Cheney's leadership, ACTA continued to focus on motivating conservative alumni to engage in curricular matters. As its website notes:

> The main threat to academic freedom today is from political intolerance on campus ... [and] alumni and trustees must make sure our colleges and universities remain forums for open debate. [Alumni] want to support their colleges, but they are often shut out of the discussion. This organization will serve as a voice for interested and concerned alums.
>
> (http://www.goacta.org)

A commitment to open debate is surely central to the academic enterprise. But it is by no means the private property of advocates of any single political hue. As we shall see shortly, libertarians and civil liberties advocates both demand that the academy remain an open forum; it is not the purview of conservative intellectuals alone.

In an attempt to provide alumni a voice, NAF/ACTA has created a number of conservative cultural products that claim that the openness needed for a healthy academic community is at peril. These reports include *The Shakespeare File: What English Majors are Really Studying* (Martin and Neale 1996), and *Defending Civilization: How Our Universities are Failing America and What Can be Done about it* (Martin and Neale 2001). As they are offered as evidence of destructive trends on campus, careful analyses of their arguments and data are warranted. Such analyses follow.

Upon its publication, and despite the fact that Shakespeare only became canonical in the mid-nineteenth century (Levine 1996), *The Shakespeare File* caused Jonathan Yardley, the *Washington Post*'s literary critic, to inveigh that, 'the lunatics are running the academic asylum', and to charge that Shakespeare was no longer required for English majors at American universities (1996: D2). While these charges certainly seem serious on the face of it, a careful analysis of the *File* suggests that its authors may have overreached in their conclusions. In constructing its assault on the undergraduate curriculum, the authors had used a curriculum revision at Georgetown University as the wedge to argue for the loss of standards. As is often the case in American higher education, the curriculum is regularly reconsidered and reformed. Such was the situation at Georgetown in 1996. After a year-long review, the University's English Department decided to amend its curricular requirements.

The outgoing requirement demanded that English majors deeply engage with two of three classic authors. Included here were Shakespeare, Chaucer and Milton. This requirement was replaced with a menu of three concentrations: studies in literature and literary history; studies in culture and performance; and studies in writing (rhetoric, genre and form). It was this change, the supposed elimination of the Shakespeare requirement, which so distressed the authors of the *Shakespeare File*. But one must look carefully here. For while it is certainly true that the requirements had changed, it is also true that even under the old regulations, English majors at Georgetown were *never* required to take Shakespeare. Chaucer and Milton would have sufficed quite nicely under the old regulations. And of course, Georgetown undergraduates did study the Bard. As Wilson reports:

> The department offers nine Shakespeare classes every year, and 17% of Georgetown undergraduates take a Shakespeare class (compared to 7% nationally) ... [Further] in the past fifteen years, Georgetown's English Department has increased its Shakespeare offerings by 300 percent.
>
> (1999: 451)

In 2001, the authors of the *Shakespeare File* returned to their concerns for the putative crisis besetting the university. In this latter jeremiad, canonical history takes the place of canonical literature. 'At this critical time in our history,' they explain, 'ACTA has launched the Defense of Civilization Fund ... [to] be used to support and defend the study of American history and civics and of Western civilization' (Martin and Neale 2001: i). With financial support from the Randolph Foundation, the William and Karen Tell Foundation, and Jane H. Fraser, the first report sponsored by the Fund received the polemic title, *Defending Civilization: How Our Universities are Failing America and What Can be Done about it* (Martin and Neale 2001).

Defending Civilization warns its readers that in post 9/11 America not only is the Bard threatened, but civilization itself is at risk. Citing polls that 92 per cent of Americans, 'favor military force even if casualties occur', and rally, 'behind the President wholeheartedly', the Report implies that this consensus should be reflected in the academy as well (Martin and Neale 2001: 1). But it is not. Rather, ACTA finds the university out of step with the majority. It sees the academy espousing, 'moral equivocation ... [and] explicit condemnations of America' (Martin and Neale 2001: 1). And with a bit of logical sleight of hand, *Defending Civilization* concludes that consensus could be realized through a curricular revision. Supporting Director Cheney's demand that, 'we need to know, in a war, exactly what is at stake', the Report demands that, 'all colleges and universities ... adopt strong core curricula that include rigorous, broad-based courses on the great works of Western civilization ... ' (Martin and Neale 2001: 7).

The logic of this argument is to contrast an *academic* demand for a curriculum based on great works of the Western canon, to a supposed *political* position on the part of left-leaning academics. Discussions concerning terrorism, ACTA argues, have been captured by these faculty who, 'BLAME AMERICA FIRST' (Martin and Neale 2001: 3). While the nation as a whole had come together in patriotic reaction against the horrors of 9/11, 'the fact remains':

> That academe is the only sector of American society that is distinctly divided in response. Indeed, expressions of moral relativism are a staple of academic life in this country and an apparent symptom of an educational system that has increasingly suggested that Western Civilization is the primary source of the world's ills ...
> (Martin and Neale 2001: 4–5)

There is something deeply troubling about this argument. It is not simply that ACTA contrasts its presumed academic position with a political one, a kind of 'apples and oranges' argument, but that the political position is framed as being unpatriotic. While there are many principled reasons to argue for privileging the Western canon in the curriculum, basing the demand on the claim that one's opponents are unpatriotic seems both illogical and untoward. Nevertheless, much of that rationale is based on data from a series of 'campus responses'. As with the document's argument, these responses also bear careful analysis.

One response, from the *Boston Globe*, describes the removal of an American flag from the desk of a department secretary by the Chair of Holy Cross' sociology department. The illustration seems to have been included to underscore ACTA's point that patriotic speech is regularly repressed at American universities. A more complete description of the episode found in a footnote to the original *Globe* article and to the libertarian Foundation for Individual Rights in Education (FIRE) suggests otherwise. Rather than arguing that academe has been taken over by extreme members of the left, the *Globe* piece describes a chilly environment on America's campuses for *all* stripes of political disputations. Nor does it depict the university as under the direction of out-of-control left-wing faculty. Both left and right are held up to ridicule.

The article rather points to the commitment to free speech held by academic leaders with a key point being made by the Director of Public Policy for the progressive American Association of University Professors (AAUP). 'We're watching these developments with a lot of concern', reports Dr Ruth Flower. 'There's a strong unity of opinion for the first time in a long time in the country, but unity doesn't allow for dissent' (Abel 2001: A7). Indeed, the unity that ACTA lauds in public opinion may turn out to be a greater threat to the academy than the supposed legions of relativist faculty. In any event, neither the *Boston Globe's* coverage of the resistance to dissent at American universities, nor its inclusion on FIRE's website seem to support the major premise of the Fund's report. On the contrary, both FIRE and the AAUP agree, across ideological grounds, that the university should be the home of dissent.

While the authors of *Defending Civilization* take a nominal stand in favour of non-conformity, they appear far more interested in motivating trustees and alumni to demand curricular consensus regardless of faculty wishes. And it appears that they may well achieve it in the future since ACTA staff members have recently been selected to train Florida's future university trustees. In fact, the authors of both the *Shakespeare File* and *Defending Civilization* were selected in the spring of 2001 by Governor Jeb Bush to instruct 145 of Florida's newly appointed university and college trustees as part of a 'dramatic reorganization of Florida's educational system ... ' (American Council of Trustees and Alumni 2001: 1).

In the absence of a copy of their trustee training manual, one cannot describe the content of these instructional programmes. Yet having reviewed ACTA's analyses of curriculum reform in *The Shakespeare File*, and of campus dissent in *Defending Civilization*, we may anticipate that their recommendations to these trustees will include strong support for the Western canon, and strong antagonism toward the pedagogy associated with a postmodern turn of mind.

Conclusion

As the above analyses of the links between capital, culture and the curriculum has revealed, substantial conservative foundation support for activist centres has led to a well-organized assault on the undergraduate curriculum in the USA. Over the past half-century these sponsored advocates have received over $19 million for conservative undergraduate newspapers, student seminars, campus guides and curriculum evaluations. While this chapter does not judge their successes, it does recognize that beneath much of its polemicist veneer the core neo-conservative position is not without merit. As Dean Catherine Stimpson of New York University's Graduate School of Arts and Sciences notes, the neo-conservative plea is for a university curriculum centred on great works of literature and history aims for commendable goals (Stimpson 2002: 37). Whether William Bennett, William Buckley, Lynne Cheney, or Diane Ravitch is making such a claim their hoped-for curriculum does focus on worthy outcomes. Despite their traditional jeremiads, the neo-conservatives long for content that will, 'create national cohesion, democratic order, and some ability to understand The Other' (Stimpson 2002: 37).

Yet, at the same time that neo-conservatives were launching their assault, the intellectual terrain had changed beneath them. As Purdue's Calvin Schrag notes, liberal learning found itself in a 'postmodern world' (1988: 1). In art, postmodernism is anti-realist; in literature it is suspicious of the rules of literary language; in science it is concerned for 'instabilities', for shifting paradigms; in philosophy, postmodernism is anti-foundationalist and suspicious of theory (1988: 4). 'More like an attitude ... a way of seeing the world and acting within it [than an easily defined area of study such as physics]' (Schrag 1988: 4), it had to be profoundly unsettling to neo-conservative sensibilities. And in many ways it was against this 'attitude' that their assault was launched.

But while unimaginable to many, the postmodern view has been remarkably useful for many twenty-first-century academics. It has, as Stimpson points out, been used to create 'a curriculum for students whose complex sense of citizenship may simultaneously include loyalty to a place of origin, the American nation-state, a faith, and a global society that connects its citizens economically and electronically' (2002: 37). These are splendid goals for the undergraduate curriculum. They are worthy of support. And if carefully nurtured, they are quite capable of resisting assaults launched against them in Gramsci's ongoing wars of cultural position.

References

Abel, D. (2001) Campuses see a downside to unity civil rights stifled, some professors say, *The Boston Globe*, 6 October, A7.
American Council of Trustees and Alumni (2001) Florida joins accountability movement, *Inside Academe* (Spring/Summer), 6(3): 1. Washington, DC: American Council of Trustees and Alumni.
Apple, M.W. (2001) *Educating the 'Right' Way*. New York and London: Routledge.
Bloom, A. (1987) *The Closing of the American Mind*. New York: Simon and Schuster.
Bok, D. (2003) *Universities and the Marketplace*. New Haven: Princeton University Press.
Buckley, W.F. (1951) *God and Man at Yale: The Superstitions of Academic Freedom*. Chicago: Regnery.
Cheney, L.V. (1992) *Telling the Truth: A Report on the State of the Humanities in Higher Education*. Washington, DC: National Endowment for the Humanities.
Collins, C. and Yeskel, F. (2000) *Economic Apartheid in America*. New York: The New Press.
Cokorinos, L. (2003) *The Assault on Diversity: An Organized Challenge to Racial and Gender Justice*. Lanham, MD: Rowman and Littlefield Publishers, Inc.
Covington, S. (1997) *Moving a Public Policy Agenda: The Strategic Philanthropy of*

Conservative Foundations, A Report From the National Committee for Responsive Philanthropy. Washington, DC: National Committee for Responsive Philanthropy.

Egen, R. (1996) *Buying a Movement: Right-Wing Foundations and American Politics.* Washington, DC: People for the American Way.

FIRE website http://www.thefire.org/offsite/globe 102601.html.

Finn, C. (2002) *September 11: What Our Children Need to Know.* Washington, DC: Thomas B. Fordham Foundation.

Gingrich, N. (1995) *To Renew America.* New York: HarperCollins.

Hohneke, T. (2003) The Conservative Restoration and the Undergraduate Curriculum: Tracing the Financial Roots and Policy Initiatives of the American Council of Trustees and Alumni. Unpublished paper, University of Maryland College Park.

Intercollegiate Studies Institute (2003), http://www.isi.org/aboutisi.html.

Kimball, R. (1998) *Tenured Radicals: How Politics Has Corrupted Our Higher Education.* Chicago: Ivan R. Dee Publishers.

Levine, L. (1996) *The Opening of the American Mind: Canons, Culture, and History.* Boston: Beacon Press.

Leo, J. (1995) How the West was lost at Yale, *US News & World Report*, 3 April, 7.

Martin, J.L. and Neale, A.D. (2001) *Defending Civilization: How Our Universities are Failing America and What Can Be Done about It.* Washington, DC: American Council of Trustees and Alumni.

Martin, J.L. and Neale, A.D. (1996) *The Shakespeare File: What English Majors are Really Studying.* Washington, DC: American Council of Trustees and Alumni.

Mayo, P. (1999) *Gramsci, Freire, and Adult Education: Possibilities for Transformative Action.* London: Zed Books.

Media Transparency, http://www.mediatransparency.org.

Pyott, P. (ed.) (1991) *The Common Sense Guide to American Colleges, 1991–1992.* Lanham, MD: Madison Books.

Ravitch, D. (2002) Education and the culture wars, in J. Miller (ed.) *Daedlalus: Journal of the American Academy of Arts and Sciences*, 5–21.

Rawls, J. (1971) *A Theory of Justice.* Cambridge: Harvard University Press.

Schmidt, P. (2003) Behind the fight over race-conscious admissions, *The Chronicle of Higher Education*, 4 April, 3.

Schrag, C.O. (1988) Liberal learning in the postmodern world. Paper presented to the Purdue University Phi Beta Kappa graduation (mimeo copy).

Stefanic, J. and Delgado, R. (1996) *No Mercy: How Conservative Think Tanks and Foundations Changed America's Social Agenda.* Philadelphia: Temple University Press.

Stimpson, C.R. (2002) The culture wars continue, in J. Miller (ed.) *Daedlalus: Journal of the American Academy of Arts and Sciences*, 36–40.

Wilson, J.K. (1999) The canon and the curriculum, in P. Altbach, R. Berdahl and J. Gumport (eds) *American Higher Education in the Twenty-First Century: Social, Political, and Economic Changes.* Baltimore: The John Hopkins University Press.

Wolfe, G. (ed.) (2002) *Choosing the Right College: The Whole Truth About America's 100 Top Schools.* Grand Rapids: William B. Eerdmans Publishing Company.

Yardley, J. (1996) For English departments, a major change, *Washington Post*, 30 December, D2.

4
Higher Education, Globalization and the Knowledge Economy[1]

Michael Peters

> The liberal university belongs to the past. The inescapable question now is whether the university will become the locus of integration or of confrontation. In both cases grave dangers may threaten the creation of new knowledge.
>
> (Alain Touraine 1974: 13)
>
> Knowledge is and will be produced in order to be sold, it is and will be consumed in order to be valorised in a new production: in both cases, the goal is exchange.
>
> (Jean-François Lyotard 1984: 4)

To say that the university is in crisis is to echo the thoughts and sentiments of a generation of post-war commentators. The word 'crisis', accordingly, has almost lost the theoretical purchase it once had and slipped into a kind of rhetoric that is now consistently invoked by writers and scholars of all political persuasions. The term crisis was used to refer to the crisis of governance of the university following the student unrest and resistance of the late 1960s. Analysis of the demands made by the student movement pointed to the need for a greater democratization of the university. It revealed the elitist functions of the university based upon the myths of 'pure inquiry' and 'objective knowledge' which operated, ideologically, to screen out different cultural and gender values that determine both what counts as knowledge and legitimate ways of pursuing it.

The term was used again during the 1970s to refer to the decline of the humanities. This was a period when increasing numbers of students in Western universities opted for science and technology and the first real pressures for universities to become more vocationally oriented began to be felt. The general shift to the Right that took place in global politics during the 1980s and the emergence of a set of policies based upon neo-liberal principles expressing both the failure of big government and a commitment to free-market solutions, heralded a double notion of 'crisis'. The first was linked to the university's survival: it was linked to problems of funding and was seen, above all, as a fiscal crisis – one of external legitimation and principally a crisis focusing upon the continued financial viability of the institution. The second centred on the curriculum and the crisis of the humanities. In the North American academy especially, this notion of crisis had been manufactured by those dedicated to a conservative cultural project.

The transformation of higher education in anglophone countries from a universal welfare entitlement into a private investment in human capital established a similar pattern shared by a number of Organization for Economic Co-operation and Development (OECD) countries. First, a transparent alignment of the university system to reflect the needs of an emerging post-industrial economy, with increasing demands for highly trained, multi-skilled, tertiary-educated workers. Second, the introduction of new forms of corporate managerialism and the emulation of private sector management styles; the corporatization of the university system – an emphasis on so-called accountability structures, including the attempted simplification of goals or purposes, and the institution of new forms of delegated authority. Third, the introduction of corporate or strategic planning and the move to institute a form of ownership monitoring in order, allegedly, to reduce the financial risk of the state. Fourth, under neoliberalism, there was an attack on faculty representation in university governance and the general attempt to discredit democratic forms of university governance on 'efficiency' grounds. Finally, the introduction of user-charges, student loans, and the creeping privatization of the system as a whole took place to varying degrees in countries like New Zealand, Australia, Canada and the United Kingdom.

The writing was on the wall by the 1980s when calls were made for a reappraisal of the university institution. Thus, for instance, the OECD Intergovernmental Conference on 'Policies for Higher Education' in 1983 referred not only to 'the crisis of performance' but, more fundamentally, pointed to 'an internal crisis of purpose'. The OECD publication, *Universities Under Scrutiny* (1987: 3) began by questioning 'the very purposes and functions of higher education in post-industrialised societies'. The OECD secretariat emphasized the mismatch between the university's self-definition and external expectations and suggested a set of policies that, at one and the same time, promoted a greater vocationalism and sense of 'appliedness', and a greater focus on efficiency, productivity and accountability.

The massification of higher education within OECD countries also involved the implementation of new financial models, which determine the manner and amount of institutional funding. This policy move was predicated on the basis of an official recognition that there is an alleged need to reduce the burden on governments to act as sole providers and that the private sector had an increasing role to play either directly or in partnership with public institutions. In some countries it also indicated that arguments that education constitutes a private good had found favour with politicians, who often believed that competition for funds increases institutional efficiency and responsiveness. Experimentation with alternative institutional funding mechanisms in OECD countries over the past couple of decades appear to follow a similar pattern. This is: the adoption and increased sophistication of institutional formulae-founding; greater financial autonomy and market freedom for institutions; an increasing proportion of income from student fees; sharper distinction between funding of research and of teaching; an increased proportion of public funding to be bid for by the institutions; and the encouragement of a diversification of funding sources with the promotion of partnerships with business. Even with the diversification of funding sources, universities have struggled to cope financially. Moreover, rapid growth in participation experienced in the last few decades forced institutions not only to compete with each other in the market for student places but also to absorb the cost of providing additional unfunded student places, at declining levels of state funding. The result has been, as the UK White Paper, *The Future of Higher Education* (see: http://www.dfes.gov.uk/higher education/hestrategy/) acknowledges, serious underfunding. The White Paper records, for instance, that funding per student fell 36 per cent between 1989 and 1997; that many of the UK's economic competitors invest more in higher education; and that the investment backlog in teaching and research is estimated at 8 billion pounds. The White Paper suggests a three-pronged long-term investment and reform strategy designed to promote research, knowledge transfer and the quality of teaching with the goals of harnessing knowledge to wealth creation and increasing participation in higher education (from the current 43 per cent to 50 per cent). While there is a recognition of the underfunding crisis and a promised increase in spending on research of 1.25 billion (compared to 2002–03) it is delayed to 2005–06, there is also a greater pragmatic emphasis on creating and encouraging a greater 'knowledge exchange' with business and regional development agencies. The discourse of 'excellence' characterizes the document – a kind of empty signifier.

The crisis of the idea of the university

In *The University in Ruins*, Bill Readings (1996: 1)[2] suggests that there is a general uncertainty as to the role of the university: university teaching staff are being proletarianized; the number of part-term contracts have increased; the production of knowledge is uncertain. His analysis is that the role of the university has shifted as the forces of globalization have become more evident:

> the University is becoming a different institution, one that is no longer linked to the destiny of the nation-state by virtue of its role as producer, protector, and inculcator of an idea of national culture. The process of economic globalisation brings with it the relative decline of the nation-

state as the prime instance of the reproduction of capital around the world. For its part, the University is becoming a transnational bureaucratic corporation, either tied to transnational instances of government such as the European Union or functioning independently, by analogy with a transnational corporation.

(Readings 1996: 3)

The emergence of the concept of culture, he suggests, should be understood as a particular way of dealing with the tensions that arose historically between the university and the state, as essentially *modern* institutions. When he writes of the university he is referring to the German model that Humboldt instituted at the University of Berlin in 1812. The notion of culture as the central legitimating idea of the modern university has come to the end of its usefulness and, accordingly, 'the story of liberal education has lost its organizing center' (Readings 1996: 10). The overall nature of the university has become corporate rather than cultural. University administrators, government officials and policy experts increasingly talk of the university's mission in terms of 'excellence' rather than 'culture'. Yet excellence is non-ideological, Readings (1996: 13) argues, (though not unpolitical) in the sense that 'what gets taught or researched is less important than the fact that it be excellently taught or researched'.

Taking my lead from Bill Readings I shall sketch my argument that three ideas of the university dominate the modern era: the Kantian idea of reason; the Humboldtian idea of culture; and the techno-bureaucratic idea of excellence. Readings summarizes the history of the modern university in terms of these three overarching ideas:

The history of the modern University can be crudely summarised by saying that the modern University has had three Ideas, the Kantian idea of reason, the Humboldtian notion of culture, and now the technological idea of excellence. The distinguishing feature of the last ... is that it lacks all referentiality – it is the *simulacrum* of the Idea of a University ... in the Kantian University [the president's] function is the purely disciplinary one of making decisive judgements in inter-faculty conflicts on the grounds of reason alone. In the University founded on culture, the president incarnates a pandisciplinary ideal of a general cultural orientation ... In the contemporary University, however, a president is a bureaucratic administrator ... From judge to synthesiser to executive.

(1996: 163)

But the founding discourses of the modern university have been permanently fractured. Under the combined pressures of globalization, managerialism and marketization, it is no longer possible to talk of the idea of the modern university or of an institution regulated and unified through the force of a single idea. The idea of the modern university based on Kant, Humboldt or Newman has become historical in the sense that the techno-bureaucratic idea of excellence has instituted an historical break or rupture with the modern. In other words, the university has become 'post-historical'. I hasten to add that my use of the term 'post-historical' is not meant to suggest an 'end of history' or the 'end of ideology' thesis. My use of 'post-historical', however, is meant to signify an 'end of modernity' and, consequently, an institutional transformation of the modern university. Universities now function as one more bureaucratic subsystem among others harnessed in the service of national competitiveness in the global economy. In the age of global capitalism universities have been reduced to a technical ideal of performance within a contemporary discourse of 'excellence'.

The point here is that the grand narrative of the university – centred on the cultural production of a liberal, reasoning, citizen subject – in the wake of globalization is no longer credible. 'The University ... no longer participates in the historical project for humanity that was the legacy of the Enlightenment: the historical project of culture' (Readings 1996: 5). The movement from cultural élite formation to the post-war massification of higher education has subjected the universalism of liberal education to criticism of its privilege based on the lines of class, gender and ethnicity. It is precisely at this point that the link between the university and the nation-state breaks down and the discourse of excellence gains a purchase. The University of Excellence replaces the University of Culture. As Readings argues:

> The economics of globalisation mean that the University is no longer called upon to train citizen subjects, while the politics of the end of the cold war mean that the university is no longer called upon to uphold national prestige by producing and legitimating national culture.
>
> (1996: 14)

Readings suggests that excellence has become the last unifying principle of the modern university. When ministry policy analysts or university administrators talk about excellence, unwittingly they bracket the question of value in favour of measurement and substitute accounting solutions for questions of accountability (Readings 1996: 119). As an integrating principle excellence has the advantage of being entirely meaningless: it is non-referential. It signifies the corporate bureaucratization of the university. Universities have become sites for the development of 'human resources'. Guided by mission statements and strategic plans, performance output is measured and total quality management (TQM) assures quality outcomes. Readings remarks:

> University mission statements, like their publicity brochures, share two distinctive features nowadays. On the one hand, they all claim that theirs is a unique educational institution. On the other hand, they all go on to describe this uniqueness in exactly the same way.
>
> (1996: 12)

He goes on to tell the true story of how Cornell University parking services received an award recently for 'excellence in parking'. The discourse of excellence is essentially contentless. It does not enable us to make judgements of value or purpose; it does not help us to answer questions of *what, how* or *why* we should teach or research; it can provide us with no direction but serves only to maintain and monitor the system in the 'audit society'.

Anyone with a passing familiarity with Readings' thesis as I have presented it must recognize the traces of Jean-François Lyotard's influence.[3] His *The Postmodern Condition: A Report on Knowledge* (1984), originally published in Paris in 1979, became an instant *cause célèbre* because Lyotard analysed the status of knowledge, science and the university in a way that many critics believed signalled an epochal break not only with the so-called 'modern era' but also with various traditionally 'modern' ways of viewing the world. It was written, Lyotard (1984: xxv) asserts, 'at this very Postmodern moment that finds the University nearing what may be its end'.

In *The Postmodern Condition* Jean-François Lyotard was concerned with grand narratives that had grown out of the Enlightenment and had come to mark modernity. In *The Postmodern Explained to Children*, Lyotard (1992: 29) mentions:

> the progressive emancipation of reason and freedom, the progressive or catastrophic emancipation of labour ... , the enrichment of all through the progress of capitalist techno-science, and even ... the salvation of creatures through the conversion of souls to the Christian narrative of martyred love.

Grand narratives are the stories that cultures tell themselves about their own practices and beliefs in order to legitimate them. They function as a unified single story that purports to legitimate or found a set of practices, a cultural self-image, a discourse or an institution.[4]

Lyotard holds that capitalist renewal after the 1930s and the post-war upsurge of technology has led to a crisis of scientific knowledge and to an internal erosion of the very prospect of legitimation. He locates the seeds of such delegitimation in the decline of the legitimating power of the grand narratives of the nineteenth century.[5] In particular, the process of European cultural disintegration[6] is symbolized most clearly by the end of philosophy as the universal meta-language able to underwrite all claims to knowledge and, thereby, to unify the rest of culture.

Since the late 1970s neo-liberalism has become the dominant grand narrative. (The publication of Lyotard's *The Postmodern Condition* coincided with the election to power of Margaret Thatcher's Conservative Government in Britain.) A particular variant revitalizes the master discourse of neo-classical economic liberalism and advances it as a basis for a global reconstruction of society. A form of economic reason encapsulated in the notion of *homo economicus*, with its abstract and universalist assumptions of individuality, rationality and self-interest, has captured the policy agendas of

Western countries. Part of its innovation has been the way in which the neo-liberal grand narrative has successfully extended the principle of self-interest into the status of a paradigm for understanding politics itself, and, purportedly, *all* behaviour and human action. In the realm of higher education policy the market has been substituted for the state: students are now 'customers' or 'clients' and teachers are 'providers'. The notion of vouchers is suggested as a universal panacea to problems of funding and quality. The teaching/learning relation has been reduced to an implicit contract between buyer and seller. As Lyotard argued prophetically in *The Postmodern Condition* not only has knowledge and research become commodified but also so have the relations of the production of knowledge in a new logic of *performativity*.

The university in the knowledge economy

The post-historical university

The crisis of the idea of the modern university has been brought about largely by changes in the nature of the capitalist system, through attempts by governments to structurally adjust their national economies to the new conditions, and by consequent shifts in the production of knowledge that leads to the de-territorialization of knowledge and intensified knowledge flows (see Delanty 1998). The new global knowledge economy is not just a universalization of capitalism after the collapse of actually existing communism, it also involves the rise of finance capitalism, supported by the emergence of new information and communications technologies, and a series of international agreements concerning the liberalization of world trade.

The 1997 Dearing Report on higher education in the UK recognized globalization as the major influence upon the UK economy and the labour market with strong implications for higher education. Analysing the Dearing Report it is possible to talk of the *globalization of tertiary or higher education*, according to three interrelated functions: the *knowledge* function, the *labour* function, and the *institutional* function. We can talk of the primacy of the knowledge function and its globalization, which has a number of dimensions: knowledge – its production transmission and acquisition – is still primary as it was with the idea of the modern university, but now its value is legitimated increasingly in terms of its attraction to and service of global corporations. Knowledge is valued for its strict utility rather than as an end in itself or for its emancipatory or enlightenment effects.[7] The globalization of the labour function is formulated in terms of both the production of technically skilled people to meet the needs of global corporations and the ideology of lifelong learning, where individuals can 're-equip themselves for a succession of jobs over a working lifetime'. The institutional function is summed up in the phrase 'higher education will become a global international service and tradable commodity'. The competitive survival of institutions is tied to the globalization of its organizational form (emulating private sector enterprises) and the globalization of its 'services'. With this function already a strong and closer alliance between global corporations and universities has developed, especially in terms of the funding of research and development, and, in some cases, the university as a global corporation with international sites for teaching and research. The latter is a trend likely to develop further with the world integration and convergence of media, telecommunications and publishing industries. The institutional form of the university depicted by Dearing, then, is one form of the post-historical university – the university as a global service corporation.

Another even more obvious example and disturbing vision of the post-historical university is provided in a commissioned paper entitled *Australian Higher Education in the Era of Mass Customisation* (http://www.dest.gov.au/archive/highered/hereview/reports/learning.pdf) by Global Alliance Limited as Appendix 11 to the West Committee's discussion paper *Review of Higher Education Financing and Policy* (http://www.dest.gov.au/archive/highered/hereview/default.htm) released in late November 1997. Global Alliance Limited (GAL) is a Tokyo-based investment bank established in 1995, which specializes in providing investment and corporate advisory services mainly to Japanese and Taiwanese companies, especially in relation to the information technology sector. GAL has investments on its own account in Internet service providers and related companies.

The GAL report proclaims both the end of 'the era of homogeneity' under state planning and the beginning of another era, which will be consumer-oriented, more diversified and exposed to international competition. The remnants of an era of state planning show that while costs of production are competitive worldwide, productivity incentives are poor and capital management requires reform. The existing providers are protected in the Australian domestic market but not for too much longer.

The report identifies the following forces for change: the reducing government fee structure, the associated shift of power to the consumer, increasing international competitive exposure and changes in the technology of production and consumption. Computers will lower costs of marketing and the provision of customer services, while at the same time promoting greater access to learning and enhancing the quality of the learning experience. Back-end systems will be automated and learning systems will increasingly apply computers so that courses can be delivered over the Internet. The effects of these forces will lead to the hollowing out of the university. The report is worth quoting at some length here:

> The vertically integrated university is a product of brand image, government policy, history and historical economies of scale in support services. If government policy is no longer biased in favour of this form, and technology liberates providers from one location, then we would

expect to see new forms arising such as multiple outlet vertically integrate specialist schools and web based universities ... Specialist service providers, such as testing companies and courseware developers will arise, as will superstar teachers who are not tied to any one university. Many universities will become marketing and production coordinators or systems integrators. They will no longer all be vertically integrated education version of the 1929 Ford assembly plant in Detroit (12).

The overall result of the effects of these combined forces of changes are an increased segmentation of markets, an increased specialization and customization of supply of courses and an increased specialization of providers. The new university business system will take the form of one of a series of possible business models: low-cost producer university; Asia middle-class web university; Harvard in Australia university; world specialist school university.

Clearly, the economic importance of education has been rediscovered as fundamental to understanding the global economy (Papadopoulos 1994: 170) and its expression in its latest phase as the knowledge economy. The OECD and the World Bank have emphasized the significance of education and training for the development of human resources, for upskilling and increasing the competencies of workers, and for the production of research and scientific knowledge, as keys to participation in the new global economy. Both Peter Drucker (1993) and Michael Porter (1990) emphasize the importance of knowledge – its economics and productivity – as the basis for national competition within the international marketplace. Lester Thurow (1996: 68) suggests 'a technological shift to an era dominated by man-made brainpower industries' is one of five economic tectonic plates that constitute a new game with new rules: 'Today knowledge and skills now stand alone as the only source of comparative advantage. They have become the key ingredient in the late twentieth century's location of economic activity.' Equipped with this central understanding and guided by neo-liberal theories of human capital, public choice, and new public management, Western governments have begun the process of restructuring universities, obliterating the distinction between education and training in the development of a massified system of higher education designed for the twenty-first century.

Knowledge economy: knowledge capitalism[8]

Among the variety of discourses of the knowledge economy, those we might characterize as third generation Chicago School economics (the economics of information, of knowledge and of education) have had perhaps the greatest impact, shaping national policy constructions of the 'knowledge economy' not only in the West – USA, United Kingdom, Ireland, Australia, Canada and New Zealand – but also in the developing world, most notably,

China and SE Asia, especially through the influence of world policy agencies. Often the link is made between technology, innovation and knowledge focusing on policies designed to assimilate the university more fully into the mode of production. The United Kingdom's White Paper *Our Competitive Future* (Department of Trade and Industry 1998), for example, begins by acknowledging the fact that the World Bank's 1998 *World Development Report* took knowledge as its theme, citing the report as follows:

> For countries in the vanguard of the world economy, the balance between knowledge and resources has shifted so far towards the former that knowledge has become perhaps the most important factor determining the standard of living ... Today's most technologically advanced economies are truly knowledge-based.
> (http://www.dti.gov.uk/comp/competitive/main.htm)

The UK White Paper also mentions that the OECD has drawn attention to the growing importance of knowledge indicating that the emergence of knowledge-based economies has significant policy implications for the organization of production and its effect on employment and skill requirements. The report suggests that already other countries, including the USA, Canada, Denmark and Finland, have identified the growing importance of knowledge and reflected it in their approach to economic policy.

The report emphasizes so-called new growth theory, charting the ways in which education and technology are now viewed as central to economic growth. Neo-classical economics does not specify how knowledge accumulation occurs and, therefore, cannot acknowledge externalities. By contrast, new growth theory has highlighted the role of higher education in the creation of human capital and in the production of new knowledge (see, for example, Solow 1956, 1994). On this basis it has explored the possibilities of education-related externalities. In short, while the evidence is far from conclusive there is a consensus emerging in economic theory that education is important for successful research activities (for example by producing scientists and engineers), which is, in turn, important for productivity growth; and education creates human capital, which directly affects knowledge accumulation and therefore productivity growth (see s. 3.4 ff 'Knowledge as the source of growth'). The report emphasizes that not only do R&D expenditures provide a positive contribution to productivity growth but also that education is important in explaining the growth of national income.

The White Paper emphasizes that 'knowledge economy' does not mean a return to interventionist strategies of the past, but neither does it mean a naïve reliance on markets. As Tony Blair expresses the role of government in the *Foreword* to the White Paper:

> The Government must promote competition, stimulating enterprise, flexibility and innovation by opening markets. But we must also invest in British capabilities when companies alone cannot: in education, in

science and in the creation of a culture of enterprise. And we must promote creative partnerships which help companies: to collaborate for competitive advantage; to promote a long term vision in a world of short term pressures; to benchmark their performance against the best in the world; and to forge alliances with other businesses and with employees.

In education at all levels there is a strong emphasis on the culture of enterprise and building skills of entrepreneurship which is not very different, if at all, from the policy emphases initiated by Lord Young under the Thatcher Government. There is an equal emphasis on the promotion of university-based research, on industry-education relationships especially in higher education, on workplace learning, and on building a culture of learning (including the establishment of individual learning accounts).

The United Kingdom's White Paper *Our Competitive Future: Building the Knowledge Driven Economy* defines a knowledge-based economy in the following terms:

> A knowledge driven economy is one in which the generation and the exploitation of knowledge has come to play the predominant part in the creation of wealth. It is not simply about pushing back the frontiers of knowledge; it is also about the more effective use and exploitation **of all types of knowledge** in **all manner of activity**.
> (emphases in the original)
> (http://www.dti.gov.uk/comp/competitive/main.htm)

The report suggests that 'knowledge' is more than just information and it goes on to distinguish between two types of knowledge: 'codified' and 'tacit'. Codifiable knowledge can be written down and transferred easily to others, whereas tacit knowledge is 'often slow to acquire and much more difficult to transfer'. The knowledge economy allegedly differs from the traditional economy with an emphasis on what I have called the 'economics of abundance', the 'annihilation of distance', the 'de-territorialization of the state', the 'importance of local knowledge', and 'investment in human capital' (see Peters 2001).

In the attempt to reposition and structurally adjust their national economies to take advantage of the main global trends, British, Australian, Canadian and New Zealand governments have begun to recognize the importance of education, and especially higher education, as an 'industry' of the future. There is an emerging understanding of the way in which higher education is now central to economic (post-) modernization and the key to competing successfully within the global economy. This understanding has emerged from the shifts that are purportedly taking place in the production and consumption of knowledge which are impacting on traditional knowledge institutions like universities (see Peters and Roberts 1999).

The role of the university is undergoing a transition in late modernity as a result of structural shifts in the production and legitimation of knowledge. The older goal of the democratization of the university has now been superseded by new challenges arising from the dual processes of the globalization and fragmentation of knowledge cultures. These arise from a range of related developments: the separation of knowledge (research) from the post-sovereign state that no longer exclusively supports 'Big Science'; the rise of new regulatory regimes that impose an 'audit society' on the previously autonomous society; a separation of research from teaching (education); the decoupling of knowledge from society and the replacement of the public by target constituencies; the functional contradiction between science and economy in the increasing specialization of knowledge and the decline in occupational opportunities; the de-territorialization of knowledge as a result of new communication technologies and knowledge flows; the crisis of scientific rationality under conditions of the risk society, reflexivity and the new demands for the legitimation of knowledge (Delanty 1998, 2003; Fuller 2000, 2003).

Conclusion: universities and knowledge cultures

Readings asks how we might re-imagine the university once we have had to relinquish the notion of culture as the unifying idea. He argues that we should not embrace the techno-bureaucratic ideal of the corporate university. He argues further that we should attempt to live in the ruins of the university without romance or nostalgia. Since Kant the university has operated as a privileged model of free and rational discussion, Readings wants to critique this notion. He offers us a new community of *dissensus* as a model for the post-historical university: not one based upon consensus and transparency but rather upon openness, opaqueness, incompleteness and difference.

I have great sympathy for Readings' view. However, rather than explore the underlying notion of community at stake – its political dimensions and exclusions – I want to take a different tack. The discourse on knowledge admits of different distinctions, which under conditions of knowledge capitalism may permit some variation at both the regional and institutional levels at least insofar as knowledge capitalism can be approached through different models: 'imperialistic' neo-liberal Anglo-American capitalism (the so-called Washington Consensus issuing in structural adjustment policies), capitalism of Blair's Third Way capitalism that emphasizes new 'public/private' synergies, French state capitalism, Scandinavian welfare capitalism, Rhine capitalism, Japanese corporate capitalism and Chinese post-socialist capitalism. Each regional model will emphasize a different approach to conceiving higher education in the knowledge economy that may depend heavily on cultural factors such as learning traditions. The importance of regional models of knowledge capitalism has not yet been studied or unpicked.

The discourses of the knowledge economy point to the new insights flowing from the economics of knowledge, the economics of information and the economics of education, whereas the concept of 'the knowledge society' helps to elucidate the concepts and rights of knowledge workers as citizens in the new economy, focusing on the subordination of economic means to social ends. In the former neoclassical economics and the revival of *homo economicus* brings together the ancient problematic of knowledge (that pre-dates capitalism and feudalism and dates from the first organized academies in Classical Greece), with the problematic of capitalism that is less than a thousand years old and only recently (since World War 2) a disciplinary formation or field. In the latter, the concept highlights the *juridical and legal infrastructure* that must accompany knowledge capitalism – knowledge and information rights of the citizen, not only rights of access to knowledge, education rights *per se*, and the rights of open and free information – a foundation of the free society – but also intellectual property rights (for example patents, copyright), the knowledge rights of the knowledge worker (human capital rights), and democratic rights concerning the governance of public science.

The term 'knowledge cultures' is crucial for understanding questions concerning the development of both knowledge economies and knowledge societies. The term points to the *cultural preconditions* that must be established before economies or societies based on knowledge can be properly understood or established. *Knowledge cultures* are based on shared epistemic practices and they embody culturally preferred ways of doing things, often developed over many generations. Simplified in the extreme, my argument is that knowledge production and dissemination requires the exchange of ideas and such exchanges, in turn, depend upon certain cultural conditions, including trust, reciprocal rights and responsibilities between different knowledge partners, and the appropriate institutional regimes and strategies. I use the term 'knowledge cultures' (in the plural) because there is not one prescription or formula that fits all institutions, societies or knowledge traditions.

If we were to admit this notion we might substitute for a single unifying idea (like 'reason' or 'culture') a constellation or field of overlapping and mutually self-reinforcing ideas of the liberal university, based on family resemblances. Let me briefly explain: first, a preservation of critical reason as a source of criticism, critique and reflection – points us moderns towards the continuing relevance of historical university ideals of self-criticism, self-reflection and self-governance. Michel Foucault captures this point when he suggests:

> the thread which may connect us to the Enlightenment is not faithfulness to doctrinal elements but, rather, the permanent reactivation of

an attitude – that is, of a philosophical ethos that could be described as
a permanent critique of our historical era.

(1996: 312)

Second, the idea of culture can be reconstructed in two senses: from
notions of self-cultivation and moral self-formation, to learning processes
(pedagogy) based on an ethical relation of self and other; and from
national culture to *cultural self-understandings* and cultural reproduction
which implies a recognition of indigenous cultures and traditional knowledges, an awareness of 'nation' as a socio-historical construction, and an
acceptance of the reality of multiculturalism. Third, the crucial shift from a
literary to *post-literary culture*. The modern Western university was a print
culture shaped by print technologies for the creation, storage and transmission of knowledge. The shift to new techno-cultures is being shaped by
digital technologies for the storage and exchange of information. We must
begin to understand the new techno-cultures in relation to the university
where the radical concordance of image, text and sound sets up new exigencies and promises for pedagogy but also new dangers.

This amounts to an historization of the ideas of the modern university as
they have developed within the Western tradition. For a single governing
Idea I substitute (the Wittgensteinian) notion of a constellation based on
family resemblances. If we were to embody these new imaginings that
reconnect us to the threads of the modern university, we may be able to
encompass and redirect the energies of the Corporate Massified Service
University towards its inherent democratic possibilities, making the most of
the historic shift from cultural élite formation to genuine open access and
democratic participation.

Notes

[1] This chapter is based on a lecture originally presented in the Winter Lectures
series, *The University in the 21st Century*, Maidment Theatre, The University of
Auckland, 25 August 1998.

[2] Both Lyotard and Readings exercised a strong direction over my thought and
both have been generous in their encouragement to me and supportive of my work.
Lyotard (1995) wrote the Foreword to the collection I edited, *Education and the
Postmodern Condition* (1995), to which Readings (1995) contributed the final chapter.
Readings invited me in 1994 to give a paper (see Peters 1996) at his multidisciplinary
seminar at the Université de Montreal called 'L'Université et la Culture: La Crise
Identitaire d'une Institution' upon which his book was based.

[3] See also Smith and Webster (1997).

[4] He says in a now famous formulation:

> I will use the term *modern* to designate any science that legitimates itself with
> reference to a metadiscourse ... making explicit appeal to some grand
> narrative, such as the dialectics of Spirit, the hermeneutics of meaning, the

emancipation of the rational or working subject, or the creation of wealth (Lyotard 1984: xxii).

By contrast, he defines *postmodern* simply as 'incredulity toward metanarratives' (Lyotard 1984: xxiv).

[5] The speculative narrative of the unity of all knowledge held that knowledge is worthy of its name only if it can generate a second-order discourse that functions to legitimate it, otherwise such 'knowledge' would amount to mere ideology. The process of 'delegitimation' has revealed that not only does science play its own language game (and consequently is both on a par with and incapable of legitimating other language games) but also it is incapable of legitimating itself as speculation assumed it could.

[6] By European cultural disintegration Lyotard is referring, first, to the collapse of the monarchies and the two world wars, and, second, what Friedrich Nietzsche calls the question of European nihilism.

[7] see Report 8, 'Externalities in Higher Education', Dearing 1997).

[8] See Peters (2002a, 2002b).

References

Delanty, G. (1998) The idea of the university in the global era: From knowledge as an end to the end of knowledge, *Social Epistemology*, 12(1):3–26.
Delanty, G. (2003) Ideologies of the knowledge society and the cultural contradictions of higher education, *Policy Futures in Education*, 1(1): at http://www.triangle.co.uk/PFIE.
Department of Trade and Industry (1998) *Our Competitive Future: Building the Knowledge Driven Economy*. http://www.dti.gov.uk/comp/competitive/main.htm (accessed 14 Nov. 2003).
Drucker, P.(1993) *Post-Capitalist Society*. New York: Harper.
Foucault, M. (1996) What is Enlightenment? in Paul Rabinow (ed.) *Michel Foucault: Ethics, The Essential Works*. London: Allen Lane and Penguin.
Fuller, S. (2000) *The Governance of Science: Ideology and the Future of the Open Society*. London and New York: Open University Press.
Fuller, S. (2003) Can universities solve the problem of knowledge in society without succumbing to the knowledge society? *Policy Futures in Education*, 1 (1): at http://www.triangle.co.uk/PFIE.
Lyotard, J.-F. (1984) *The Postmodern Condition: A Report on Knowledge*, translated G. Bennington and B. Massumi, Foreword by F. Jameson. Minneapolis: University of Minnesota Press.
Lyotard, J.-F. (1992) *The Postmodern Explained to Children, Correspondence 1982-1985*, translated and edited by J. Pefanis and M. Thomas. Sydney: Power Publications.
Lyotard, J.-F. (1995) Foreword: Spaceship, in M. Peters (ed.) *Education and the Postmodern Condition*. Westport, CT and London: Begin and Garvey.
National Committee of Inquiry into Higher Education, http://www.leeds.ac.uk/educol/ncihe (accessed 14 Nov. 2003).
Papadopoulos, G. (1994) *Education 1960–1990: The OECD Perspective*. Paris: The Organisation.
Peters, M.A. (ed.) (1995) *Education and the Postmodern Condition*. Westport, CT and London: Begin and Garvey. Foreword by J.-F. Lyotard.

Peters, M.A. (1996) Cybernetics, Cyberspace and the University: Herman Hesse's *The Glass Bead Game* and the Dream of a Universal Language in *Poststructuralism, Politics and Education*. Westport, CT and London: Bergin and Garvey.

Peters, M.A. (2001) National education policy constructions of the 'knowledge economy': Towards a critique, *Journal of Educational Enquiry*, 2(1), May, (http://www.education.unisa.edu.au/JEE/).

Peters, M.A. (2002a) Universities, globalisation and the knowledge economy, *Southern Review: Communication, Politics and Culture*, 35(2):16–36.

Peters, M.A. (2002b) Universities, globalisation and the knowledge economy: An essay in the new political economy of knowledge. Paper presented at SRHE Annual Conference 2002, *Students and Learning: What is Changing?* University of Glasgow, 10–12 December 2002.

Peters, M.A. and Roberts, P. (1999) *University Futures*. Palmerston North, NZ: Dunmore Press.

Porter, M. (1990) *The Competitive Advantage of Nations*. New York: Free Press.

Readings, B. (1995) From emancipation to obligation: Sketch for a heteronomous politics of education, in M. Peters (ed.) *Education and the Postmodern Condition*. Westport, CT and London: Begin and Garvey.

Readings, B. (1996) *The University in Ruins*. Cambridge, Mass and London: Harvard University Press.

Smith, A. and Webster, F. (1997) *The Postmodern University? Contested Visions of Higher Education in Society*. Buckingham: SRHE and Open University Press.

Solow, R. (1956) A contribution to the theory of economic growth, *Quarterly Journal of Economics*, 70:65–94.

Solow, R. (1994) Perspectives on growth theory, *Journal of Economic Perspectives*, 8:45–54.

Thurow, L. (1996) *The Future of Capitalism: How Today's Economic Forces Will Shape Tomorrow's Future*. New York: Morrow.

Touraine, A. (1974) *The Post-Industrial Society: Tomorrow's Social History, Classes, Conflicts and Culture in the Programmed Society*, translated by L. Mayhew. London: Wildwood House.

World Bank (1998) *World Development Report: Knowledge For Development*. Oxford: Oxford University Press.

Part 2
Languages of Reconstruction

5
Training the Imagination to go Visiting

Jean Barr and Morwenna Griffiths

Jon Nixon's chapter in this Part (Chapter 7), 'Learning the Language of Deliberative Democracy', explores languages of hope in relation to the discourses of deliberative democracy. Ours also considers this theme of finding languages of hope. Like his chapter, ours makes people central. It explores a neglected area of epistemology: knowing people. It suggests that we take a critical perspective on the metaphors we live and then reconfigure them to think again about the public and private spaces in the universities where we work.

This chapter explores, in the context of university education, the nature of a public space that can accommodate and reconstruct 'public knowledge'. We understand 'public space' to be a *social* space of interaction, rather than a location in physical or cyber space (though it may be that too). We understand 'public knowledge' to be that knowledge which is articulated and/or expressed by all, including those people who are routinely excluded from traditional public spaces. People require public spaces in which they can discover, construct, develop and reinterpret knowledge of various kinds, and, in some cases, use the knowledge to help resolve practical problems they face. The nature of these spaces is changing as society (including its schools and universities) evolves. We point out that the traditional theoretical frameworks of political philosophy are unable to deal with the complexity of social space in today's society. They depend heavily on the notion of the public 'forum' (or sphere), that is, a space available to all citizens – accessible to them and usable by them. This notion is inadequate even within the limited context of higher education and its communities.

In criticizing traditional frameworks we draw on feminist and other writings which move on from critique to the more positive project of reconstructing knowledge and pedagogy. We use real examples not just as illustrations of our argument but as concrete embodiments of our case and in order to encourage less confining frameworks, processes and metaphors for organizing our work in higher education. The examples are drawn from our own experiences. They are offered both as reasons for hope and as aids to the imagination. They point, too, towards greater risk-taking than is encouraged in the current atmosphere of university teaching and research.

Public spaces and their uses

The story is told again and again, for example, by Jürgen Habermas, of a public sphere gained (by the liberal bourgeoisie of the nineteenth century) and lost (in the age of consumerism, the mass media and the intrusion of the state into the intimacy of the family); it is re-iterated by Sennet, about cities, in *The Fall of Public Man* and critiqued by Robbins in *The Phantom Public Sphere* (see Habermas 1962, recently translated; Sennet 1974; Robbins 1993). The question we must ask of course is: for whom was the social entity of the 'city' once more public than now? Was it ever open to scrutiny and participation by the majority? If so, where were the workers, the women, gays, black people? Rosalyn Deutsche believes that those who most lament the loss of the public sphere (conceived as unitary) may be suffering from a form of agoraphobia, panicking at the openness of a truly democratic public sphere, requiring a security blanket against uncertainty (Deutsche 1996: 327).

The rise and fall of the educated public, says MacIntyre, coincided with the rise and fall of the philosophy of common sense as taught in the universities (MacIntyre 1987). MacIntyre acknowledges that this public was very exclusive (and it certainly was – of the working class, women, Catholics – anyone, it would seem, whose ability to reason in the required disinterested, from-first-principles way could not be guaranteed). He is referring specifically to the Scottish Enlightenment, but the point can be made more generally, although any particular 'educated public' will work its own exclusions: Protestants, perhaps, or Jews, or Arabs, or gays. Despite this acknowledgement, MacIntyre still argues:

> It is only through the discipline of having one's claims tested in ongoing debate, in the light of standards on the rational justification of which, and on the rational justification afforded by which, the participants in debate are able to agree, that the reasoning of any particular individual is rescued from the vagaries of passion and interest.
>
> (1987: 24)

One is tempted to ask who would want to be a member of such a bloodless and exclusive club of rational, ascetic, Christian Scotsmen who can write such sentences. Certainly, any small community such as this, sharing a common culture and sense of purpose *could* of course believe in its own universal character and disinterestedness ('the power of the best argument'). But surely we cannot.[1]

The bourgeois notion of the public sphere which has been outlined by Jürgen Habermas on numerous occasions requires *bracketing* inequalities of status, proceeding in deliberation and discussion *as if* they do not exist. Yet, to proceed in this way – as if inequalities between the participants do not exist – is unlikely to foster *participatory* parity; on the contrary, it is much more likely that such 'bracketing' (which is how most seminars proceed in universities) will work to advantage dominant groups and to disadvantage subordinates. It is hard to imagine any possible participatory parity between the Home Office, the tabloid press and asylum seekers already in Britain, let alone any would-be refugees, facing danger in their own countries. Even for refugees with a university education, fluency in English, and the help of lawyers, parity must remain a chimera, logically as well as in fact, because the Home Office and the tabloid press are institutions that are set up precisely to work as powerful interest groups, not as reasonable individuals.[2] As Iris Young insists: 'The ideal of the civic public as expressing the general interest, the impartial point of view of reason, itself results in exclusion'. Specifically: 'By assuming that reason stands opposed to desire, affectivity and the body, the civic public must exclude bodily and affective aspects of human existence' (Young 1987: 59–66).

Similarly, as Nancy Fraser has suggested, unequally empowered social groups develop unequally valued cultural styles, and the workings of political economy reinforces this imbalance by denying to them equal access to the material means of equal participation, including education (Fraser 1993). We agree. Consider, we would add, the continuing impact of the Bantu Education Act, in South Africa. More than ten years after apartheid ended black South Africans are less able to access their legal rights to education than their white compatriots (McGregor 2003). Consider how few working-class women contribute to 'public' debates on higher education policy (Morley and Walsh 1995; Leonard 2002).[3]

Some feminists have made stronger claims. They have scrutinized the notion of reason as impartiality and detachment which holds sway in education and which reappears in many theorists of democracy, including Habermas. According to Habermas, the force of the better argument is what wins in his rational 'ideal speech situation'. Iris Young contests this on the grounds that *what counts* as acceptable reasons, good grounds and so on, must be understood as *itself* contestable. Further, according to Young, a model of democratic education based on discussion, though important, is limited; we need, in her view, a more open notion of communication than mere deliberation, one which does not exclude emotions as beyond the pale, for example, and one which assumes a starting point of distance and difference (even conflict and struggle) rather than togetherness and sameness (Young 1990). This draws attention to the fact that efforts to make the world a more just place depend a lot on developing people's capacity to relate to others as well as on refining people's capacity to discern rational principles of argument and to abide by a particular set of ground rules when engaging in it.[4]

What kind of public discussion?

If traditional models of discussion are inadequate, what can be put in their place? The writing of Hannah Arendt on the nature of political life is suggestive here.

Hannah Arendt believes that plurality and conflict are conditions of public life. Arendt's notion of plurality does not denote incommensurable differences, only their irreducibility to a common measure or standard. She proposes storytelling as an alternative way of constructing knowledge and as a way of engaging people in a kind of critical thinking which is different from an argument. According to Arendt, what is normally intended by the notion of critical thinking (impartial, detached) fails when it comes to seeking to understand unprecedented events because such events bring to light the 'ruin of our categories and standards of judgement'. Such events demand, in her memorable phrase, 'thinking without a banister' (Arendt 1994). They demand explicitly judgemental storytelling, aimed at teaching the kind of critical understanding which Martha Nussbaum has described as consisting in 'the keen responsiveness of intellect, imagination and feeling to the particularity of a situation' (Nussbaum 1986: 191).

Thus, in *The Human Condition*, Hannah Arendt (1958) writes about totalitarianism in such a way as to move her audience to engage with her in thinking, 'what we are doing' (Disch 1996: 140). In Arendt's view of critical thinking philosophy takes second place to poetry. This is because, for her, it is not abstraction but considered attention to particularity that accounts for 'enlarged thought'. Being critical, for Arendt, does not call for disinterest, detachment or withdrawal from political commitment. Instead, it requires 'training the imagination to go visiting' and this is done by means of stories. By storytelling, she asks, 'how would you see the world if you saw it from my position?' The reader or 'visitor' is offered a bridge and invited not merely to assimilate different perspectives but to converse with them and to consider how they differ from their own. Deliberate 'distancing', making the familiar strange, is also required for critical thought, believes Arendt. By means of taking the imagination visiting I am both distanced from the familiar and taken to unfamiliar standpoints. Serious heartfelt differences remain even where they do not preclude a useful degree of mutual understanding. Similarly, Cockburn draws on a careful analysis of her observations of women's peace groups working across difference, to articulate 'rooting' and 'shifting' as key concepts in developing understandings across difference. The groups she studied were located in places where identity and difference 'is a killing matter' (Cockburn 1998; Cockburn and Hunter 1999): Belfast, Bosnia and Israel/Palestine. Yet the women were able to construct enough mutual understanding and common ground to work with each other on the practical problems that faced them. Each woman stayed 'rooted' in her own position, while 'shifting' towards other women in the dialogue by recognizing their specific positionings, and her own unfinished knowledge about them.

The recommendation to 'train the imagination to go visiting' is offered as a social model of rationality which involves a commitment to disputation. It is suggestive for those interested in a reconstituted higher education. Where her imagination takes her is to a place where conflict is ubiquitous, where actors are explicitly partisan and where what is involved is 'taking sides for the world's sake' (Arendt 1968: 8).

According to Arendt, 'civic mindedness' can too often be a façade which suppresses dissent; for her, it is the spaces people inhabit together as citizens which unite them in a political community; it is not a set of common values: 'We call this reality the "web" of human relationships, indicating by the metaphor its somewhat intangible quality'. And, 'for all its intangibility, this in-between is no less real than the world of things we visibly have in common' (Arendt 1958: 183). It is the 'space between' them which they share, not some quality *in* them or some common beliefs which unites people.

Undoubtedly, plurality is the political principle par excellence for Arendt: people bring together their interests and points of view and these are tested, influenced and expanded but not thereby transformed into unanimous agreement. Similarly, Iris Young proposes a notion of 'differentiated solidarity'. She explains: 'Most uses of the term "solidarity" assume some sort of fellow feeling or mutual identification, as do its synonyms, such a "community"' (Young 2000: 222). However, in our complex and plural societies, she maintains, ideals of inclusion 'must rely on a concept of mutual respect and caring that presumes *distance*: that norms of solidarity hold among *strangers* and those who in many ways remain strange to one another' (our italics). The basis of such solidarity is quite simply that people live together – in a specific locale or region or, more widely, the world – whether they like it or not.

This plural, political process depends on the creation of public spaces for collective discussion and deliberation where citizens can test and expand their views, a public culture where people's self-centred perspectives are constantly challenged – but not obliterated – by the multiplicity of perspectives which make up public life. This then requires the creation of institutions and practices (like those traditionally developed within adult education, including university-based adult education) where the perspectives of others, of diverse groups and communities, can be articulated and expressed in their own right and in their own terms. Such a requirement 'affirms the need for group-based organization and voice at the same time that it expresses openness to listening to others and engaging with them in shared public spaces' (Young 2000: 225).

Arendt stresses the spatial quality of politics and public life: people must be able to see and talk to one another, to meet together in a public space so that both their differences and their commonalities can emerge, and so become subject to democratic debate. In this Arendt shares a metaphor with liberalism (which continues to be the dominant perspective in Western societies). Both views draw on the metaphor of the public square which is contrasted with the private spaces of the houses where citizens live. Arendt describes this view very clearly: 'The distinction between a private and a public sphere of life corresponds to the household and the political realms, which have existed as distinct separate entities at least since the rise of the ancient city-state.' (Arendt 1958: 28).

She also shares with liberalism a view that a public space is one that is open to all who are able and willing to engage in rational argument. However, there is an important difference. Arendt acknowledges real continuing differences and disagreements. Liberalism, on the other hand, depends on the triumph of the rational argument: 'rational men will agree'. It is a view that is still widespread. Annick Cojean articulates this liberal position when she writes, in an article bemoaning the obstacles being put in the way of a well-informed public debate in the UK and US concerning the build up to war with Iraq (such as systematic disinformation and the failure of politicians to get down to the grassroots to ask some simple questions): 'One would be surprised to note that it is by exploring the differences that we find the most similarities' (Cojean 2003).

Ways of understanding public spaces

In what follows, we consider how political-public space has been understood (a) in terms of the distinction between private and public; and (b) in terms of the metaphor of the public 'forum' or 'sphere'. This is not only of theoretical interest. Our purpose is to use a critique of the current concepts of public space to construct a concept (or set of concepts) which would provide a framework which points up, rather than obscures, possibilities within higher education for the accommodation and reconstruction of 'public knowledge'. We are particularly interested in the spaces in and around institutions of higher education where women, gays, black people, migrants, working-class people, Asian people – and any other of the many groups currently under-represented in the class of people creating, articulating and expressing knowledge.

The distinction between private and public

The sharp distinction made between public and private space is central to the usual concepts of public space used in our societies. This remains true for currently influential versions of liberalism including Rawls (1972), in the Anglo-American tradition, and Benhabib (1992), a feminist strongly influenced by Habermas.[5] That it is a mistake to make this sharp distinction can be seen from reflection on everyday experiences of scholarship, teaching, learning and researching, in our own institutions of higher education. Such activities depend on there being a number of spaces where individuals meet to formulate and reformulate their understanding of the world, and to devise, learn and practise their skills: in short to 'produce' knowledge in all the many senses of that word, related to gaining and expressing factual information, understanding, wisdom and skills. Yet these spaces are not quite public. They are not equally open to all; neither are they quite private, in the sense that they are open to individuals by virtue of *what* they are (for example students, chemists, deans), rather than *who* they are (for example Jean Barr, Morwenna Griffiths, Melanie Walker or Jon Nixon) (Arendt 1958).

A familiar and helpful example of the complexity of the divisions between public and private spaces is to be found in the university department. A university department is a place of work, where people are to be found in virtue of their role there – though it is not co-terminous with its physical location (as Ryle (1971) remarked of Oxford University). It can be described by contrast to the home, and is the 'work' part of the work/life balance. On the other hand, it is clear that some of the worry about that balance comes about precisely because one seeps into the other. Doreen Massey describes how in a context of competitive workaholism in current academic life women endlessly try to juggle incompatibilities between work and home demands, whilst men working in the 'High-Tech' industries she studied (and, by extension, she suggests, in the academy) spoke of 'minds being elsewhere' when playing with their children, but not vice versa, whilst at work (Massey 2001).

Even when the department is viewed as a public place in relation to the home, it is, at the same time, not so public in relation to the university as a whole, nor to various policy-making bodies – in the UK the funding bodies and central government – nor to various local communities or institutions (for example in business, the arts, local government, schools, hospitals and the law). A department's discussions about teaching or research are not open to the rest of the university, except in carefully worded reports or minutes. Discussions are certainly not open to the general public. (Going to the press is a serious matter, as is the content of websites.) Nor are they open to policy-makers (anecdotes abound about successful performance in front of inspecting bodies and how wool was pulled over eyes).

This complexity of public places in relation to the private is sometimes described as a set of concentric circles, of increasing openness as they become more public. But this is a false description. A university department is rarely the place to encounter educational policy-makers and their discussions in the public space of coming to know what is happening in higher education. Ordinary members of university departments are rarely included, even as observers in discussions among educational policy-makers. Ask any member of staff trying to discover what might be going on among the movers and shakers in the ministry, let alone trying to contribute to their knowledge about higher education.[6]

Metaphor

The distinction between private and public mirrors the metaphor used to describe the space in which public debates occur: the forum of ancient city-states as contrasted with the private houses of citizens. This narrowly physical conception of political-public space may have been adequate once but it has outlived its usefulness. It may well have been true that the (male, free) citizens of ancient times could congregate in a single space in which any of them could make their presence felt. However, such spaces no longer exist, even for a single university.

The boundaries defining a university are fluid, fuzzy and difficult to draw. At first sight it may appear that the staff and students of a university make up a small community roughly the size of many ancient city-states. But the community is not so self-contained. Those deeply interested in the teaching, learning, scholarship and research of any given university include all those who might benefit from it, or wish to do so. Consider again the local schools, hospitals, law firms and businesses. Consider all those people who visit from time to time (in person, through e-mail, through the Internet) to visit the library, engage in dialogue or simply learn from its tutors and support staff. Consider all those institutions in partnership with the university, locally, nationally and internationally: they are in partnership precisely because of their interest in knowledge. In this context there is a very limited application for the metaphor of a universally accessible 'forum' or a 'sphere', even in the attenuated form of, say, an academic council, or a university e-mail system.

Why make such a fuss about a metaphor? As Maxine Greene says: 'A metaphor is what it does. A metaphor, because of the way it brings together things that are unlike, re-orients consciousness, which customarily connects things that are like' (Greene and Griffiths 2002: 85). We want to work with this idea that thinking metaphorically can reorient consciousness. At the same time we remain mindful that thinking with old, stiff, outworn metaphors can fix thinking in unhelpful directions. This raises the question as to how new metaphors might be invented, whether metaphors can be 'timely', and how and why some metaphors come to be seen as illuminating or a hindrance. The feminist philosopher Jean Grimshaw, in an illuminating article on 'Philosophy and the feminist imagination', draws on the work of George Lakoff and Mark Johnson.

Lakoff and Johnson (1990) point out that much of our everyday language which we may think of as cut and dried and 'literal' is in fact metaphorically structured, in that one sort of thing is conceptualized in terms of another. Examples they discuss are 'Argument is war', 'Time is money', 'Love is a journey'. Some can be seen as kinds of 'root' metaphors in the sense that they underlie a whole host of everyday ways of thinking. 'Argument is war' is like this in that it underlies other terms such as 'winning', 'strategy', 'weak points' and so on. These are *metaphors we live by*, according to Lakoff and

Johnson, in that they provide us with open-ended 'gestalts' which organize and help construct our experience to such an extent that they have become 'common sense'. By drawing attention to their root metaphor ('Argument is war') which we do not in fact use explicitly as a metaphor, such expressions are de-familiarized and we are thereby invited to reflect on how they affect the ways we think and the ways we behave (Grimshaw 2000).

Jean Grimshaw asks us to 're-metaphorise the familiar', to see it as strange, by asking us to consider a new metaphor for the processes of discussion and argument, 'Argument is horticulture'. We are to imagine ourselves faced with statements such as:

We need to water this argument.
This idea needs pruning.
We'd be clearer if we re-potted these thoughts.
These ideas need putting into the sunlight.
This theory won't be ripe until the autumn.
This book doesn't have deep enough roots.

Of course any 'non-ordinary' meanings and metaphors would have to catch on, and given the academic 'cringe' factor, the horticultural one is unlikely to do so in our universities. Grimshaw acknowledges:

> Linguistic agency cannot be thought of as an abstract autonomy; our utterances are produced and sedimented by histories which we do not create, and have effects which we cannot ultimately determine, predict or control, and of which we may be unaware. But *within* this history and unwittingness, I believe there is a space for the conscious and intentional operation of feminist imagination, for experimental engagements with metaphors and styles and forms of discourse.
> (Grimshaw 2000: 204–5)

Feminists have been amongst those who are most interested in freeing up old patterns of thinking, behaving and relating. The project recommended here by Grimshaw, to investigate the role which metaphors might play in the 'feminist imagination' is suggestive for our project in this paper. For it helps point towards 'loosening up' thinking about the public sphere/public spaces in ways which may be more helpful and more 'timely' than traditional, sedimented ways.

Following Jean Grimshaw's suggestion, we present a new metaphor of public space, in the hope that it will help in the task of freeing up ossified patterns of understanding the democratic possibilities of public space in universities. More exactly, it is less a new metaphor, than an old one with a feminist makeover. We invite reconsideration of the metaphor of 'the body politic'.

In its more traditional forms, the body politic is one in which the head rules, while each of the members play their various parts. This is a metaphor of a bounded body ruled by hierarchies. The feminist philosopher, Donna Haraway, in a series of books and articles gives a richer – and a more startling – notion of the body. This is a notion of a body as network, as connected, as constructed both by discourse and by the materiality of new technologies. Haraway draws together two ideas governing biological discourse about bodies: the immune system and the cyborg. The immune system, she says, is understood:

> Not as a system of work, organized by the hierarchical division of labour, ordered by a privileged dialectic between highly localized nervous and reproductive functions, but instead as a coded text, organized as an engineered communications system, ordered by a fluid and dispersed command-control-intelligence network.
>
> (1991: 211)

She goes on to explain that this discourse has: 'Destabilised the symbolic privilege of the hierarchical, localised, organic body.' She argues: 'Bodies have become cyborgs – cybernetic organisms – compounds of hybrid techno-organic embodiment and textuality. The cyborg is text, machine, body, and metaphor – all theorized and engaged in terms of communication' (Haraway 1991: 2,12). Similarly, Christine Battersby (1998) criticizes traditional philosophers' conceptions of the body as she rather draws our attention to bodies that bleed; to leaky bodies that have no fixed or impermeable boundary; to bodies that are fluid and changing rather than fixed and immutable.

These metaphors provide us with a rich set of possibilities for understanding the public spaces in the networks that go beyond any traditional bounds of universities. They point to the leaky bodies politic that constitute our familiar world of institutions of higher education. They make it easier for us to discern some of the spaces in and around universities where public knowledge is alive and well. They allow us to rethink the spaces where knowledge can travel both ways through various forms of dialogue and expression.

The first example comes from North America. Ross Gray works at the University of Toronto and is also the co-director of a cancer centre. He works closely with groups of patients, drawing out from them their fears and understandings of their health problems. He is careful, as he describes, to work with them, not on them, as would happen with classical research subjects. This then opens the way to carrying out a collective exploration of ways of expressing what they have (collectively) learnt in drama – which is used for health education more widely in North America. The research-based drama about breast cancer, *Handle with Care?*, was performed across Canada about 200 times. He is now working with a new drama on prostate cancer, *No Big Deal*. (See Gray and Sinding 2002; Gray 2003.) One of us (Morwenna) heard about this project at an academic conference in Canada. Getting knowledge from conference presentations is academic life as normal. But consider: this is knowledge gained from drawing on spaces far beyond the traditional, which has now been incorporated into the academy. At the same conference another academic described how her approach to her research had been transformed by coming across Gray's work. Meanwhile, once back in England, Morwenna e-mailed one of her research students (who lived in another town and lectured at a different university) to tell him about it. He ordered the books for his own library – and for all she knows he still e-mails Gray across the Atlantic. A public space, a web of relations has been created; it is a space of a cyborg body politic, dependent for its creation and maintenance on both face-to-face contact and the technologies of phone, e-mail, word-processing – even mass air travel.

Cynthia Cockburn, a university-based sociologist, also shifts productively between the university and the knowledge to be found beyond its formal boundaries. She used her university position and knowledge to fund a project, part-research, part-development, part-activist, in which she worked with women in Bosnia, Belfast and Israel/Palestine. Earlier in the article we quoted her explaining that these are places where differences of identity may be lethal. The groups she worked with operate as collectives across the boundaries of such identities. Cockburn learnt from and contributed to these groups (Cockburn 1998; Cockburn and Hunter 1999). The collaboration was more than a rational and verbal exchange of views – though it included many verbal and rational exchanges of views. The project included producing an exhibition of photographs, and visits by the women to observe and to live closely with women from the other countries for short periods of time. The exhibition was intended to be of use to the activist communities who might support the various projects. At the same time knowledge collectively made across the academic/activist boundary has been used to inform academic projects. For example, it has informed this one: we cited this work earlier in this article. It reached our attention through a mix of cross-university cyber links, of face-to-face conferences and seminars, and through traditionally printed books and desktop published material. As with the previous example, a cyborg body politic has been created in this web of relations. It depends on technologies for its existence.

A final example comes from knowledge gained, developed and expressed as part of doing a PhD. Jean Rath's doctorate (Rath 1999) evaluated a course which trained rape counsellors. This was not an evaluation in which the university-based worker tried to take an external objective stance. It was not just that as a rape counsellor herself, she was an outsider-insider. A major part of the project of creating the thesis was taken up with her exploration of ways she could find to work with rape counsellors to express what it means to do the job. For instance, rather than present their words as short quotations, as is usual in qualitative evaluation, she turned their words into poetry (keeping the words and the order, and working closely with the women). These powerful evocations of experience were then part of the academic knowledge she could use, did use, in academic settings: papers, seminars. Other aspects of this academic knowledge included highly theoretical discussion of the limits of knowledge and its expression. But the poems also entered the space of the rape counsellors and the rape counselling training, and had a separate life and purpose there. In short this doctoral thesis uses the public space of esoteric postmodern theory, while it intersects with the public space of rape counselling centres, to construct knowledge for both, drawing on both, differently expressed in each space, but unorthodox in both. Again, as with the previous examples, this network of relations would not have been possible without a range of technologies. Indeed the thesis as a whole is best read in its electronic versions.

In this article we have stressed plurality and imagination in thinking about the role of universities as producers, purveyors and guardians of what we have called 'public knowledge'. We have stressed the involvement of many publics and many forms of engagement in re-thinking (re-imagining) notions of public space which have held sway until now. It is our belief that traditional meanings and sedimented metaphors restrict and contain and that the time is ripe for new thinking which will open up rather than close down possibilities for the creative development of new understandings of the world (as well as practical solutions to urgent problems). Our argument is that academics cannot do this on their own but have to learn to engage with communities, individuals and groups outside the academy. Specifically, we have suggested that the requirement is for higher education practices in which the perspectives and insights of diverse groups and communities can be treated in their own terms and where the knowledge developed is not just about information or even 'critical intelligence' but is about our sense of ourselves and the world, and, a much-neglected aspect of epistemology, knowing people.

In the current context, the danger we face of a privatized university system is not a distant possibility, given the prominence of market criteria in higher education as in the wider society. Faced with this, a new, committed approach to higher education is urgently required, one which reaches out in dialogue and partnership with its wider community (local and international) and which, in resisting the equation of 'community' with 'business community', acknowledges that we live in a deeply troubled world. In such a world, the possibility of engaging the university with the whole community, bringing to bear rigorous intellectual enquiry and creative imagination into the whole range of areas of importance to humankind is surely vital.

Nicholas Maxwell gets it right, we think, when he writes in a letter to the Guardian (2003: p. 23):

> Academia as it exists at present ... betrays both reason and humanity. The proper rational task of academia is to help humanity learn how to tackle its conflicts and problems of living in more cooperatively rational ways than at present. A rational and responsible academia would act as a kind of people's civil service doing openly for the public what actual civil services are supposed to do in secret for governments.

Notes

[1] Related to this, David Noble has written a fascinating account of how the advent of ascetic culture among Christian clerics from the late medieval period 'has led to male dominance over the practices and institutions of higher learning' and continues to exert a 'subtle influence' even today (see Noble 1992: back cover). He shows, through painstaking historical research (insisting that 'the history of ideas is not the same as the history of people' (Noble 1992: 3)) that the usual story of Western science (told in 'secular retrospect') as *in opposition* to religion, as, that is, a dramatic *departure from* clerical (Catholic and Protestant) tradition and authority, is simply wrong, and ahistorical. 'Western science evolved only half human, in a world without women' is the dramatic opening sentence of his book, which is at pains to underline the *strangeness* of the resulting state of affairs, whilst coming to appear so *normal*. He contests, too, the common assumption that women have always been excluded:

> an assumption that rests on the allegedly enduring legacy of ancient Greece, with its homosocial Platonic academies and Aristotelian misogyny (xv)

And he provides an account of anticlerical social struggle as a corrective to this common ahistorical assumption of continuity, as well as to the fatalism it engenders. In his final chapter he describes women's permanent entry, in the nineteenth century, into what *was* by then a world without women,

> only to be confronted by another clerical restoration, in the form of a male scientific professionalism that betrayed the same misogynistic and, indeed, monastic habits of the clerical culture it superceded (xvi).

[2] The argument is sharply made in Stephen Frears' 2003 film *Dirty Pretty Things*. A line summarizing the anger behind the film is delivered by an actor playing just such a refugee, a Nigerian doctor, who had worked in the USA, to an English van driver: 'You did not notice us because you do not see us. We are the ones who clean your rooms, drive your taxis and suck your cocks.' The line is as it has been remembered and may not be quite accurate.

[3] There is more detail about this systematic lack of parity in Griffiths (2000).

[4] See Gaita (2002), which locates the roots of our capacity for justice and virtue in love and intimacy.

[5] The public space is not necessarily a unitary space. For instance, Benhabib argues that Habermasian public space could be construed as plural. Since it is constructed by discourse, 'in principle there can be as many publics as there are discourses concerning controversial norms' (1992: 119). She gives the example of the ' "public" sphere of the pornography debate' as distinct from the ' "public" sphere of the foreign policy debate' (1992: 119). However, the sharp distinction between 'private' and 'public' remains.

[6] See Smith (2001) for an account of how he was offended by Dearing's failure to understand what university teaching means to a university teacher: certainly not 'facilitation' or 'delivery'.

References

Arendt, H. (1958) *The Human Condition*. London and Chicago: University of Chicago Press.
Arendt, H. (1968) *Men in Dark Times*. New York: Harcourt Brace Jovanovich.
Arendt, H. (1994) Understanding and politics, in J. Kohn (ed.) *Essays on Understanding 1930–1954*. New York: Harcourt Brace.
Battersby, C. (1998) *The Phenomenal Woman*. Cambridge: Polity.
Benhabib, S. (1992) *Situating the Self: Gender, Community and Postmodernism in Contemporary Ethics*. Cambridge: Polity Press.
Cockburn, C. (1998) *The Space Between Us: Negotiating Gender and National Identities in Conflict*. London and New York: Zed Books.
Cockburn, C. and Hunter, L. (1999) Transversal politics and translating practices, *Soundings: A Journal of Politics and Culture*, 12. London: Lawrence and Wishart.
Cojean, A. (2003) in *The Guardian G2*, 13 February, p.7.
Deutsche, R. (1996) *Evictions: Art and Spatial Politics*. Cambridge, Mass and London: MIT Press.
Disch, L.J. (1996) *Hannah Arendt and the Limits of Philosophy*. Ithaca: Cornell University Press.
Fraser, N. (1993) Re-thinking the Public Sphere, in B. Robbins (ed.) *The Phantom Public Sphere*. Minneapolis: University of Minnesota Press.
Gaita, R. (2002) *A Common Humanity*. London and New York: Routledge.
Gray, R.E. (2003) *Prostate Tales: Men's Experiences with Prostate Cancer*. Harriman, Tennessee: Men's Studies Press.
Gray, R. E. and Sinding, C. (2002) *Standing Ovation: Performing Social Science Research About Cancer*. Lanham, Md: Altamira Press.
Greene, M. and Griffiths, M. (2002) Feminism, philosophy and education: Imagining public spaces, in N. Blake, P. Smeyers, R. Smith and P. Standish (eds) *Blackwell Guide to the Philosophy of Education*. Oxford: Blackwell.
Griffiths, M. (2000) Collaboration and partnership in question: knowledge, politics and practice, *Journal of Education Policy (Philosophical Perspectives on Education Policy)*, 15(4).
Grimshaw, J. (2000) Philosophy and the feminist imagination, in S. Ahmed, J. Kilby, C. Lary, M. McNeil and B. Skeggs (eds) *Transformations: Thinking Through Feminism*. London and New York: Routledge.
Habermas, J. (1962) *The Structural Transformation of the Public Sphere*. Cambridge, Mass and London: MIT Press.
Haraway, D. (1991) *Simians, Cyborgs, and Women: The Reinvention of Nature*. London: Free Association Books.
Lakoff, G. and Johnson, M. (1990) *Metaphors We Live By*. Chicago: Chicago University Press.
Leonard, D. (ed.) (2002) *The Politics of Gender and Education*. London: Institute of Education, University of London.
MacIntyre, A. (1987) The idea of an educated public, in G. Haydon (ed.) *Education and Values*. London: Institute of Education, University of London.
Massey, D. (2001) Blurring the boundaries: High-Tech in Cambridge, in C. Pechter, M. Preedy, D. Scott and J. Soler (eds) *Knowledge, Power and Learning*. London and Milton Keynes: Paul Chapman in association with the Open University.
Maxwell, N. (2003) Letter to *The Guardian*, 25 March, p.23.
McGregor, L. (2003) Share in the future, *The Guardian Education*, 11 February.

Morley, L. and Walsh, V. (eds) (1995) *Feminist Academics and Creative Agents for Change*. London: Taylor and Francis.

Noble, D. (1992) *A World Without Women: The Christian Clerical Culture of Western Science*. Oxford and New York: Oxford University Press.

Nussbaum, M. (1986) *The Fragility of Goodness*. Cambridge: Cambridge University Press.

Rath, J. (1999) *Getting smarter? Inventing context bound feminist research/writing with/in the postmodern*. PhD thesis. Warwick: University of Warwick, Department of Continuing Education.

Rawls, J. (1972) *A Theory of Justice*. Oxford: Clarendon Press.

Robbins, B. (1993) The Public as Phantom, in B. Robbins (ed.) *The Phantom Public Sphere*. Minneapolis: University of Minnesota Press.

Ryle, G. (1971) *Collected Papers*. London: Hutchinson.

Sennet, R. (1974) *The Fall of Public Man*. New York: Random House.

Smith, R. (2001) The demand of language: the justice of the différend, in *The School Field (Special Issue: Social Justice in/and Education)*, XII (1/2), 43–54.

Young, I. M. (1987) Impartiality and the civic public: Some implications of feminist critiqueness of moral and political theory, in S. Benhabib and D. Cornell (eds) *Feminism as Critique*. Minneapolis: University of Minnesota Press.

Young, I.M. (1990) *Justice and the Politics of Difference*. Princeton: Princeton University Press.

Young, I.M. (2000) *Inclusion and Democracy*. Oxford: Oxford University Press.

6

Sitting Uneasily at the Table

Judyth Sachs

Over the past ten years I have participated in a variety of quality assurance (QA) and quality improvement (QI) activities at two universities. Both of these experiences have been significantly different in their orientation, how quality has come to be defined, and the role I played in implementing quality assurance and quality improvement initiatives across the institution. While both of the activities were concerned with developing a 'quality culture' across the institution, the political contexts at the time had a significant effect on how these activities were conducted and findings reported. Significantly, at the time of both activities there were strong pressures for external accountability. The early 1990s signalled the first wave of government interest in QA in Australia with visits to universities by panels of academics. Importantly, the ranking of university performance had a reward/penalty component. The rankings were such that the more highly ranked universities were allocated extra funds. More recently, the second wave of QA is being conducted by panels of the Australian Universities Quality Agency (AUQA) with no funding allocation associated with the report of the panel.

This chapter has two provocations. This first is that it provides an opportunity for me to reflect on my experiences of QA and how in my current position I find myself contributing to the institution's quality assurance initiatives in a collegial set of processes rather than the more orthodox managerial ones. The second is my work on the development of an activist form of teacher professionalism (Sachs 2003) and my attempts to model this type of professionalism in my work as Chair of the Academic Board.

While at Griffith University, from 1993–95, I coordinated a university-wide project that was concerned with specific quality initiatives in three faculties: The Queensland College of Arts (QCA), The Faculty of Education and the Arts (EDA) and The Faculty of Engineering and Environmental Science (ENS). The overall project adopted a developmental orientation which was reflected in all its practices, rather than a technical rationalist approach characterized by heavy reliance on hard appraisal processes, through which change was to be bureaucratically mandated and imposed (Sachs 1995). The outcomes of the latter demanded compliance because of bureaucratically mandated penalties for non-compliance.

The three projects involved staff from the faculties working with me to develop quality improvement practices ranging from the development of new assessment strategies at the QCA, to the implementation of a school-university partnership strategy at EDA and examining the effectiveness and appropriateness of the model of the Graduate School of Environmental Sciences and Engineering. The defining feature of these projects was that they were developed in response to emergent needs and issues identified by faculty staff. My job was to facilitate the development of a quality culture and a set of quality improvement measures that were documented and reported to the central University as well as to the Commonwealth who funded the project.

This initiative was a collegial activity supported by the staff development unit of the Faculty of Education. Structurally it did not have a reporting or accountability line into a central management portfolio of the University. As a courtesy, reports were forwarded to the Pro Vice-Chancellor (Quality Assurance). This information was used to contribute to the University's QA portfolio.

More recently, as Chair of the Academic Board at the University of Sydney, I have had a role to play in the development of quality assurance/quality improvement activities across the University. In this position my work towards the University's QA agenda has been in three capacities: i. Chairing Academic Board Faculty Reviews of Teaching and Learning and Research Training; ii. membership of the Quality Advisory Coordinating Group; and iii. contributing to the writing of the University Self Audit portfolio required in preparation for the visit in June 2004 by a panel of the Australian Universities Quality Agency.

In thinking about this I have become aware of the paradox that even though the Chair of the Academic Board is not seen to be part of management in a structural sense, as Chair I contribute to management functions and practices of the University in responding to externally driven accountability measures. Furthermore, the practices of an activist academic professional could well be seen to be counter to the requirements of a contemporary university. Indeed, this is why on occasion I sit uncomfortably at the table – the tension for me is to maintain my independence and not be captured by managerialist agendas that are shaping contemporary university policies and practices or to be seduced by the influence and access to information that this position affords.

Accountability and higher education

Nixon et al. (2001: 229) observe that 'Higher education is undergoing a series of complex overlapping changes, which are profoundly affecting its organisational structures, traditional practices, and the way in which its institutions and those who work within them are viewed by the public'. For Rowland (2001: 3) this has meant that 'The obsession with so-called standards has transformed the products of higher education and the lives of those who work in it as learners, teachers and researchers'. In practice the increasing demands for external accountability and the development of systems of verification to ensure institutional compliance is a feature of much institutional work whereby a great deal of staff time is taken up with monitoring, responding to and reporting on aspects of the university's performance. Furthermore, at the University of Sydney in this new climate the Academic Board now has a central role to play in the development of a review strategy across the university.

In this chapter I suggest that the development of audit cultures (Strathern 2000) and systems of verification can be seen as a response to the development of risk consciousness (Ericson and Haggerty 1997) or risk anxiety (Wilkinson 2001) across the public sphere of Western society. Wilkinson (2001: 91) maintains that the 'conceptions of the risk-anxiety relationship are politically motivated to persuade us towards a favoured perspective on the trustworthiness of expert opinion as well as the moral acceptability of the statistically improbable event of disaster'.

Contemporary public sector reforms and the ensuing policies in the UK, Australia and the USA have led to the development of 'the audit society' and 'audit cultures', with an emphasis of regimes of verification (Power 1997; Strathern 2000). For Power (1997: 122) auditing is now:

> ... a programmatic idea circulating in organisational environments, an idea which promises a certain style of control and organisational transparency. From this point of view audit may be less a rational response to the need to reduce transactions costs and more a temporarily congealed taste or fashion which escapes a conscious design ... The underlying social theory is more that of routine or institutionalised practice rather than rational choice, cognitive congealment rather than efficient adaptation.

Under the strictures of an audit society surveillance and inspection go hand in hand. Regulation, enforcement and sanctions are required to ensure compliance. Of its professionals it requires self-ordering, not based on individual or moral judgement, but upon meeting externally applied edicts and commands. It requires 'regulatory mechanisms acting as "political technologies" which seek to bring persons, organisations and objectives into alignment' (Shore and Wright 2000: 61). Indeed, a major aspect of Academic Board reviews of faculties is to investigate compliance with various Academic Board policies. In essence this in itself is a risk management strategy and demonstrates the concern with the legal ramifications if policies are not observed and put into practice.

The development of risk consciousness across public and private spheres alike has been a consequence of these determinations. Likewise audit can be seen as a response to risk consciousness. For Caplan (2000: 23) 'one aspect of risk management is that, in its name, control can be asserted by governments and other bodies over populations'. Indeed, as Douglas (1992) has rightly observed, the discourse on risk is politicized and the language of risk is reserved as a specialized lexical register for political talk about the undesirable outcomes. For universities these could refer to unsatisfactory research and publication outcomes and productivity, poor outcomes in graduate employment or reports by students that teaching is of poor quality.

By its very nature risk is about the exercise of power and control – who has the power to make decisions about what constitutes risk and what kind of strategies or regulatory frameworks are to be put in place to ensure compliance. Risk is manifest in discourses circulating across institutions, especially those around QA, and becomes instutionalized within the everyday practices of the institution by a system of rules, regulations and policies. The strong and sustained push for accountability required by governments and various risk management and quality assurance methods developed within universities, and their accompanying policies to ensure that this is done, can be seen in this light.

Risk and audit then go hand in hand. In Australia, as elsewhere, the audit explosion has emerged from deep structural changes in organizational governance. Those of us who have experienced external or even internal audits will concur with Power's (1997: 142–3) observation that 'audits may turn organisations on their heads and generate excessive pre-occupations with, often costly, auditable processes. At the extreme, performance and quality are in danger of being defined largely in terms of conformity to the processes.'

Nevertheless, governments appear to retain their commitment to use risk technologies such as audit visits as a means of overseeing the governance and management of universities and making judgements about their performance. The Australian Universities Quality Agency (AUQA) can be seen as a government response to issues of quality and risk. The Academic Board Reviews of Academic Quality Assurance Systems and the Board's review of Faculty Teaching and Learning Plans and Faculty compliance with the University goals expressed in the University Strategic Plan can be seen as an institutional response to joint pressures of risk and audit.

AUQA as a response to risk

AUQA was formally established by the Ministerial Council on Education, Training and Youth Affairs (MCEETYA) in March 2000. It operates independently of governments and the higher education sectors under the direction of a Board of Directors.

AUQA is responsible for:

- Conducting quality audits of self-accrediting Australian higher education institutions and State and Territory Government higher education accreditation authorities on a five-yearly cycle;
- Providing public reports on the outcomes of these audits;
- Commenting on the criteria for the recognition of new universities and accreditation of non-university higher education awards, as a result of information obtained during the audits of institutions and State and Territory accreditation processes; and
- Reporting the relative standards and international standing of the Australian higher education system and its quality assurance processes. As a result of information obtained during the audit process.
  (http://auqa.edu.au/aboutauqa/auqainfo/body_mainshtml)

Audits are whole of institution's audits based on self-assessment and on-site visit. AUQA panels investigate the extent to which the institutions are achieving their missions and objectives. They assess the adequacy of the institutions' quality assurance arrangements in the key areas of teaching and learning, research and management, including the institutions' overseas activities. They also assess the institutions' success in maintaining standards consistent with university education in Australia.

Comments have been mixed about the visits. On the one hand negative comments have been made about the financial costs, not only of hosting the audit teams but also the preparation of the audit portfolios. In some institutions estimates of between AUS$450,000 and AUS$1.5 million have been suggested. More significant though has been the institutional and administrative disruption caused by preparation for AUQA visits because they take resources away from core university business. On the other hand, there have been positive comments about how the preparation of the reports has enabled a more systematic approach to a critical examination of an institution's performance. For some institutions this has become a strategy for cross-institutional change and renewal, acting as an externally imposed trigger.

To date some 18 academic institutions have had visits from AUQA panels. The reports are public documents and can be found on the AUQA website. At the time of writing this chapter the University of Sydney had been informed that it was to be visited in June 2004. The self-review document has to be completed and submitted to AUQA by March 2004.

The development of the University of Sydney self-review portfolio will draw strongly on the Academic Board Review Reports. A decision was made early in its development for the Academic Board activities to be an integral aspect of the University's quality assurance strategy. It is through this process that the work of the Academic Board becomes firmly associated with the managerial functions of the institution and the position of Chair of the Academic Board and Chair of most of the Faculty Review panels complements this. The 'independence' of the Chair from management then comes into question.

The Academic Board – managing but not management

In the *Review of New Zealand Tertiary Education Institution Governance*, Edwards (2003: 50) observes that 'the last decade or so has seen the relative power of Academic Boards across many countries diminish as entrepreneurial and fiscal policies become important for tertiary institutions'. She goes on to argue that 'attitudes appear to be switching back toward the value of strong Academic Boards' (50). Within the Australian context the role and power of Academic Boards have certainly reflected this trend. There is a general orthodoxy that they should be at the centre of providing academic policy and advice to university governing bodies and Vice-Chancellors, be proactive and effective in contributing to academic policy, be independent and balanced in their membership and in their deliberations, and have visibility in and the confidence of the university community. A major responsibility of the Chair is to ensure that these activities are happening, and that they are seen to be happening.

Autonomy and independence are very important to most Academic Boards. Most Academic Boards and their chairs or presidents also recognize that, along with autonomy and independence, there comes the privilege of showing responsibility and duty to the University as a whole (McConkey 2002). To act in the best interests of the university is an unspoken dictum.

At the University of Sydney, the Academic Board advises the Senate and Vice-Chancellor on all matters relating to or affecting the University's teaching and research activities, and its educational programmes. Two of its functions are to coordinate and maintain an overview of the activities of faculties and to participate in a formal and regular programme of review of academic activities of faculties. The recent activities on quality assurance come within these two functions.

Structurally the Academic Board stands apart from university management. Its role is the development, monitoring and evaluation of policies as these relate to the academic and research aspects of university activity. It is a collegial structure comprised of the Board itself, which at present has a membership of 62 representing various ex-officio and elected staff and student constituencies. There are six committees of the Board, which deal specifically with Teaching and Learning, Research, Graduate Studies, Undergraduate Studies, Library and Academic Staffing. At various times working parties are constituted to develop discussion papers, investigate issues or revise specific Academic Board policies. These usually report back to the committee that commissioned the work.

Unlike chairs or presidents of Academic Boards at some other universities, the Chair of the Academic Board at the University of Sydney does not participate in the senior management activities of the University, but often has to respond to and oversee the managerial initiatives of the University administration. The Chair is an ex-officio member of the Senate (the University's governing body) and member of the University Finance Committee – a committee of Senate, the Senate/ Sports Liaison Committee and is Chair of the Senate Student Appeals Committee (Exclusions and Readmissions). The Chair of the Board is also a member of the Vice-Chancellor's Advisory Committee (VCAC), the Quality Advisory Coordinating Group (QACG) and other university-wide committees. Unlike other universities, the Chair of the Academic Board is not a member of the Senior Executive Group (which includes the three Deputy Vice-Chancellors (DVCs), the Chief Financial Officer and the three College Pro Vice-Chancellors (PVCs)) or the Budget Advisory Committee.

Accordingly, there is some structural ambiguity in the position, especially as the responsibility for overseeing compliance with academic policy across the University puts the Chair of the Board often between a rock and a hard place. For my purposes here my Scylla can be seen to be my independence from senior management and my Charybdis is maintaining my professional autonomy when the expectation is that this work contributes to a managerial function of quality assurance.

Because it is led by academics this collegial approach to quality assurance has served to improve the perception of the work of the Academic Board and its relevance as a mechanism for academic decision-making. Previously it had been seen as 'rubber stamping the decisions of its committees'. A submission to the Review of the Academic Board commissioned in 2001 suggested, 'The reason why the Academic Board is seen to merely rubber stamp recommendations of its committees lies in members' perceptions of a lack of power or authority in the Board'. The reviews make the Board more visible in the eyes of academics and lend a strong academic function.

Academic Board reviews at the University of Sydney

The Academic Board Resolution *The Management and Evaluation of Coursework Teaching* states that the Academic Board's policy structures are intended to encourage the maintenance and development of high standards of teaching, scholarship and research. To be confident that the policy structures properly sustain academic quality assurance and are appropriate to the University's needs, the Board must monitor their implementation and effectiveness. Much of this monitoring is effected through the annual reviews of Academic Quality Assurance Systems and the Board's review of Faculty Teaching and Learning Plans.

To fulfil its functions, the Academic Board coordinates and maintains an overview of the academic activities of faculties and similar organizational units. The Board's annual reviews of Academic Quality Assurance Systems and the Board's review of Faculty Teaching and Learning Plans are designed to ensure that this overview is maintained consistently across the University, so that the Academic Board is in a position to offer informed and accurate advice to Senate and the Vice-Chancellor.

The Academic Board Reviews are informed by seven principles.[1] These include inter alia:

Principle 1
The University's approach to quality assurance and improvement is 'academic led'. In practice this means:

- That there is widespread involvement of academic staff in working parties and Academic Board structures where quality issues are discussed and quality improvement policies and procedures are formulated;
- That the University promotes a view of quality improvement as an integral part of the academic enterprise;
- That quality improvement shall be driven by staff who are active in teaching and research rather than considered as an additional activity;
- That quality improvement applies the same criteria of excellence to academic activities and to quality improvement; and that it judges its performance in both areas against the standards appropriate to internationally competitive research-intensive universities.

Principle 2
The Academic Board coordinates and maintains an overview of the academic activities of faculties. The Board's annual reviews of teaching, learning and research training systems and of Faculty Teaching and Learning Plans are designed to ensure that this overview is maintained consistently and constructively across the University.

Principle 3
Reviews will be conducted regularly and systematically, following the Academic Board Resolution *The Management and Evaluation of Coursework Teaching*. Before undertaking reviews of Faculty academic and award courses, members of review teams will receive training.

Principle 4
The aim of the review process is to enhance and improve teaching, learning and research training practices of the University. It will be led

by the needs of the University, but will also help faculties prepare for AUQA audits.

Principle 5
The review process is formative and collegial. The aim is to provide constructive feedback on the quality of a faculty's teaching, learning and research training processes, resulting in the sharing of information and open collegial dialogue about the quality of academic activities. Points of good practice and recommendations for improvement identified in the reports will be circulated to facilitate the sharing of good practices.

Principle 6
In order to take into account the diversity, variation and complexities of teaching and learning across the University, faculties with a number of departments and schools are encouraged to develop their own quality review processes to evaluate teaching and research training in these departments and schools. This will enable more thorough assessment of the faculty's teaching, learning and research training practices at the time of the review.

Principle 7
The review team will act ethically and according to principles of natural justice, equity and fairness. No member of a pool of reviewers shall be on the review team for the faculty of which s/he is a member. Other persons will disclose any potential conflict of interest in the faculties being reviewed.

The Academic Board Reviews are organized around five phases. During the first phase the faculty prepares a self-evaluation report on teaching, learning and research training. This is sent to the central quality assurance officer who then distributes it to members of the Review Panel. Phase two involves the analysis of the Self Evaluation Report and the Faculty Teaching and Learning Plan. Questions are developed by the team to 'drill down' into the 'fit' between stated objectives, processes and outcomes. The third phase involves a day visit to the faculty to interview the Dean, members of the Faculty Executive, academic and general staff and students (undergraduate, postgraduate and research). At the end of the visit the Chair of the Review Committee (usually the Chair of the Academic Board or nominee) provides an oral report back to the Dean relating to areas of commendation and recommendation for improvement. Stage four occurs when a draft report is sent back to the faculty for comment and accuracy. The final phase involves the report being presented to the Teaching and Learning Committee of Academic Board. At this stage the report becomes a public document and is put up on the Academic Board website.

During late 2001 and 2002 review teams visited 17 faculties. Each team member had a series of questions that were asked to the various interview groups. To ensure consistency the same suite of questions were asked to each group on the day. In what follows I will make some observations about the process and outcomes of the Phase one reviews.

Some observations and achievements

The overall response from staff after the first round of reviews has been positive. In particular, the majority of academic staff have been appreciative of the collegial nature of the review visits. That these are peer reviews has contributed to a greater 'buy in' from staff – senior management, academic and administrative. Territorial or discipline disputes that might otherwise erode a sense of collegiality have not been evident. If anything, there is a greater appreciation of the complexity of the University but more importantly of the individual and collective achievements of staff.

Hand in hand with the collegial nature of the review, and perhaps scaffolding their apparent success, is the view held by staff that as a QA strategy the emphasis is not on staff making judgements about their peers, rather it is about advising and supporting them. Indeed, while many reports were critical of some faculty practices, these were presented in a way where the orientation for improvement, and suggested strategies to achieve this, possibly neutralized what could have been otherwise seen as a negative or judgemental comment. Furthermore, the mere fact that there were no members external to the University on the panels was a deliberate strategy to reinforce a peer approach to quality across the University.

Nevertheless, on occasion there was a tension between the necessity of providing a rigorous process with what could be seen by some as a 'soft' collegial one. What marked this process as being different from previous QA regimes was that staff had confidence in the process which was seen to be transparent and improvement oriented. This was largely due to the fact that during its development there had been significant consultation across the University and the feedback gained during this time was incorporated into the policy documentation and the accompanying implementation process. There had been discussions at the faculty level, which was fed back into the University Teaching and Learning Committee, an Academic Board Forum and the Academic Board meeting itself. In addition to this all staff who participated as members of panels had to undergo a one day training session where they were introduced to the principles informing the process and developed skills in reading the self-evaluation reports critically, focusing on what was left out, claims that were not supported with evidence and asking probing questions. Questions were to be focused and concerned with broader issues rather than the minutiae of detail.

The alignment of academic and managerial processes is an integral part of the QA processes currently in train. Ramsden (2003) refers to this as an attempt at harmonization, where mandated academic policies are complemented by voluntary recognition and reward processes, while resource related management strategies are combined with review and policy processes underpinned by collegial imperatives.

It would be remiss not to talk about the intensification of academic work that is accompanied by the QA strategy at the University. The review visits were undertaken on already heavy work schedules – regrettably there were no opportunities or resources for staff to be bought out of either teaching or administrative commitments. The issue of workload was apparent across various levels of the University. At the faculty level the preparation of the Self Evaluation Reports increased the workloads of the Deans and members of his/her executive. For the Chair of the Board it meant chairing the majority of review visits; for the PVC (Teaching and Learning) it was through staff associated with that office that the organization of the visits and then the writing of the review reports and finally, for individual academics at least two days was spent away from their other academic tasks in participating in at least two reviews. Interestingly despite this staff believed that the process and experience enhanced their understanding of the complexity of the University and provided them with ideas and strategies that they could take back to their own faculty, especially with regard to their own future faculty visit.

The QA processes implicit in the Academic Board reviews also helped to open up lines of communication across the University. Here the Academic Board acted as a conduit through which information was communicated and circulated to management, staff and students. Much of this information was about 'best practice' which could be transposed across to other faculties. It also fostered communication between staff in faculties and the development of collegial networks between staff participating in the review panels. This probably would not have occurred without the impetus of the Academic Board reviews.

Another reason for this QA being accepted by academic staff was that the process was seen to be facilitative and improvement oriented rather than punitive. Unlike many QA initiatives this was not used as a 'shaming' strategy to ensure compliance. One of its singular benefits from a faculty point of view is that it provides an opportunity for a group of peers to help identify problems and then provide suggestions as to how these might be addressed or solved. Moreover, the identification of areas of commendation provided a form of affirmation and recognition to faculties of the areas where they were doing well.

While students were not involved in the review panels (this was discussed during the development of the processes and the decision was made to have academic only membership), they commented positively about the review process. They expressed gratitude that the University was wanting to improve its performance across areas of teaching and learning and research training. At the end of each student session the chair asked them 'why did they come to the session?' There was a consistent response back that they were proud to be students at Sydney and wanted to contribute to the maintenance of its good name.

The final comment is how the Academic Board review visits contributed to a process of institution building. The systematic strategy of faculty visits, undertaken in a collegial, but rigorous and non judgemental, manner helped to facilitate among staff a view that the University was endeavouring to improve both its practices and its performance across a number of areas. While these visits contributed to the development of the University's AUQA self-review portfolio, this was not their prime purpose. It was a sense of pragmatism that saw these data used for the QA requirements of AUQA and not that this pending visit was driving the QA strategy.

Sitting uneasily at the table

Thus far I have presented a description of the QA processes that I have had to implement and monitor in my role as Chair of the Academic Board. In what follows I reflect on my own reactions and perceptions of being 'betwixt and between' – that is, not being part of management but often having to do the work of management especially as this relates to quality assurance processes and procedures.

Let me first begin with my own perceptions of professionalism that this work has made me confront both in my own practice and also that of colleagues. It is clear that I have had to develop a view on my own practice as a senior member of the University. Given my own commitment to an activist teaching profession I have attempted to model this type of approach in my work as Chair of the Board. This has required more of a public presence of the Chair of the Board across the institution. Perhaps it was fortuitous that the Board reviews helped to facilitate this. My strategy of commissioning an external review of the operation and structure of the Academic Board and the then Academic Forum also brought into focus the role and purpose of an independent Academic Board and the role of its Chair during a period of systemic change and uncertainty. In this sense I was acting as a champion for a strong and active Academic Board.

To say that my two and a half years to date as Chair has been easy would not be accurate. I have taken certain risks in attempting to revitalize the work and operations of the Board. I have had some successes but also have been bruised on other occasions. Indeed, trying to maintain a balance between managerial imperatives and dicta and a strong and autonomous Academic Board is best described on occasion as being a risky business. The Academic Board visits have certainly improved the relevance of the Board in the eyes of many of my academic colleagues. These visits have taken the Board into faculties which previously had not been the case. If anything, faculties came to the Board for approval of new courses and policies. They have facilitated new and different types of politics, practices and relationships between faculties and across the institution.

The type of professionalism I have sought to model has been collegial and activist. I have been an advocate of issues of equity and social justice. I have attempted to practice what Guttman and Thompson (1996) have referred to as deliberative democracy where deliberation should extend throughout the political process. Deliberative democracy asks its citizens and officials to justify public policy by giving reasons that can be accepted by those bound to it. Through the structures, processes and relationships that I have developed during my tenure as Chair, I have attempted to do this. Thus, the processes of review have had as their focus the improvement of faculty performance rather than purely an audit of activities. This disposition to seek mutually justifiable reasons expresses the core of the process of deliberation (Groundwater-Smith and Sachs 2002).

A key dimension of participatory democracy for an activist academic professionalism is citizen participation, which for Rimmerman (2001) requires increased citizen participation in community and workplace decision making. Central to my argument here is Rimmerman's claim that in a true participatory setting, citizens do not merely act as autonomous individuals pursuing their own interests, but instead, through a process of decision, debate and compromise, they ultimately link their concerns with the needs of the community. In this instance debates have moved beyond sectional or discipline-specific interests toward a more institution-wide focus.

While I accept that the development of an activist academic professional is not easy, nor is it straightforward, it is something to aspire to as it works towards common goals and interests of the various stakeholders within a university community. Fundamentally its principles and practices are negotiated, collaborative, socially critical, future oriented, strategic and transparent.

Of course the acid test of the sustainability of deliberative democracy as a foundation of the Board and an activist academic professional as its Chair is yet to be tested. My successors will have the challenge or choice of whether or not to continue this type of work.

One of the greatest paradoxes has been how a potentially invasive and managerial initiative as QA reviews has achieved other institutional political work. Furthermore, while the challenge of trying to serve two masters (university management and government) could dilute the institutional building opportunities that QA can afford, the processes and the relationships thus far developed have fortunately not been compromised in its implementation.

In the current environment of government and public scrutiny of universities, the idea of the Chair of an Academic Board being co-opted by management is not beyond imagination – indeed, I have seen it happen to my colleagues in other universities. While on occasion I do sit uneasily at the table with management through my QA responsibilities I have been able to ensure that an academic voice is heard rather than a purely managerial one. My liminal status, being betwixt and between, is both a strength and source of weakness. By not being invited to sit at the table on occasions I do not have access to certain types of information, nor do I have the opportunity to participate in discussions that have strong academic implications. Indeed, to mix my metaphors I have to take comfort in between a rock and a hard place – and indeed at present university life is that!

Note

[1] Guidelines for Faculty Reviews of Teaching, Learning and Research Training. Academic Board document, July 2002.

References

Caplan, P. (2000) *Risk Revisited.* London: Pluto Press.
Douglas, M. (1992) *Risk and Blame.* London: Routledge.
Edwards, M. (2003) *Review of New Zealand Tertiary Education Institution Governance.* Wellington: Ministry of Education.
Ericson, R. and Haggerty, K. (1997) *Policing the Risk Society.* Toronto: University of Toronto Press.
Groundwater-Smith, S. and Sachs, J. (2002) The activist professional and the reinstatement of trust, *Cambridge Journal of Education,* 32(3):341–58.
Guttman, A. and Thompson, D. (1996) *Democracy and disagreement.* Cambridge, Mass: Belknap Press of Harvard University.
McConkey, K. (2002) The Academic Board: purpose and place. Invited paper presented at the National Conference on University Governance, Adelaide, 9–11 November.
Nixon, J., Marks, A., Rowland, S. and Walker, M. (2001) Towards a New Academic Professionalism: a manifesto of hope, *British Journal of Sociology of Education* 22(2):227–44.
Power, M. (1997) *The Audit Society: Rituals of Verification.* Oxford: Oxford University Press.
Ramsden, P. (2003) *Learning to Teach in Higher Education,* 2nd edn. London and New York: Routledge Falmer.
Rimmerman, C. (2001) *The New Citizenship: Unconventional Politics, Activism and Service.* Boulder, CO: Westview Press.
Rowland, S. (2001) *Higher Education: Purposes and Roles.* Paper presented at British Education Research Association Conference, University of Leeds, 13–15 September.
Sachs, J. (1995) Bridging the gap between quality improvement and quality assurance: a project at Griffith University, *Journal of Institutional Research in Australasia* 4(1).
Sachs, J. (2003) *The Activist Teaching Profession.* Buckingham: Open University Press.
Shore, C. and Wright, S. (2000) Coercive accountability, in M. Strathern (ed.) *Audit Cultures.* London: Routledge.
Strathern, M. (ed.) (2000) *Audit Cultures.* London: Routledge.
Wilkinson, I. (2001) *Anxiety in a Risk Society.* London and New York: Routledge.

7
Learning the Language of Deliberative Democracy

Jon Nixon

> Given the scorn Socrates heaps on the idea of grovelling to save one's life, there seems little reason to suppose that he is lying when he emphasises his own ignorance of the correct definition of the virtues, of a positive account of moral truth. The sole form of wisdom he does claim is, famously, the awareness of his own lack of positive knowledge of the good: 'I am only too conscious that I have no claim to wisdom, great or small'. His radically imperfect 'human wisdom' consists in knowing what he does not know, in realizing that he does not possess anything like the moral expertise claimed by the sophists, politicians, and poets. It is this negative wisdom – the sense of one's own relative ignorance of what virtue is and what the 'best life' looks like – which serves as the basis and goad of Socrates' philosophical activity.
>
> (Villa 2001: 18)

This chapter introduces some of the resources necessary for developing a language of reconstruction based on the principles and precepts of deliberative democracy. These resources are drawn from the ongoing work of various writers who are seeking to understand what it means to live together in difference within the context of 'a runaway world' (Beck and Beck-Gernsheim 2002). Although these writers do not form a clearly defined 'school', I refer to their ideas under the general category of 'new Aristotelianism', because for all their differences they take as their starting point precepts that I take to be part of a common Aristotelian legacy: that goodness lies in practice, that practice must be defined in terms of the contingent circumstances within which we find ourselves, and that those circumstances are deeply and inextricably social.

The aim is to establish neither a closed framework of ideas nor a programmatic framework for action, but to develop a mode of what Walker (2003) has termed 'bivalent theorizing'; a mode of theorizing, that is, whereby individual flourishing and organizational structure must be included within the frame of understanding. I argue that the theoretical import of notions such as 'recognition' and 'deliberation', 'authenticity' and 'connectedness', lies precisely in their sense of bivalence: their capacity for conceptual linkage between matters of both principle and practice, and issues of both structure and agency. We can only work our way through this bivalence by developing within our specific institutional settings relationships which the Aristotelian notion of 'perfect friendship' may help us realize more fully; relationships, that is, by which we can begin to reconstruct the institutional conditions necessary for learning to flourish.

Towards a 'new Aristotelianism'

Villa's (2001) gloss on Socrates' defence (as reported in Plato's *The Apology*) to the public charge, brought against him in 399 BC, of being a menace to society deserves careful consideration. According to Villa, Socrates does not deny 'the good', but asserts his incapacity to offer a positive account of what constitutes 'the good'. Socrates' claim to 'virtue' is his unswerving commitment to questioning his own and others' taken-for-granted assumptions regarding what 'goodness' is and what 'virtue' is. 'The good society', according to this reading, is a society which has the capacity to question its own account of moral truth and, in so doing, to rid itself of its own illusions. The basis of Socrates' philosophical activity is 'dis-illusionment': not the Romantic notion of 'disillusionment' as loss of hope, but a notion of 'dis-illusionment' as the means whereby we strip away false assumptions.

A key question for us, as indeed for Villa, is how the Socratic notion of 'negative wisdom' relates to a continuing tradition of Aristotelian thought that places the moral emphasis on right action. This is a particularly urgent question, since the resurgence of neo-Aristotelian thought within the recent writings of communitarians and virtue theorists has emphasized the need for increased civic engagement and social commitment. According to these accounts the only answer to the multiple ills of contemporary society – consumerism, social fragmentation, moral nihilism, voter apathy, and so on – is to be found in a renewed commitment to the shared principles and values that constitute the resources of 'social capital'. From this benignly conservative perspective the Socratic emphasis on 'dis-illusionment', which would of course seek to question those principles and values, might well be seen as a lingering menace.

If Socratic 'negative wisdom' is a stumbling block to the communitarians, it is a major obstacle to those who peddle the tired orthodoxies of post-modernism. As Nussbaum (1997) has remarked, 'it is fashionable today in progressive intellectual circles to say that rational argument is a male Western device, in its very nature subversive of the equality of women and minorities and non-Western people' (pp.18–19). However, Nussbaum goes on to argue, 'in order to foster a democracy that genuinely takes thought for the common good, we must produce citizens who have the Socratic capacity to reason about their beliefs ... To unmask prejudice and to secure justice, we need argument, an essential tool of civic freedom' (p.19). Far from being exclusive, the Socratic 'method' is potentially inclusive and deeply democratic. What is of overriding importance in the implementation of that 'method' is the acknowledgement of the universal capacity to think:

> Socrates does not apply to the ignorant and recalcitrant many an expert knowledge available only to the few; rather, he attempts to open the philosophical vocation to everyone. This is not to say he harbors the unrealistic expectation that the majority will become philosophers. It *is* to say, however, that he thinks neither age nor civic status is a bar to the kind of self-examination he has in mind. What matters is not class, status, education, gender, or even freedom but the capacity to think.
>
> (Villa 2001: 28–9)

Now, as always, the pursuit of 'negative wisdom' is beset by those who claim to know what moral truth is and those who deny its possibility. The 'new Aristotelianism' is located at this symbolic crossroads. It does not deny 'the virtues', but seeks to redefine them as dispositions towards moral truth. We cannot assume we know what that truth is, but nor can we assume our human incapacity to grasp it. The virtuous life is the life that embraces that epistemological and moral tension. The virtues are not moral end-points but the practical means by which we orientate ourselves towards 'the good society'. They are the means by which we cultivate in ourselves those dispositions that enable us to live in association with others. In an increasingly pluralist world, a world shot through with difference, the notion of the virtuous life is of paramount importance. We may and indeed do differ radically in our notion of what constitutes moral truth. The key question is, can we live virtuously while entertaining those differences?

Insofar as we believe that we can, we adopt what Arendt (1998) calls 'care for the world'. Caring for the world means being of the world, and acknowledging that one is of the world, while maintaining one's own critical distance from the world and recognizing the right of others to do likewise. The capacity to 'stop and think', as Arendt puts it, is crucial. Without a willingness to act from that human capacity, citizenship becomes unthinking loyalty with no regard for the values that support it. All that stands between the loyal citizen and the 'banality of evil', according to Arendt in her dispatches from the Eichmann trial, is the possibility of that capacity being actualized (see Arendt 1963). Dissidence, by this reckoning, is sometimes a necessary condition of citizenship – as, indeed, it was for Socrates.

In the last of the three speeches (reported in Plato's *The Apology*) to the 501 citizens of Athens before whom Socrates was arraigned, he refused to offer as was his right an alternative to the death penalty for himself. He did so on the grounds that he could deny neither his philosophical calling nor the authority of the Athenian constitution. His death thereby became the symbolic affirmation of the two absolutes that shaped his life and legacy: his belief in philosophy, as he understood and practised it, and his belief in 'the good society' as he inferred it from the Athenian way of life. Growing between these absolutes was his intuition that each was dependent upon the other: that 'the good society' requires a deeply questioning citizenry and that the purposefulness of such a citizenry lies in the hope of building 'the good society'.

Aristotle's elaboration of the virtues would have been impossible without this Socratic insight; without, that is, the death of Socrates with all the symbolic weight it has had to bear. The Aristotelian insistence on the virtues as dispositions that are developed as they are brought to bear on, and shaped by, human practice is fundamentally Socratic. Of course, Aristotle provided us with an ethical system for thinking about and distinguishing between the virtues, and elaborated that system in such a way as to develop a kind of typology of virtuous action, but the idea of the virtues as intrinsic to human practice, a way of being and acting in a world of tragic unpredictability, carries many of the hallmarks of Socratic thought; not least of which is the belief that the virtuous life does not come ready-made as a legacy of received wisdom. It requires the constant exercise of judgement with regard to right action in particular circumstances. Such a perspective allows us an opportunity to reconceptualize the notion of moral purposefulness and to rethink both the moral bases and the relational conditions of learning.

Moral purposefulness

> Another space is vitally necessary.
> (Berger 2001: 214)

Given the unpredictability of human circumstance, the evaluation of any life must be both formative and summative. None can assume that goodness has been achieved, until the final closure of the human life: the best can become the worst as unpredictability takes its toll. Nevertheless, to live 'the examined life' is to engage morally with that unpredictability and to increase the likelihood of benign closure. Whatever virtue there is, and whatever hope in virtue there may be, can only be achieved in the face of contingency, incommensurability, and the deep unpredictability of human existence. The fashioning of human life through right action, and through wise judgement regarding what constitutes right action, thereby becomes supremely important. The virtuous life cannot be read off from tradition, dogma, creed or community, although each of these may provide guidance. It can only be constructed through the living of it.

The unity of the virtues does not spring, then, from their formal or schematic coherence, but from the coherence that each of us achieves in attempting to live a virtuous life: the choices we make from the options that are open to us. MacIntyre, who has the distinction of being claimed quite erroneously by both communitarians and postmodernists, analyses this coherence in terms of what he calls 'the unity of a human life'. His interpretation of the virtues, and of the Aristotelian tradition, is central to our argument and requires at this point in the development of that argument some elaboration.

MacIntyre's (1985) *After Virtue: A Study in Moral Theory* is a key text within the 'new Aristotelianism'. It is a complex and densely argued text, which defies easy summary. The particular line of argument which concerns us here, however, is his attempt to define the nature of the virtues. Before outlining this line of argument it is important to acknowledge what many see as a deep strain of pessimism in this work: his insistence on the failure of the 'Enlightenment project'. MacIntyre refuses to celebrate that failure, which he sees as both a moral and epistemological failure inherent in the breakdown of late modern society. Nevertheless, he reclaims for this 'after-virtue' society a notion of the virtues which survives his own pessimism and indeed provides resources for hope.

MacIntyre makes three major moves in developing his argument regarding the nature of the virtues. First, he offers a definition of the virtues which privileges the notion of practice: 'a virtue is an acquired human quality the possession and exercise of which tends to enable us to achieve those goods which are internal to practices and the lack of which effectively prevents us from achieving any such goods' (1985: 191). A virtue, he insists, is a 'quality', or disposition, which is 'acquired' rather than given and whose acquisition enables us to achieve certain 'goods' which he claims are 'internal' to certain kinds of practices. The achievement of those 'goods' requires particular qualities, or dispositions, which are in turn enhanced through that achievement. *I become virtuous through the practice of virtue.*

Second, he argues that the actions that comprise practice are only intelligible if viewed in the context of what he calls 'the unity of a human life'. Intentionality and purposefulness are what give our actions meaning and moral import. If we extract those actions from the contexts within which agents construct their intentions and purposes, then the actions become unintelligible and meaningless. The intentionality and purposefulness of the agent provide human life with its unity and ensures that the virtues cohere within that unity. Of course, the intentions and purposes are always fought out against the unpredictability and contingency of the human world, but without intentionality and purpose the virtues cannot cohere. They fall apart. *I grow in virtue as I see my own life, and that of others, in narrative form.*

Third, he argues that 'the unity of a human life' is dependent upon traditions of practice that provide continuity between past, present and future. The intentions and purposes that guide action are part of the traditions within which we practice: health care or athletics, engineering or administration, pottery or hospitality. None of us – health care worker or athlete, engineer or administrator, potter or host – starts entirely from scratch. Each of us inherits a complex past and, through our present agency, contributes to the legacy of the future. We do so through traditions of practice that are handed down to us and that we hand on. *I grow in virtue as I struggle with the continuities and discontinuities inherent in the tradition within which I practice.*

There is, then, always reciprocity in the process of becoming virtuous. The reciprocity refers to my relation to my own practice, my relation to the contexts and situations within which I practice, and my relation to the continuing traditions within which my practice is located. The motor which drives these virtuous reciprocities is my own agency: my own developing sense of purposefulness and intentionality. Since, however, I am in this respect at least no different from you, or another, we must acknowledge the importance of engaging with other purposes and other intentions. The recognition of those other purposes and intentions is, therefore, of supreme importance in sustaining reciprocity. Without such recognition the reciprocity stalls and the potential 'unity of a human life' collapses into disunity: the virtues fall into disarray or simply turn their back on us.

So recognition is itself part of the virtuous circle and requires its own practices and traditions. The 'new Aristotelianism' provides, in its insistence on deliberative modes of thinking and interaction, a set of practices and a tradition within which incommensurable differences of purpose and intention can be engaged and examined. Deliberation is a form of thinking-not-yet-finished which always seeks to argue beyond the point of seemingly ultimate disagreement. It carries the precepts of Socratic 'negative wisdom' into the public forum, the supreme moral theorist of which remains Aristotle. He adds a new dimension to the meaning of 'negative wisdom': a public dimension; a dimension that acknowledges the super-complexity of difference; a social dimension beyond the exclusivities of the symposium.

Aristotle's public space was of course a comparatively easy matter: it excluded slaves, women, migrant workers. It was not only male-dominated, but exclusively male and exclusive also in its definition of male citizenship. Our aspiration towards a more egalitarian and inclusive public sphere is a much more difficult affair, for it poses the supremely important but awkward question of how we are to live together in a world of multiple difference. The metaphors of the assembly and the agora, as the formal and informal forums of public exchange, are now of course hopelessly anachronistic. We live in a world of public and private pluralities, within which the distinction between the private and the public still holds, but is globally dispersed. Worldwide news coverage brings the public forum into my own intimate space, while intimate documentaries allow me to enter the private space of other lives and other households. Public space is increasingly characterized by what John Berger (2001: 210) calls 'a kind of spatial delirium'.

We need ways of understanding these processes whereby hitherto private spaces attain public significance and hitherto public spaces close in on themselves: ways of understanding how to act out our citizenship. We also, crucially, need ways of understanding how in an increasingly professionalized society, professionals in the non-profit-making and public sectors can remake and rethink the plurality of the public sphere. The 'new Aristotelianism' may, I suggest, help us discover those ways: through its reconnection with notions of 'recognition' and 'deliberation', 'authenticity' and 'connectedness', and its insistence on the complicated linkage, at the level of lived experience, between these binaries. Moral purposefulness, according to that tradition, is not a rationally pre-specified end-point which we then devise the technical means of attaining, but a formative process which requires the ongoing exercise of deliberation. It requires, in Dunne's (1997) apt phrase, a turn 'back to the rough ground' of uncertain, practical judgement.

Pedagogies of recognition

In his seminal essay, 'The politics of recognition', Taylor (1994) draws a distinction between 'a system of hierarchical honour' in which 'one person's glory must be another's shame, or at least obscurity' and the Hegelian notion of 'a politics of equal dignity'. In his dialectic of the master and the slave, Taylor argues, Hegel 'takes it as fundamental that we can flourish only to the extent that we are recognized. Each consciousness seeks recognition in another'. So, he argues, 'the struggle for recognition can find only one satisfactory solution, and that is a regime of reciprocal recognition among equals'. A 'politics of equal dignity' requires a 'regime of reciprocal recognition' (pp.48–50). Such a perspective points us in the direction of a notion of learning as morally grounded practice: learning as a kind of turning to the world; a kind of 'care for the world' (Arendt 1998).

The notion of 'recognition', as theorized for example by Calhoun (1995), Honneth (1995), Phillips (1995) and Taylor (1994), in analyses developed in the mid-1990s, is central to the response by contemporary social theorists to the question of how we are to live together in difference and virtue. Developed in the aftermath of the Cold War, which in some quarters was being hailed euphorically as the end of history, this theorizing of 'recognition', as Fraser (1997) pointed out, established a new moral and political agenda. It is an agenda which gains increasing relevance in the post 11 September 2001 world within which we now live: a world of immense danger, unpredictability and threat. (A world not dissimilar to the one in which Aristotle wrote and thought.)

As Taylor (1994) suggests, the response raises new and unprecedented questions for the democratic state and for civil society. Should the state, as Dworkin (1977) and Rawls (1971) have suggested, exercise control in procedural terms, thereby privileging procedural notions of democratic practice over substantive notions of what constitutes the good society? Or should it declare its hand and acknowledge that in an increasingly multicultural world liberalism is also a fighting creed? Such questions take on a renewed urgency within the situation we now find ourselves. How can the state arbitrate between conflicting interest groups within and beyond its own state boundaries when it is itself embroiled in the conflicting interests? On the other hand, how can it preserve its liberal and democratic substance when, in the face of diametrically opposed values, it fails to engage in the struggle?

Whichever way we answer these questions, one thing is certain: the 'struggle for recognition', as Honneth (1995) puts it, requires new modes of deliberative thinking and democratic participation by the citizenry of the state. What is at stake is neatly summed up in Touraine's (2000) crucial question: 'can we live together?'. In order to do so we must undoubtedly learn, speak and think across our differences and in recognition of our equal worth. The problem is not, in other words, a problem that can be left to the state (although, as Westwood (2002), reminds us, the state may be a significant component of particular 'regimes of recognition'). It is, rather, one which as Young (2000) reminds us is central to the survival of a civil society that transcends state boundaries and national loyalties. It is a matter, ultimately, of how we can learn to live together, not necessarily in harmony but certainly in recognition of our differences.

Young (2000) provides some useful pointers as to how we might begin to develop pedagogies of recognition around the themes of plurality and participation. Participation is conditional upon a commitment to both the substantive and procedural aspects of deliberative discourse. As a participant I should have both an interest in what is being talked about and a disinterested regard for what others think and say. Were I not to be interested in respect of the topic, or not to be disinterested in respect of others' perspectives on that topic, then my participation might rightly be challenged. Of course, my interest, and capacity for disinterestedness, may well develop as the discourse develops. What is at stake is not my commonality or sameness, but my capacity to bring to the deliberative forum my differences as they bear upon our common problem of being able to live together in difference. *Pedagogies of recognition acknowledge different perspectives and trajectories.*

That commitment, argues Young (2000), involves a further recognition of the ways in which participation finds form in different modes of public address. Deliberative discourse, particularly within the university setting, is associated with a particular tradition of rational argument and public oratory. However, communication and expression take many forms, almost all of which should arguably be part of the discursive plurality that constitutes such discourse. Story and anecdote are particularly rich resources. The hierarchy of rhetoric has been significantly flattened over the last 50 years, partly as a result within the UK of the tradition of public broadcasting. But the authenticity of the messy narrative (the story, the autobiography, the biography, the anecdote, etc.) needs still to be upheld against the presiding influence of the tidy syllogism. What is at stake is not the survival of a particular form of public language, but my capacity for expression and receptivity in respect of diverse forms of communication. *Pedagogies of recognition acknowledge these communicative and expressive differences.*

Finally, Young (2000) reminds us that emotion and feeling are integral to reason. Recognition and deliberation require, and are conditional upon, an acknowledgement of emotional and affective attachments. We do not become reasonable by divorcing ourselves from these attachments; our reason, rather, depends upon these attachments for its commitment and focus. Insofar as we know about love, or compassion, or justice, we do so because we have loved, and grieved, and suffered. We cannot set these loves, griefs and sufferings to one side. They are integral to our thinking and to our rational discourse one with another and must be admitted to that discourse. They constitute our authenticity and our integrity. What is at stake is my presence as a mindful and sentient being in the deliberative process. *Pedagogies of recognition acknowledge the depth dimension of learning.*

The depth dimension

Nussbaum (2001) has explored the last of these themes in her recent study of the emotions. She argues for what she terms a revised neo-Stoic theory of the emotions as intrinsic to intelligence. The emotions, she argues, are not alien forces to be tamed, endured or pacified, but highly discriminating responses to what is of value and significance to the agent experiencing those emotions. She traces the intelligence of the emotions to the need we all have in infancy to reconcile ourselves through recognition and reciprocity to the world of objective reality. Our emotional lives, she argues, are necessarily ambivalent because we are from infancy having to reconcile our own helplessness to a world of objects over which each of us has at best limited control. Learning to recognize the other is a cradle-to-grave task; and, insofar as we continue to go on learning, it remains a supremely difficult task. It is, however, the one task that defines our humanity and that enables us to flourish as human beings.

The complex process of practical reasoning through deliberation emerges from this shared experience of living our own lives together with others. It is a matter of discovering both our own authenticity and of connecting with the authenticity of others. What has to be acknowledged is the emotional intensity of that process of connectivity. To live the good life is no easy matter. It is a continuation of those 'upheavals of thought', as Nussbaum characterizes them, that infants experience as the contingencies of the outside world borne in upon their own helplessness: the human animal being characterized by a relatively prolonged state of infant dependency coupled with a unique mental capacity. Deliberation, we need to remember, is always like that. It is always difficult. There is no point at which we 'grow up'. We are always to some extent little children negotiating a difficult passage between our own identity and that of others. To conceive of deliberation as some kind of rationalist pursuit divorced from our own emotional lives is to wholly misconceive its relation to the way in which our life histories are shaped by the struggle for recognition: the struggle, that is, for recognition through authentic engagement.

Through the virtues we acknowledge that what we share one with another is the need for recognition. We also learn to acknowledge, through the virtues, that each of us needs to be recognized, and thereby achieve authentic engagement, in different ways. The complexity of this process explains the disunity of the virtues: through courage I assert my own claims, or those of my clan, to recognition; through compassion I assert the right of others to recognition; through patience I mediate between these seemingly irreconcilable claims. Sometimes we have to choose, or have chosen for us, the appropriate virtues that would seem at the time to measure up to the moral requirements of the time or the circumstance. It is not the virtues that provide coherence, but our own moral purposefulness as agents in a world of incommensurable difference and unpredictable contingency. For most of us most of the time, the virtues are an ethical rag bag from which we weave our moral careers.

This complex process of achieving agency and authenticity within the complex interconnectivities of social engagement is precisely what learning is all about. Learning is not what we do once we have achieved agency and authenticity; it is the means whereby such agency and authenticity is achieved in the first place. In turning to the world, I at once connect with the world as object and at the same time gain the measure of my own subjectivity as intrinsic to that world. I acknowledge, that is, not only my own capacity to learn and to go on learning, but the capacity of others to do likewise. Learning is the means by which I both flourish as an individual and connect as a social being. It is the means by which I contribute to the making of a society, the goodness of which depends not only upon my actions but also upon my dispositions. Learning, so conceived, is an essential component of 'the good society'.

The conditions of learning: 'perfect friendship'

> What Aristotle seems to be saying is that if we understand the psychodynamics of friendship in the narrow sense, we thereby also understand the nature of other human associations. All human associations are forms of friendship, even if only imperfectly.
> (Hutter 1978: 115)

What, then are the conditions of learning that can enable and enrich the good society? Returning to Walker's (2003) notion of 'bivalent theorizing', we are reminded that human flourishing is always a matter of both structure and agency: structure without a notion of human agency topples over into determinism; agency without a notion of institutional structure teeters towards romantic anarchism. In addressing the crucial question regarding the conditions of learning, we require a conceptual focus that, in its acknowledgement of reciprocity and mutuality as the moral bases of learning, avoids the shortfalls of these dichotomous modes of thinking. The Aristotelian notion of 'perfect friendship' provides us with a means of achieving such a focus, by reasserting the primacy of relationship as a key element of both institutional structure and moral agency.

In the *Nicomachean Ethics* Aristotle was clear that 'perfect friendship' is founded on equality of attitude and belief insofar as these constitute the basis of virtue. He also acknowledged, however, that friendships differ in kind and quality. Friendship may, for example, be tactical and therefore provisional and conditional: a kind of strategic alliance based upon the mutuality of either self-interest or pleasure. Friendship, in either of these two senses, is a matter of being part of the club, part of the enclave. Pahl (2000: 21) neatly summarizes this set of distinctions in terms of 'friends of utility, friends of pleasure and friends of virtue'.

Much hinges on this set of distinctions, not least the notion of equality. 'Friends of utility' and 'friends of pleasure' are likely to be useful and pleasurable to one another precisely because of their economic and social commonality: who has access to which influential networks; who can afford to dine out at which fashionable restaurants. However, 'friends of virtue', who may be diversely positioned in terms of their economic and social conditions, may still be useful and pleasurable to one another since the 'perfect friendship' to which they aspire morally re-orientates 'the useful' and 'the pleasurable' towards 'the good': 'perfect friendship, which has virtue as its base and aim is also pleasant and useful. It combines all three aims, since the good in character, when friends, also find each other's company pleasant and useful' (Hutter 1978: 108).

'Perfect friendship', Aristotle maintained, is between equals who have their own and each others' best moral interests at heart. Such friendship is neither provisional nor instrumental, but unconditional in terms of what is good for oneself and the other: it is both inward-looking and outward-reaching. It is premised on the assumption that we become better people through the reciprocity afforded by our shared aspiration to help one another in doing so. That is why, as Pahl (2000: 79) puts it, 'friends of virtue' are also 'friends of hope' and 'ultimately friends of communication': 'our friends who stimulate hope and invite change are concerned with deep understanding and knowing'.

The notion of 'perfect friendship', as referring to a kind of relationship that privileges the recognition of equal worth, is central to our understanding of the conditions of learning. Such relationships are a precondition not only of the deliberative process whereby we ascertain what constitutes right action for ourselves and others; they are also the means by which such processes endure and enjoy some albeit fragile security. They inform our agency, while at the same time providing us with relational structures within which to recognize the agency of others. Thus, as Stern-Gillet (1995: 50) puts it, 'friendship plays a unique and crucial role in the noetic actualisation of moral agents'. What Aristotle understood by 'perfect friendship' becomes a means of rethinking, from the bottom up, what we aspire to in terms of the institutional conditions of learning.

'Perfect friendship' may, however, require closely guarded formalities to ensure that the principle of 'what is good for the other' is held in supreme regard. There are necessarily asymmetries in the relation between teacher and taught, and indeed between colleagues (with regard to knowledge of the field, breadth of experience, and so on). It is only by acknowledging those asymmetries that the relationship between teacher and taught can begin to move towards the common ground that constitutes learning. In the context of any such relationship, 'perfect friendship' is almost always an aspiration and very rarely an achieved state: what Hutter (1978: 104–5) calls 'a theoretical searchlight' or 'a guiding norm' by which actual friendships can be evaluated. It is a teleological concept which enables us to grasp, ontologically, the underlying purposefulness of the kind of relationship which Giddens (1993: 194) has characterized as 'pure' in its adherence to 'the imperative of free and open communication'.

To conceive of 'perfect friendship' as the ground and horizon of relationships within which individuals can learn together is to admit that such relationships are not just 'professional relationships' but also 'human relationships': they require deep rather than just surface recognition and a mode of deliberation that acknowledges colleagues and students as unique persons with varied backgrounds and trajectories. The notion of 'perfect friendship' points, then, in the direction of questions that have a direct bearing on issues relating to academic practice, institutional management, and academic identity:

- What kinds of pedagogical, scholastic and collegial practices support those modes of deep recognition that are implicit in the notion of 'perfect friendship'?
- How might universities be organized and managed in such a way as to privilege these modes of deep recognition and so develop organizational structures that are sensitive to the requirements of 'perfect friendship'?
- What are the implications of the notion of 'perfect friendship' for the way in which I conceive of my own identity as a professional academic and orientate myself towards the identity of others?

Each of these questions is a framing device for including alternative concepts, values and outlooks into a broader language of reconstruction for thinking and talking about universities in 'a runaway world'; concepts, values and outlooks grounded, that is, in the evolving and highly contested tradition of deliberative democracy. Until as academic workers we develop some such language of reconstruction, our professional and institutional practices and the organizational structures within which we operate will continue to be highly vulnerable to what Dunne (1997) refers to as 'the lure of technique'. Developing a deliberative *language* of reconstruction is, as the following chapters in this section seek to illustrate, integral to the democratic *practice* of reconstruction.

Conclusion

The 'new Aristolianism', as I conceive it, provides us with a discursive framework within which to challenge many of the callow assumptions that dominate the current debate on academic professionalism. First, it challenges the view that learning outcomes can be pre-specified and that it is a prime task of academic professionals to draw up and adhere to such pre-specifications. If learning is constructed through deliberation, then its outcomes are necessarily unpredictable. Second, it challenges the idea that learning is an isolating (as opposed to solitary, which it often is) activity. Deliberation involves interaction, with other learners, with texts, and with other traditions of thought. Third, it challenges the notion that learning is somehow compartmentalized from what Williams (1958) called 'a whole way of life'. Learning is where we are now as we move beyond our origins to new beginnings (which always involve others).

We require a language which allows us to re-engage as moral agents with the purposefulness of learning. The 'new Aristotelianism' provides bits and pieces of a lexicon with which to set about this task. It is not the terminology itself that requires promotion, but the simple and very old idea that there is some kind of a connection, albeit tentative and fragile, between being a learner and becoming a good person. That connection, notwithstanding its vulnerability, is perhaps where we need to start in re-constructing, at precise points and within specific sectors, 'the good society'. But we do need to rethink it all the way down and to rebuild it all the way up: through our re-descriptions of our ends and purposes and our re-engagement with the deliberative processes by which those ends and purposes may be fulfilled.

References

Arendt, H. (1963) *Eichmann in Jerusalem*. New York: Harcourt Brace.
Arendt, H. (1998) *The Human Condition*. Chicago: University of Chicago Press.
Beck, U. and Beck-Gernsheim, E. (2002) *Individualization: Institutionalised Individualism and its Social and Political Consequences*. London, Thousand Oaks and New Delhi: Sage Publications.
Berger, J. (2001) *The Shape of a Pocket*. London: Bloomsbury.
Calhoun, C. (1995) *Critical Social Theory: Culture, History, and the Challenge of Difference*. Oxford, UK and Cambridge, MA: Blackwell. (Chapter 7: 'The politics of identity and recognition', 193–230).
Dunne, J. (1997) *Back to the Rough Ground: Practical Judgement and the Lure of Technique*. Indiana: University of Notre Dame Press.
Dworkin, R. (1977) *Taking Rights Seriously*. London: Duckworth.
Fraser, N. (1997) *Justice Interruptus: Critical Reflections on the 'Postcolonialist' Condition*. Cambridge: Polity Press.
Giddens, A. (1993) *The Transformation of Intimacy: Sexuality, Love and Eroticism in Modern Societies*. Cambridge: Polity Press.

Honneth, A. (1995) *The Struggle for Recognition: The Moral Grammar of Social Conflicts.* Cambridge: Polity Press.

Hutter, H. (1978) *Politics as Friendship: The Origins of Classical Notions of Politics in the Theory and Practice of Friendship.* Waterloo, Ontario: Wilfred Laurier University Press.

MacIntyre, A. (1985) *After Virtue: A Study in Moral Theory*, 2nd edn. London: Duckworth.

Nussbaum, M.C. (1997) *Cultivating Humanity: A Classical Defence of Reform in Liberal Education.* Cambridge, MA and London: Harvard University Press.

Nussbaum, M.C. (2001) *Upheavals of Thought: The Intelligence of Emotions.* Cambridge: Cambridge University Press.

Pahl, R. (2000) *On Friendship.* Cambridge: Polity Press.

Phillips, A. (1995) *The Politics of Presence.* Oxford: Oxford University Press.

Rawls, J. (1971) *A Theory of Justice.* Cambridge, MA: Harvard University Press.

Stern-Gillet, S. (1995) *Aristotle's Philosophy of Friendship.* Albany: State University of New York Press.

Taylor, C. (1994) The politics of recognition, in A. Gutman (ed.) *Multiculturalism: Examining the Politics of Recognition*, 2nd edn. Princeton: Princeton University Press. (Lecture inaugurating the founding of Princeton University's Center for Human Values, 1990. First published by Princeton University Press, 1992.)

Touraine, A. (2000) *Can We Live Together? Equality and Difference*, translated by D. Macey. Cambridge: Polity Press.

Villa, D. (2001) *Socratic Citizenship.* Princeton and Oxford: Princeton University Press.

Walker, M. (2003) Framing social justice in education: what does the 'capabilities' approach offer?, *British Journal of Educational Studies*, 51(2):168–87.

Westwood, S. (2002) Complex choreography: politics and regimes of recognition, in S. Lash and M. Featherstone (eds) *Recognition and Difference: Politics, Identity and Multiculture.* London, Thousand Oaks and New Delhi: Sage Publications.

Williams, R. (1958) *Culture and Society 1780-1950.* London: Chatto and Windus.

Young, I.M. (2000) *Inclusion and Democracy.* Oxford: Oxford University Press.

Part 3
Pointing to Hope

8
Pedagogies of Beginning

Melanie Walker

'I'm beginning, on my own two feet – I'm beginning ... '[1]

Introducing pedagogy

This chapter sets out to map what I am describing as 'pedagogies of beginning', taken from the character of Beatie Bryant, a working-class woman, in Arnold Wesker's (1964) play *Roots*. For Beatie, having been discarded by Ronnie, the romantic intellectual, her 'beginnings' take shape as she starts to find her own voice in the closing moments of Wesker's play. Thus we hear Beatie declaring: 'D'you hear that? D'you hear it? Did you listen to me? I'm talking ... I'm not quoting no more ... listen to me someone'. Finally Beatie triumphantly avows: 'It does work, it's happening to me, I can feel it happening, I'm beginning, on my own two feet – I'm beginning ... ' (Wesker 1964: 148).

As Basil Bernstein (2000: 12) says, 'To know whose voice is speaking is the beginning of one's own voice'. At issue is that higher education needs pedagogical languages and practices that are about this kind of learning – critical, democratic, moral and ethical – as much as they are about 'key skills' or 'deep' individual learning. We need ways to talk about teaching and learning which raise questions about how pedagogy enables an educated citizenry, which asks questions about how we might live our lives well, as well as what careers we might follow. Moreover, as Nixon (2002: 8) sharply reminds us, the current language of clients, delivery, measurable outputs and so on, 'is not just a different way of talking about the same thing. It radically alters what we are talking about.' 'It constitutes', he argues, 'a new way of thinking about teaching and learning. Ultimately it affects how we teach and learn.' Therefore I want to put the case for pedagogical actions of the kind instead where we create the spaces where freedom 'can come out of hiding, as it were, and make its appearance'

(Arendt 1968: 169). The 'new beginnings' of teaching and learning then generate 'infinite improbabilities'; 'historical processes are created and constantly interrupted by human initiative' (Arendt 1968: 170).

I therefore offer instances of student learning which, I argue, point optimistically to hope, while not claiming that these instances necessarily build into larger patterns of educational change. The empirical cases are offered because developing our conceptual frameworks about pedagogy – what ought to be done – is necessary and important even if insufficient for structural change. As Geertz writes in reference to a *Peanuts* cartoon, in which Lucy is asked by Charlie Brown for advice, she replies: 'I don't give advice. I just point to the roots of the problem' (2000: 24). In teaching and learning in higher education what matters is also the 'So what do we do about it?' question. This is not to say that these pedagogic stories that follow in themselves constitute a remaking or transformation of higher education institutions. Our actions for justice need to correct both inequities in education and the structural and institutional frameworks that generate them. But the instances here do at least signal counter-cultural pathways, if not yet the entire landscape. This chapter thus seeks to point to hope in two interrelated ways – by producing a 'counter memory' (Said 2002) in the form of a pedagogical language of beginning, and by offering examples of when and how we might recognize 'beginning' at work in student learning.

In all this, the point to be emphasized is that pedagogy (or teaching and learning as it is called in the UK) is not neutral or 'uncontaminated' by the context in which it operates but acts as a complicated carrier for relations of power and privilege (see Bernstein 2000). For example, Skeggs describes being a working-class student in higher education in England:

> My first real recognition that I could be categorized by others as working class happened when I went to university (an upper/middle-class university that often felt more like a finishing school) and I was identified in a seminar group as 'oh, you must be one of those working class people we hear so much about'. I was absolutely mortified. I knew what this meant – I had been recognized as common, authentic and without much cultural value. The noisy, bolshy, outspoken me was silenced... I did not want to be judged and found wanting.
>
> (1997: 130)

As Skeggs points out, in her case it was middle-class standards and members of the middle class who instigated these judgements. Who is recognized and recognizes themselves as of value matters because our students are not blank slates but carriers of socially inflected autobiographical experiences; as are we ourselves. Pedagogy and pedagogical relationships privilege certain identities over others and some ways of interacting or being over others, and these mirror in some way broader unequal social and political circumstances, in this case structures of social class and gender. In turn such experiences construct differences in our inner lives: what we aspire to do and be and what we turn away from – as belonging to higher education communities, or marginalized within them, or excluded altogether. Learning in this view is complex: both intellectual and emotional, both individual and interactional, both about subject knowledge and self development. It is both about trajectories of social biographies and situated educational experiences. What conditions and practices of learning might then work to shape pedagogic identities which are enabling of 'beginning' – expanded and new horizons of possibility?

Fostering capabilities

My first claim for pedagogies of beginning is that such approaches foster the development of student capabilities. Here I have in mind Nussbaum's (2000) expansive 'capabilities' approach which is concerned with 'what people are actually able to do and to be', informed by the idea of 'a life that is worthy of the dignity of the human being' (2000: 5). In other words, the pedagogical implications of fostering capabilities would be an ethical concern with human flourishing for each and every student. She details ten capabilities. While she argues that all are of central importance, and while all point in some way to education, some do so more directly than others. Four capabilities out of the ten are of special importance for higher education pedagogy – (i) practical reason; (ii) senses, imagination and thought; (iii) emotions; and (iv) affiliation. The capability of practical reason involves 'being able to form a conception of the good and to engage in critical reflection about the planning of one's life'. The affiliation capability involves 'being able to live with and toward others, to recognise and show concern for other human beings, to engage in various forms of social interactions; to be able to imagine the situation of another and to have compassion for that situation; to have the capability for both justice and friendship ... having the social bases of self–respect and non-humiliations; being able to be treated as a dignified being whose worth is equal to that of others'. Senses, imagination and thought involves thinking, reasoning, imagining, searching for meaning, and so on, while the emotion capability includes being able to love, care, be cared for, or to experience justified anger (see Nussbaum 2000: 78–9).

Here is an example of the interwoven development of these capabilities in an instance of higher education pedagogy. Alison Phipps teaches an honours level course in German Popular Culture (see Phipps 2001 and Walker 2002). She tries to start from the students' own experiences and perspectives on Germany and German popular culture, to problematize these and to develop student reflexivity which enables them to understand 'that they have choices to make'. Classes are participatory; students work together in small groups of five and in whole class plenaries to discuss questions and problems which relate to popular German films and texts and to different theories of popular culture so that students have 'lots of different ways of looking'. Students are expected to read the theoretical background and to work on the case study before each class. They meet in their small groups between classes to discuss questions which require them to relate the theories to the case studies. The first hour of each class takes the form of a plenary with each of the groups feeding back in turn on their task as it relates to the case study and the theory. Others ask questions, make notes and add their opinion. The teacher's role here, as described by Alison herself, is as chairperson, trouble shooter and devil's advocate. But she also works to 'scaffold' student's learning. Alison explains: 'I am trying', she says 'to engender a love of ideas and the relevance of ideas and theories. I'll try and give them three points of view from three different authors and say "These are three different ways of looking at culture. This shows how complex the term is and the important thing to remember when reading these texts is that's it's about complexity and that you won't necessarily understand it the first time you read it through"... I tell them it's alright to be confused ...' (quoted in Walker 2002: 52).

The second hour of the course is in two parts. Alison introduces the next theory of popular culture, supplementing material that the students have already considered, with examples and discussion and critique. The students then discuss this new theory in their groups and then begin to apply it to the case studies. Iteration is an important element of the course, as is space in small groups and in plenaries for open questioning and the exploration of ideas. The content of the course demands effort and students are heard to complain about lectures and seminars that are 'too difficult', 'go over their heads', because argues Alison, 'they haven't yet found a way of establishing a relationship to the material, of forging a dialogue with a demanding text'. But, she is convinced as a teacher that the university is the place of the 'too difficult'; in forging 'a critical relationship' with difficult texts, students expand their own perspectives (or their capabilities).

A feature of their course thus is the collaborative discussion, including their disagreements, of theories of popular culture in small groups and then applying the ideas to case studies in a way which requires them to deconstruct their taken for granted assumptions about the world, and reconstruct and imagine alternatives:

Peter: It [theory] makes you really aware of what you're doing and what's happening
[...]
Jon: It makes you recognise what you're doing. It's not so much, I don't know, that it makes you change what you're doing, but it makes you recognise what you're doing and makes you think about why you're doing it. It goes back to like sitting watching this film where I knew what was going to happen at the end anyway. I'd never seen it before but it's just that it's so predictable and things and it's because I've seen fifty or however many films that follow these patterns.

Peter: I think it could change your vision of the world if you really want to, it might change that. . . . that's why I find it sometimes scary. [. . .]

Jon: the point is I don't think I actually had a view of society before. Society was there, it was what I lived in but I didn't really have a view of why it was like that. I think that's what gives you a sort of different way to look and see, you know, why things are the way they are and why are people the way they are. Whereas before I don't think I really thought a lot about that. I probably moaned about certain aspects of society but I never really had any idea what society was.

(quoted in Phipps 2001: 141–2)

Over time, students construct learning communities which are hard work, collaborative, respectful, enjoyable, critical and participatory, and which enable their access to esoteric knowledge and to academic success:

Jane: I think sometimes somebody would understand something then if you didn't understand it they can explain it to you. If different people are learning different things at different times you can kind of explain, share what you've learned with other people and they tell you what they think and you can kind of build up something from that. We had so many different books that we could read as well. Everyone was reading different books and different theories and because you'd found out different things in your own interviews you would use different theories. So each person would be using a different theory maybe something you didn't know much about because it wasn't applicable to your data, they could explain it to you and so you could share.

Helen: But do you not think as well it was the fact that we were in the same groups all the way through and we started off just discussing things that nobody knew anything about so we were all in the same boat. And as we got more information and knowledgeable about different things, we kind of worked through a lot of things and helped each other, and you never once think 'Well I know it and I'm not going to tell anyone'.

(quoted in Walker 2001: 17–18)

In my next example, Mike Gonzalez's second year undergraduate class in Hispanic Studies works independently for six months in small groups of between four and six on a history project (see Gonzalez 2001 and Chapter 11 of this book). The students include young men and women, older mature students, and students from the UK, Ireland, Continental Europe and Latin America. After initial brainstorming, students form topic groups, which in the past have included themes as diverse as Barcelona – its history and culture, dictatorships in Latin America, the hispanic influence on contemporary culture in the USA, Spanish film and soap operas. They are then pretty much left to their own devices. Nonetheless, Mike recognizes that his wide-ranging expertise is essential, but he tries to deploy his expertise in ways which do not paralyse all initiatives in the students, or instil a fear of their own ideas or of expressing them. He describes this early process as a 'provocation' to learning in which he 'lights a touch paper and retires to a discreet distance!'

Student interviews suggest that self-directed learning around topics which catch student interest enabled these students to engage with the Hispanic world in a rich and complex way. They all expressed great 'pride' in their work, sharing it with the other groups, but also with family and with friends. In the best sense, working on the project aroused their passions. All the groups developed a critical view on their topics, for example learning about political oppression in Chile in ways which surprised them:

> Veronica: I was surprised by how torture chambers are transformed into shopping malls, which is crazy really. That's just an attempt to destroy the past totally, that shocked me a lot.
> Caroline: I was kind of expecting but I didn't realise the extent to which the US was involved with so much of it ... now I know and I'm glad I know.
> Dan: I wasn't expecting to hear such sad stories about a place where I had so much fun and it just goes to show that although I lived there for six months you only see the up side and you rarely get to know what's behind it.
> (focus group interview with Melanie Walker, 27 April 1999)

The group who worked on the Cocaine Trade developed their own critical view of this trade and its huge profitability. Johannes comments:

> It's just like, as Jamie says, a commodity in the world, so it's like these poor peasants they don't think about some crack addict in the US or how much they might harm them. To them they don't think about that, it's about money ... especially in a poor country [Columbia] ... they wouldn't be growing cocaine if coffee was more profitable ... Western governments ... ought to concentrate on the question of why people want to use drugs so much ... like maybe something's wrong with the society.
> (focus group interview with Melanie Walker, 28 April 1999)

As Johannes explained: 'I think it's better in this case to find your own truth and your own opinion'. Through their encounters as thinking and doing subjects, these students actively make and own historical knowledge under conditions of critical reflection, showing concern and respect for each other, experiencing senses, imagination and creative thought in the enjoyment as much as the difficulty of learning in this way, and engaging their emotions (amazement, pleasure, uncertainty, pride in the work, curiosity to know more, and so on) as part of their learning.

The implications for teaching and learning in these instances is that prespecified learning outcomes cannot capture all the learning that happens on a course. The further point here is that teaching and learning involves dependence and interdependence; it is relational. As one of Alison's students commented on the apparently simple matter of knowing each others' names: 'I think the fact that we all know each other's names. I find that in a lot of classes there are people in the classes that I do not know their names at all, which is awful... whereas Dr Phipps always says your name ...' (quoted in Phipps 2001: 138). Or as another student says of how the course had both changed her thinking and her opinion of university because of the confidence she has developed in finding her own voice: 'Before the course I probably wouldn't have spoken much in the tutorial because I had the impression that anything I said wasn't good enough, you know, I was frightened to come out with something that would sound good and I couldn't do it ...' (quoted in Phipps 2001: 142).

Such approaches are ethically concerned with the learning of each and every student, and with learning as a process which enables purposeful human flourishing. Instrumental learning, technicist conceptualizations of 'group work', exercising power to humiliate or exclude or being made afraid to speak out would not then be part of pedagogical practice.

- *The first principle, then, is that pedagogies of beginning foster capabilities (of practical reason, senses, imagination and thought, emotions and affiliation).*

Enabling deliberative dialogue

What we also see at work in these instances is deliberation, which Young (2000) characterizes as involving collective problem-solving through processes of critical dialogue, inclusion of diverse experiences and perspectives and 'reasonableness', that is the willingness to listen to others whose views, histories and experiences differ from one's own. Deliberation opens out a potentially transformative space in which, through democratic dialogue with others different from oneself, we gain new ideas which enable our critical reflection on the partiality of our own positions, prejudices or ignorance. Deliberative processes, Young argues, provide 'the epistemic conditions for the collective knowledge of which proposals are most likely to promote results that are wise and just' (2000: 30). Unlike utilitarian 'key skills', or technique-driven conceptions of 'team work', deliberative discussion, democratically conducted, offers a pedagogy of critical dialogue – developing the confidence to defend a point of view, while taking into account the perspectives of those who differ from oneself. Young's agonistic conceptualization recognizes that collaboration is both a powerful way to learn but also difficult in practice. It both requires and makes possible the development of students' capabilities. In this our processes serve as 'outcomes' which allow for unpredictability (where the process will take us cannot and should not be pre-determined) and the forging of human connection and responsibility across diverse biographies in a pedagogical *agora* characterized by agency, attentive dialogue and action.

In my next instance a group of final year town planning students at Sheffield University are reflecting on their course on protection of the environment, specifically here about designated national parks. The lecturer, Tim Richardson, is concerned that as a profession, town planners fail 'to strongly engage with the deepest value conflicts that surround their work' to which there are seldom 'easy' solutions. Instead, he is concerned that students learn that the planning process is 'inherently political', saturated with value conflicts and that they explore what kinds of practices then need to flow from this awareness. The point is that students learn both technical skills and a critical understanding of the planning process as democratic and participatory, rather than one driven by powerful 'experts'. The approach chosen in this particular course requires that students take up 'stakeholder' positions towards environmental issues, which sometimes are not their own, using a dialogical process to address and understand diverse and conflicting points of view. The discussion-based sessions take on the different scenarios which students might encounter in actual professional situations – for example, a public meeting, or a closed doors round table conference – and in which the rules for engagement work differently. They must struggle with other stakeholders to get their own views heard and to persuade others. Because the students themselves hold different views on what constitutes the best approach to particular environmental issues they have to work hard to listen to each other. As Kevin explained:

> One of the good things of working in groups is that the two people I worked with came from different viewpoints to me. The one was very conservation minded and he had what I consider some quite strange approaches to dealing with issues of conservation, like he'd look at conservation in economic terms. He'd try to put a [economic] value on the landscape. The other person, her approach was very much more concerned about social issues, but at the same time balancing social issues with conservation, and I came with the view point that it's a national park but at the same time people have to live there, you've got to allow development.
> (focus group interview with Melanie Walker, 19 April 2002)

The course attempts to enable them also to learn how to build consensus in contexts of value conflict. 'If we understand what we mean by consensus', says their lecturer, 'can we use that to look critically at what we've just been through ... in each [planning] context there's a different relationship which you have to keep your eye on and all of these things are really things that hopefully allow the students to create their own insights into the processes, not just the issues, but the processes that are used to explore these conflicts' (interview with Melanie Walker, 1 March 2002). Students learn how to deliberate across differences to build a creative consensus. The pedagogical process made them realize that:

quite often there are conflicts between different people's points of view and that perhaps you can't reconcile the conflicts but you can manage them and by trying to get local communities involved with the planning process you can better work out what different people's view points are and then from there try to mitigate and compensate some of the things that people will lose through the planning process by having to make concessions to other parties and create balance in the process.
(focus group interview with Melanie Walker, 19 April 2002)

This process of active dialogue was, students said 'far more engaging' because 'if people are asking you awkward questions you're forced to think about the issues and you're forced to come up with solutions, and you're forced to work through issues and come to conclusions and compromises with other people'. The students learn that 'there are value judgements, there are different ways of doing things ... It made you think about things differently and it makes you realise that just coming in with the same opinion every time and looking at things in the same way every time, stifles innovation and it stops you perhaps from being as good as you could be if you were willing to have a more open mind and look at things in a different way and take on board other people's opinions ... ' (focus group interview, 19 April 2002). Students commented that they had realized how their own value judgements make it difficult for them to understand the perspective of others with different perspectives and interests because 'we already have a reaction lined up in our minds'. What they had to learn through deliberation was a considered empathy by defending positions which they found unsympathetic to their own points of view, and the value of 'rough and ready' compromises rather than situations 'where nobody backed down'.

Mike Gonzalez's students were similarly required to engage with each other – agreeing and arguing over conflicting interpretations, taking leadership roles, taking responsibility for organizing and doing the work – including some of the more tedious bits – and, engaging as knowledge producers. 'We did it ourselves' emerged as a common refrain, as did notions of 'learning in a different way'. Deliberation was not straightforward. Desmond wryly commented that 'there were times when we lost the plot a bit ... I think we learned what we could do ourselves and we didn't really need lecture notes and things like that; we could go away and do it ourselves, produce it ourselves. So we learned about what we could do basically'. Chris added, 'It was different from lectures where it's very ordered and structured; you could go off on a tangent and if it didn't work out there wasn't any pressure on you. You don't have to conform to it, you just go back to where you were and try something else and in that way it was good. You do have moments when you're thinking "Where's this going, I don't know what I'm doing and I don't know what anybody else is thinking", but because you've got this deadline a long way away you've got enough time to research things, to try things out, and that was the best thing about it for me.' Finally, Stephanie suggested: 'Everybody brings ideas forward but it's less a confrontation it's not really "I really want to do this", it's more "Well what do you think about this?" ' (quoted in Gonzalez 2001: 179–80).

Mike Gonzalez comments in this way on these kinds of deliberative dialogues:

> This process and its educational outcomes (both tangible, less obvious and unexpected) show that the acquisition of knowledge does not require years of obedience and submissive apprenticeship to those who 'know'. On the contrary it can occur within a group of peers who are learning to interrogate new knowledge, or as we might say, to do research. Knowledge is socially acquired and should be socially held and socially made meaningful. Students establish their own learning communities in the course of the project through their interactions with each other and with the process in which they are engaged. They create and enact experiences, knowledge and ways of knowing in relation to a topic and goals that have meaning for them. Their own knowledge, cultures and discourses become available as resources for all.
> (Gonzalez 2001: 175)

- *The second principle then is that pedagogies of beginning create public spaces for deliberative dialogue as integral to learning and critical knowledge-making.*

'Training the imagination to go visiting'

Woven into capabilities development and deliberative processes, must also be authentic recognition of the 'other', what Nussbaum might describe as the affiliation capability, and Young as the importance of dialogue across difference. Fraser (1997) explains that for participation to be enabling of capability development, we need to recognize and value the variety of difference and the cultural resources students bring to learning. Repeated encounters, she reminds us, with non-recognition and disrespect by the culturally dominant Other produces a negative internalized self-image, for example, 'the hidden injuries of class' which includes non-recognition of working-class cultures and experiences. Higher education is then less 'a practice of freedom' (hooks 1994), and more a practice of rejection and silencing. From this argument, it follows that recognition from others is essential to the development of a successful and powerful learning identity, to self-confidence, self-esteem and self-respect, precisely because our identities are always produced with and in relation to others. But, following Young (2000), a simple reversal of perspectives is ultimately impossible precisely because we are all different. It risks those with more power appropriating the experiences of others with less power, a kind of passive empathy which leaves ones' own self-understandings in place. What is required is closer to Arendt's injunction to 'train the imagination to go visiting', that is 'being and thinking in my own identity where actually I am not' (1968: 241) and the 'enlarged mentality' this makes possible. As Arendt explains: 'The more people's standpoints I have in mind while I am pondering a given issue, and the better I can imagine how I would feel and think if I were in their place, the stronger will be my capacity for representative thinking and the more valid my final conclusions, my opinion' (1968: 241). It would also be similar to Yuval-Davis's (1997) notion of 'tranversal politics' involving an authentic 'rooting' in one's own identity while 'shifting' to understand the perspectives of others.

I would argue that in the three cases already noted, we have instances and examples of students working hard to understand the perspectives of other students. Here we have two students from the German Popular Culture course, one a young Scot from a working-class background, the other a French exchange student. They demonstrate in this brief excerpt that they are able to form a conception of the good through a critical consideration of knowledge and reflective self-knowledge in respectful interaction with each other:

> Jon: Everybody comes with their own and thinks 'That's it, that's what I got out of it and I can't get any more out of it' but then some else will say 'Yeah, well, but you've not got this or what did you think about that?' and I'd be like 'I don't get that at all out of it.'
> Peter: I'm actually surprised to see how well it works. I mean it's quite amazing when you think about it, because we are so different. I know we might come from different backgrounds and have different experiences and eventually it works and I'm amazed to see what others do.
>
> (quoted in Phipps 2001: 144)

They are, in effect, taking up positions as active participants in a conversation about the 'good' society, listening to, accommodating each other, but also expressing disagreements as they try to tease out the prevailing consensus about how society works. They are quite simply re-making themselves.

The difficulty is how one acts when pedagogy comes up against values which are deeply antithetical to democratic life, for example hidden or overt racism, sexism, classism, or other forms of discrimination and prejudice. How, then, might a lecturer confront sexist, racist or classist attitudes that students bring to learning as part of their own biographies? Similarly, how do we, as university teachers, confront our own taken for granted assumptions and positionality, inflected as it is by lived experiences also of class, race and gender embedded in our own educational and teacher biographies? What pedagogies of beginning at the very least do, is to acknowledge that education is a practice which involves both the acquisition of knowledge through higher learning, and learning how to be. Moreover, pedagogies of beginning acknowledge that students do not arrive at university as blank slates but are carriers of complex socially shaped learner and learning identities, acquired in formal and informal contexts.

What are manifest as personal identities and biographies are then always the product of historical and social experiences and available social resources (Rees et al. 1997). The implication for higher education is that we need to pay attention to the learning identities that we aspire to engender in our students.

This chapter argues that universities ought to provide conditions for all students to learn and to acquire critical knowledge and expansive skills in social settings. This goes beyond notions of 'transferable skills', even though these may well be part of critical knowledge acquisition, and includes qualities of intellectual growth, imagination, creativity and emotions. It encompasses drawing on such developing qualities to learn through social relationships and arrangements in which students are offered opportunities to communicate respectfully with others, and to express their perspectives on social life in contexts where others listen. Students ought to be offered the opportunity to cultivate a critical narrative imagination, thinking what it might be like to be in the place of a person with a different view from themselves, to take intelligent account of such stories, and to understand why the story matters to its teller.

- *The third principle therefore is that pedagogies of beginning 'train the imagination to go visiting', valuing learning from and with others the same as (we have a shared humanity which makes communication possible) and different from oneself.*

Preserving 'newness'

Hannah Arendt (1977: 196) argues for conditions of newness ('natality') as well as plurality (dialogue, recognition, difference, affiliation) as integral to the project of learning. In her view, education 'is the point at which we decide whether we love the world enough to assume responsibility for it and by the same token save it from that ruin which, except for renewal, except for the coming of the new and the young, would be inevitable'. She argues that teachers should not 'strike from their [students'] hands their chance of undertaking something new, something foreseen by no-one, but to prepare them in advance for the task of renewing the common world' (1977: 196). Arendt would thus refuse the idea of predicting the future needs of the economy, for example, and tailoring a 'relevant' education accordingly. Instead Arendt was concerned to emphasize the unpredictability of the future and the possibilities of change, renewal and a better life through human agency, lodging the future in the hands of students, and making possible acting on the future differently. As Arendt explains: 'The problem is simply to educate in such a way that a setting-right [of the world] remains actually possible, even though it can, of course, never be assured' (1977: 192).

Thus Mike Gonzalez (2001) describes his voice as being present in meetings with student groups, but he works to restrain his own interventions to get dialogue underway at the start, trying not to allow his own 'verbal density' to overwhelm the less experienced students. Early on in his teaching of town planning, Tim Richardson encountered resistant feedback on a lecture course in which he and a colleague tried to 'push at the students, to challenge them' about serious environmental issues 'in quite a forceful way', 'just taking the whole thing head on and almost pushing a message at the students'. Put another way, they tried to take from the students the possibility that they might create something entirely new. Interestingly they encountered a 'wall of defence' from the students – 'they just tried to ignore some of the stuff we were putting across to them'. This experience led him to develop more interactive and dialogical problem-based approaches – enabling the new, the unpredictable, the unexpected. His position on the planning dilemmas with which students must grapple is:

> to leave it open for the students to look at it how they want... there's a lot of room for interpretation and debate, it's not hard and fast, I'm quite open about where it goes... In a sense what the course is doing is setting out the tools that I've used in developing [my own] position... if any of the students want to they can use those analytical tools and say 'Well no, actually we can construct the whole thing differently', and it is open to them to do that.
> (interview with Melanie Walker, 1 March 2002)

This is not to say that the students find this a comfortable process; they are, he says, 'constantly looking for closure on issues'.

Pedagogies of beginning would therefore work to foster lecturer and student capabilities which create new capability sets for each person, expanding the opportunities available to them – to become a lawyer, a reflective teacher, a mathematician, and engineer, and so on, but also to become people holding critical knowledge, emotional intelligence, and greater opportunities for well-being and quality of life. While Arendt argues for conditions of natality, we should nonetheless bear in mind that education is a value-saturated activity embedded with often competing versions of the good life, for example individuals as consumers, or individuals as democratic citizens. Thus conditions and processes of democratic dialogue, multiple perspectives, respect and recognition for others different from oneself would also act to develop students' capacity to judge how it might be appropriate to exercise the abilities they are developing through higher education. But as Arendt cautions, we could not as teachers guarantee or impose on students how they might choose to act, at best we might hope through higher learning to 'develop the judgement of the person to be able to value in which way it is appropriate to use capabilities' (Saito 2003: 29).

- *The fourth principle of pedagogies of beginning is thus to 'preserve newness'.*

Professional learning

But it is also important to note that in each case these lecturers have constructed pedagogic professional identities for themselves somewhat against the grain of managerialist discourses or technicist accounts of teaching and learning. In each case, pedagogy is constructed through a relationship between the teacher and his or her ethical stance, the subject, and the students. These are lecturers working rigorously and creatively to enable students' access to knowledge, to discourse communities and to confident learner identities. They begin to produce counter-cultural pathways which place educational practice at their centre, as they turn the gaze of inquiry and learning onto their own professional practice. Because pedagogy is relational and interactional, the lecturers also change and are changed by their encounters with students as they learn professionally from students and in dialogue with each other (see, for example, Walker 2001, and Chapter 11 of this book). Quintin Cutts, who teaches computer science, comments that he 'gained considerable insight' into pedagogical practices both generally and across a range of subject areas from his colleagues in their collaborative action research project (see Chapter 11). As a result, he now better understands how such ideas might be incorporated into his own discipline. Thus, he says:

> Whether we like the currently popular phrase 'lifelong learning' or not, we are still confronted by it. Everything we do changes us and requires an openness to the new learning available. The students, whose cycle of change is the most evident, are challenged to adopt responsibility for themselves and their learning beyond that of their schooldays. My colleagues, my department, academia as a whole are all challenged to accept the changing nature of higher education and to make a stand for our fundamental beliefs. And myself? I am challenged repeatedly to learn that there is no right answer to the many dilemmas in life, and to acknowledge my ability to search for a worthwhile path nonetheless.
>
> (Cutts 2001: 127)

We learn professionally from our students and from each other. Judy Wilkinson (see Wilkinson 2001: 78), who teaches mathematics to engineering students, describes how arts and science disciplines need to learn from each other; how engineering might learn from the language of postmodernism and the humanities from quantum and chaos theories so that cross disciplinary ideas 'can illuminate the present [human] condition'. For her, the collegial action research collaboration 'widened my academic perspective' and also 'honed my teaching skills' (quoted in Walker 2001: 47). She commented on another occasion: 'You have to accept being a learner yourself and putting yourself in the position of learner...' (quoted in Walker 2001: 192). And because our values shape the pedagogical decisions we make, as much as the contemporary policy and institutional climate, we ought to work at developing our professional judgements regarding the worthwhileness and educational quality of what we offer our students.

- *Thus the fifth principle for pedagogies of beginning is that reflexive professional learning and a renewed academic professionalism on the part of university teachers is required.*

Beginning

What is sought in recounting these examples is not perfection or prescription in teaching and learning. Practices of capability development, democratic deliberation and recognition take us part of the way in opening up counter-cultural pathways. They show that individual change is a beginning and that moments of transformation point to hopefulness, even if they will also only take us only so far. Besides, we also do not want to be paralysed where institutional conditions seem so unpropitious. Change must start somewhere, and, on the whole, I think that we prefer to describe or critique the world as it is and are less successful in thinking about how our actions today build an educational world of tomorrow – the struggle for counter pedagogies is hard work, but we can only make the road by walking, as the Spanish poet Antonio Machado reminds us. At least when we try to act on our principles for pedagogies of beginning (higher education for tomorrow) we are faced with the gap between our theories and our practices (trying to work in higher education as it is today). The gap is a hard one but also helps us to see the moments and possibilities for something different, more rather than less just. Our achievements are always precarious and our pedagogies fragile. Nonetheless, what these cases attempt, as much writing on critical pedagogy fails to do, is to open out the gap between the 'ought' of critical pedagogy and the 'is' of how it might be done in a real classroom. The stories here offer, at the very least, moments of transformation where different pedagogical relationships and different views on what is knowledge are present, even as the normalizing scripts of the institution and society pull in the opposite direction.

Like Beatie Bryant in *Roots*, we might hope that our students would also say: 'I'm beginning, on my own two feet – I'm beginning'. We might hope that in some way our teaching enables their chance 'of undertaking something new, something foreseen by no-one' and works 'to prepare them in advance for the task of renewing the common world' (Arendt 1977: 196). The teaching question becomes something like: How do I/we teach in ways which foster the ethical and democratic political imagination of our students so that they are able to see the world from other points of view, understand themselves in relation to the world, and grasp their own agency in relation to knowledge and action in an uncertain world?

Note

[1] My thanks to Jon Nixon for drawing my attention to Beatie Bryant and her story in his inaugural lecture at the University of Sheffield, 15 May 2002; see Nixon (2002).

References

Arendt, H. (1968) *The Origins of Totalitarianism*. London: Harcourt Brace.
Arendt H. (1977) *Between Past and Future*. Harmondsworth: Penguin Books.
Bernstein, B. (2000) *Pedagogy, Symbolic Control and Identity*, rev. edn. Lanham: Rowman and Littlefield.
Cutts, C. (2001) Engaging a large first year class, in M. Walker (ed.) *Reconstructing Professionalism in University Teaching: Teachers and Learners in Action*. Buckingham: SRHE/Open University Press.
Fraser, N. (1997) *Justice Interruptus. Critical Reflections on the 'Postsocialist' Condition*. New York and London: Routledge.
Geertz, C. (2000) *Available Light*. Princeton: Princeton University Press.
Gonzalez, M. (2001) Learning independently through project work; in M. Walker (ed.) *Reconstructing Professionalism in University Teaching: Teachers and Learners in Action*. Buckingham: SRHE/Open University Press.
hooks, bell (1994) *Teaching to Transgress. Education as the Practice of Freedom*. New York/London: Routledge.
Nixon, J. (2002) *Education, Leadership and Civil Society*. Inaugural Professorial Lecture, University of Sheffield, 15 May 2002.
Nussbaum, M. (2000) *Women and Human Development. The Capabilities Approach*. Cambridge, MA: Cambridge University Press.
Phipps, A. (2001) Towards alternative performance indicators; in M. Walker (ed.) *Reconstructing Professionalism in University Teaching: Teachers and Learners in Action*. Buckingham: SRHE/Open University Press.
Rees, G., Furlong, J. and Gorard, S. (1997) History, place and the learning society: towards a sociology of lifetime learning, *Journal of Education Policy*, 12(6):485–97.
Said, E. (2002) The public role of writers and intellectuals, in H. Small (ed.) *The Public Intellectual*. Oxford: Blackwell.
Saito, M. (2003) Amartya Sen's capability approach to education: A critical exploration, *Journal of Philosophy of Education*, 31(1):17–34.
Skeggs, B. (1997) Classifying practices, in P. Mahony and C. Zmroczek (eds) *Class Matters. 'Working-Class' Women's Perspectives on Social Class*. London: Taylor and Francis.
Walker, M. (ed.) (2001) *Reconstructing Professionalism in University Teaching: Teachers and Learners in Action*. Buckingham: SRHE/Open University Press.
Walker, M. (2002) Pedagogy and the politics and purposes of higher education, *Arts and Humanities in Higher Education*, 1(1):43–58.
Wesker, A. (1964) *The Wesker Trilogy: Chicken Soup with Barley, Roots, I'm Talking About Jerusalem*. Harmondsworth: Penguin Books.
Wilkinson, J. (2001) Introducing a mentoring programme, in M. Walker (ed.) *Reconstructing Professionalism in University Teaching: Teachers and Learners in Action*. Buckingham: SRHE/Open University Press.
Young, I. M. (2000) *Inclusion and Democracy*. Oxford: Oxford University Press.
Yuval-Davis, N. (1997) *Gender and Nation*. London: Sage.

9

The New Media in an Old Institution: Implementing Change/Containing the Potential for Transformation

Rob Walker

> [Through their research role] universities have a fundamental connection with change in society ... However, as organisations, they have been characterised as conservative and reluctant to change. The circumstances of the past decade or more have been that new computer and communications technologies, together with a melange of social, demographic and economic changes, have torn the fabric of the traditional university. Nowadays, universities are seen to be stitching together various activities and approaches in order to cope with, or maybe to be seen to be coping with, the challenges of the times.
>
> (Evans and Nation 2000: 1)

No discussions of the state of the contemporary university can overlook the impact that communications and computing technologies (CCTs) have had on the way that universities present themselves to the outside world or to their students. It is rare to find any recent major statement of policy, any mission statement from an institution or any programme handbook, that does not at least mention the educational use of the Internet, flexible course delivery and electronic access. Indeed, the university home page itself has rapidly become the university façade, the front page of the prospectus and first line of publicity aimed at potential students and the public.

Yet it seems that much of this technological impact has been rhetorical and symbolic rather than marking any real transformation of organizations or of professional practice. Indeed, it could be argued that education as a whole, and higher education in particular, has been slow to adopt the new media and its associated technologies and cautious, not to say conservative, in applying them and implementing them beyond a fixed range of clerical and administrative functions. Slowly, it seems, universities have added computer applications where they fit existing practice and provision, but they have resisted their impact where real change to teaching/learning and its management threatens. It is only in fringe activities (like, until recently, distance education) that universities have looked ahead to newly emerging technologies, novel applications and the new educational possibilities that lie beyond the immediate organizational horizon. For the most part, despite organizational rhetoric, we work with previous generation technologies and well-worn applications, which in turn are mostly derived from industry, commerce and the military.

Compared with the commercial sector, where there have been major changes in organizations and transformative adoption of technologies, education has until now remained relatively unchanged. Until now, it has kept its conventional staffing levels, management structures, roles and hierarchies, it has added CCTs to its administrative and research tasks (rather than transforming them) and it has limited the use of technologies in teaching and learning to an enhancement role. To give a single anecdotal instance, my own institution has decreed that, in order to ensure equity, students must receive in hard copy any information that might have a bearing on their assessment. In practice this is taken to include any course handouts, changes in rooms or times of meetings and information about assignments or exams. This at a time when e-commerce has accustomed us to life without the printed document and when most students think of the Internet as old technology and use as their first line of communication the text message. This institutional response is not atypical and while students have successively colonized gaming, the Internet and mobile phones, the academy has routinely responded conservatively and with strategies of control and denial, resorting to moral panic when faced with evidence of Internet plagiarism, students using its systems to access pornography or any suspicion that its systems are being used for illegal purposes.

It appears that the images and discourse of technology in higher education polarize around binary poles. From an administrative perspective there is the high-gloss vision of a virtual future, in which students have easy, direct access to high-quality resources and the best teachers, wherever they are to be found in a global intellectual economy, and then there is a dark side inhabited by hackers and cheats. From an academic point of view there is the appeal of a teaching medium that makes teaching more like research as against the threat of 'diploma mills', offering cheap access to qualifications through the mechanism of the web and call centre tutorials.

The Illinois seminars

During the 1998–9 academic year, the University of Illinois, in response to a growing concern from its administration and among its academic staff, convened a seminar series to investigate the increasing impact of educational technology on (and in) its teaching programmes.

The concerns about technology and education that were emerging at this time spread much more widely than Illinois, but the response that the

University of Illinois made was probably unique. At this time, in most institutions (and more widely in the UK through a number of significant infrastructure projects funded by JISC), CCT programmes were rolled out through university budgets by a combination of service departments – computer services, libraries and teaching and learning units, usually with a few enthusiastic academics and staff developers tagging along. Budgets and decision-making increasingly centred on these service departments, and in doing so redefined academics as customers and clients. But against this trend, the University of Illinois took a scholarly approach to what they saw primarily as an academic problem, and more than this, they documented their response for public access. The Report of the seminars, and links to the papers, continue to be available on a university website and provide a valuable resource in terms of understanding the debates around technology and education as well as providing a useful source for those interested in this recent (and often undocumented) history (University of Illinois 1999).

The mid-and late 1990s was a time when significant changes were in the air: a number of new higher education institutions were forming in the USA that were dedicated to offering large-scale distance programmes, and which were perceived by some large state institutions as a threat to their home markets (Blumenstyk 1998). More threatening still was the emergence of discussions at some high-status universities (Harvard, MIT, Johns Hopkins, for instance) in which they considered whether they might market or franchise some of their courses worldwide on the Internet. Perhaps for the first time there was talk of 'branding' in the provision of university education as university façades came to include the website as well as the ivy-covered and sandstone walls. Also at this time, Gates, Disney and Murdoch were reported to be investing heavily in acquiring the ownership of intellectual property rights as their advisers and media industry commentators predicted that the Internet would continue to grow apace and that 'content would become king'. The universities were not unaware of the threats that this implied and the Carnegie Commission initiated a study ('Vision 2010') into the future of the university in the USA which produced some apocalyptic scenarios (Carnegie 1995). All in all, there were increasing signs on campus that the collapse of the distinctions between education, entertainment and publishing, predicted some years previously by Nicholas Negroponte (Brand 1987), were finally being realized.

The implications for education clearly represented a significant threat to the status quo and suggested the need for radical change in a wide range of cultural institutions. University of Illinois president, James J. Stukel, saw the threat and helped promulgate the need for a new vision:

> ... the Internet, and the technology which supports it, may well constitute the third modern revolution in higher education. The land-grant movement in the Nineteenth Century brought access to higher education to the middle class. The community college movement of the Twentieth Century brought universal access to higher education.

> The technology revolution of the Twenty-first Century can bring access to all beyond the bounds of time and place ...
>
> Towards full realization of our enduring core values, the University of Illinois will lead nationally in creating, assessing, transferring, and integrating advanced technologies, in our research, teaching, outreach and operations.
>
> (Stukel 1997, quoted in University of Illinois 1999: 5)

The full impact of the envisaged change on large-scale established institutions like the state universities is hard to imagine, for while the 1990s saw major changes in the organization of business and commerce, the impact of downsizing, outsourcing and increased attention to a customer service orientation are not easily transferable to more than a cosmetic level in academic organizations. Not least because conventional universities make huge investments in cultural capital over long periods of time and have cultures imbued with notions of scholarship and intellectual independence that resist management solutions. Unlike the industrial and commercial sector (or government itself), the organizational mechanisms of recruitment and staff turnover do not provide an easy route to cultural change, nor is the rapid prototyping and implementation of organizational change easy to secure. The absence of easy indicators ('the bottom line') has, until the recent growth of audit cultures in HE, also been difficult to establish and achieved only by strong central government control.

In summarizing the need for the seminar series, the convenors of the Illinois seminar began from President Stukel's statement of his sense of mission and linked this to the concerns of faculty. This they interpreted primarily in terms of a concern about the quality of teaching:

> On the crest of the computer revolution, and especially with the advent of the Internet, the academy is asking how technology might be utilized to improve the teaching and learning of university students. How can high quality 'teaching at an Internet distance' or 'online teaching' be assured? Just where does the traditional 'face to face' classroom sit in the sea of information technology?
>
> (University of Illinois 1999: 5)

But close to the philosophical debate was a fear of what the impact of the technology was likely to be, not just on the processes of learning and teaching but on the future of the institution itself:

> Taken to the extreme, will bricks and mortar be wholly replaced by fibre optic cable and PCs? In the last chapter of *Learning Networks*, co-authored by four of the pioneers of computer-mediated communication (Harasim et al. 1995), the authors imagine such startling possibilities as statewide closure of community college systems.
>
> (University of Illinois 1999: 5)

It was clear from the start of the Illinois project that the concerns were not just technical but educational, albeit in a context that had heavy political overtones and occasionally veered towards a sense of panic. In education we easily forget that the technologies we take for granted – not just the chalkboard and the OHP but the classroom and the lecture theatre, the notion and practices of simultaneous instruction, of classroom recitation and the use of the essay and the multiple choice test, are themselves social inventions that were contemporaneous with an earlier technological revolution. As Stukel himself suggested, in the current revolution no less than the survival of the institution appeared to be at stake. But, as in any crisis, threat stimulated a flow of institutional adrenalin which meant that there was a clear sense of excitement in the air, not unlike the excitement created around a big research programme. The Report quoted one associate dean, who became a member of the seminar, as saying that his motive for being involved was that, 'I deal with practical issues every day. I want to do the fun stuff!'

At the University of Illinois, as in many similar debates in other institutions, and more widely in professional, academic and policy circles, the rapid growth of the new media mobilized and disturbed established and previously sedimented institutional positions. Those on the left and the right, the conservatives and the progressives, the administrators and the teachers, were all drawn into the debate. Arguments and discussions that had long been dormant, or had become localized within small organizational or academic niches, suddenly bubbled to the surface in new forms. New advocacies emerged, often from unexpected alliances or from those who were previously at the institutional margins. New rhetorics appeared (and were quickly learnt!) and old, often forgotten discourses were revived, given a fresh gloss and a new purpose (not least the term 'pedagogy' itself).

The Illinois seminars are instructive because they focused a debate that was ubiquitous but diffuse. This was not a research group that made a new breakthrough, a project that suggested new directions for policy and practice, or the site of a brave new technological invention. What was discussed at Illinois was very like what was being discussed elsewhere, and for those at the cutting edges perhaps a little behind the game, but it was a public discussion that picked up on issues and concerns being voiced in many universities at the time. The seminar brought together some of the key thinkers, critics, researchers and practitioners and the organizers provided a report that captures the state of discussion at a critical moment, just before the widespread adoption of virtual learning environments (VLEs) and just before the collapse in the value of Nasdaq shares and the end of the e-consumer investment bubble.

In the event, as most universities plunged straight into policy decisions and management solutions, the University of Illinois attempted to step back, to take a thoughtful and research-driven perspective on the issues:

... [The] then Vice President of Academic Affairs Sylvia Manning proposed a scholarly study of 'Teaching at an Internet Distance (TID),' or the pedagogy of online learning, in the form of a faculty seminar. The seminar mode, as opposed to a committee, was adopted to emphasize the learning to be experienced by its members. The seminar was not to focus on practical matters like security or software. The 'seminar should avoid matters of governance, personnel policy and technical issues such as registration. It should focus exclusively on pedagogy and the quality of the educational experience, including both student and faculty satisfaction.' (Manning 1998) From the beginning, hardware, software, and technical support were assumed to be free of any shortcoming, so that the discussion would remain entirely on pedagogy. And yet, from this fundamental consideration of pedagogy there should arise some practical guidelines for those faculty wishing to implement online teaching (Manning 1998; Regalbuto 1998b).

(University of Illinois 1999: 6)

A representative group of 18 people was assembled, representative not just of elements of the organization but using the criteria that members of the seminar be 'outstanding and highly committed teachers', that there was an academic balance, and a roughly even split between the 'converted' or online-using or advocating faculty, and 'sceptical' or online-doubting professors, or those who were 'sitting on the fence'.

The seminars met over the course of the year, in face-to-face retreats and via videoconference. The invited speakers were people from inside and outside the university, many of whom were key figures in the field, again both advocates and sceptics. The list of seminar speakers and links to their presentations are given below in Table 1.

Table 1. Seminars presented to the TID Faculty Seminar

---
23 September 1998   Prof. Linda Smith
Library and Information Science, University of Illinois at Urbana/Champaign
Teaching in LEEP 3
(www.vpaa.uillinois.edu/tid/meetings/092298)

---
3 November 1998   Prof. Curtis Bonk
Counseling and Educational Psychology, Indiana U.
Electronic Collaboration Theory, Research, and Pedagogy: Stories from Indiana University
(www.vpaa.uillinois.edu/tid/meetings/110398)

---
17 November 1998   Prof. John Etchemendy
Dept. of Philosophy and Symbolic Systems, Stanford
Technology to Enhance the Classroom, Not Replace It
(www.vpaa.uillinois.edu/tid/meetings/111798)

1 December 1998   Prof. Janice Newson
Sociology, York University, Ontario.
Distinguishing the Hype from Practice: Inquiring into the Pedagogical Claims of Computer Mediated Instruction
(www.vpaa.uillinois.edu/tid/meetings/120198)

15 January 1999   Prof. Mark Gelula
Medical Education, University of Illinois at Urbana/Champaign
In Teaching, Enthusiasm is Perception, Not Personality
(www.vpaa.uillinois.edu/tid/meetings/011599)

2 February 1999   Profs. David Hansen and Nick Burbules
Education, University of Illinois, Educational Policy Studies, UIUC
Good Teaching
(www.vpaa.uillinois.edu/tid/meetings/020299)

19 February 1999   Prof. Linda Harasim
Communication, Simon Fraser University, Vancouver BC
What We are Learning about Online Learning: Lessons from the Virtual-U Field Trials
(www.vpaa.uillinois.edu/tid/meetings/021999)

12 March 1999   Prof. Andrew Feenberg
Philosophy, San Diego State University
Distance Learning: Promise or Threat?
(www.vpaa.uillinois.edu/tid/meetings/031299)

2 April 1999   Prof. David Noble
History, York University, Ontario.
The History of Correspondence Schools
(www.vpaa.uillinois.edu/tid/meetings/040299)

13 April 1999   Prof. Pat Shapley
Chemistry, University of Illinois at Urbana/Champaign
Online Instruction of Chemistry 331

It was around David Noble's seminar that the politics of change crystallized. Noble's critical histories of educational technology are well known among education academics (Noble 1979, 1995), in which he has shown how many of the innovations we have adopted in education have their origins in the military-industrial complex. In the mid-1990s, Noble became involved in debates around the increasing use of web technologies in education when his university became the centre of a debate about academic autonomy and institutional intellectual property rights. The debate focused on a major employment issue which resulted in a long strike with, on the one side, the employers requiring academics to provide websites to support their teaching (and in some cases censoring what was provided), and on the other, individual professors arguing that the decision to provide web-based material should be an academic judgement and that the products of their work belonged to the academic community as a whole, not just to the institution.

Noble's first paper on this issue was published in the online journal, *First Monday*, a Danish e-journal highly respected within the distance education community, where it led to a series of critiques and counter claims. Noble followed this up with a second and third paper, extending the arguments and documenting cases elsewhere in the universities (David Noble's collected papers have been usefully collated on a website and collected together in book form, see Noble 1999). So behind the seemingly innocuous title of his Illinois seminar paper, lay a radical history and the expectation that he would argue strongly for academic control over the use of the web for teaching purposes.

An end to the tyranny of distance?

At the same time, but not directly connected to the Illinois debates, Otto Peters, a German academic, was developing a new line of thinking about similar issues. Peters had played a key role in the establishment of the Fern Universitat (the German Open University) as its founding rector, and was acknowledged as one of the key theorists of distance education. Having been a strong advocate for distance education for many years, he began arguing that distance education was facing its demise, not because of any intrinsic failings, but because in a context in which a growing mass education system was becoming increasingly dependent on digital technologies, the mainstream was increasingly incorporating distance education as part of its move towards 'flexible delivery'.

Peters saw some dangers in this development, in that distance education had always stood for educational values not always well represented in the mainstream. In particular, distance education generally takes a strong position on open access, on the need to take issues of instructional design seriously and in its emphasis on the need to attend to the learning needs of its students. In this context, Peters argues that the educational need in contemporary and emerging societies is for new forms of pedagogy and curriculum.

In the future, there will be greater emphasis placed on the ability [of students] to:

- learn and continue to learn independently and autonomously;
- communicate to others deliberately and on a differentiated basis;
- collaborate with others in a group;
- show social sensitivities;
- accept social responsibility;
- be ready and willing to be flexible, and to have experience of flexibility. (Peters 2000: 11)

To take this agenda seriously, Peters argues, is to require a transformation in the universities as institutions:

> ... the university of the future will have to be the result of a fundamental process of transformation in which it changes into a university that mainly enables self-studying in all its forms oriented towards the research process. The university supports this and in the end makes it into the foundation of its curricula and teaching. A strict orientation to research must in fact be presupposed for all three forms of learning.
> (2000: 15)

The three forms of learning that Peters identifies are: 'guided self-study and self study', 'studying in a digital environment' and 'taking part in teaching events at traditional universities' (though he warns that the latter should not be taken to mean attending 'traditional lectures', but rather engaging in a range of discussion based and tutorial activities).

Peters implies that, in looking to the future for universities, distance institutions provide a more appropriate (and tested) educational model than the conventional face-to-face ('f2f') model (though some object to this term, arguing that the lecture hall can hardly be seen as more 'face-to-face' than the web-based videoconference). 'To sum up', he writes:

> ... learning and teaching at university must be oriented to a much greater extent than ever before to the principles of continuing education and life long learning. It must have an egalitarian character and be open as well as student-, practice-, and future-oriented. It will have to proceed with flexible teaching and learning programmes which impart not only cognitive, but also communicative and collaborative competence. Along with classical expository teaching and receptive learning, autonomous and self-controlled learning should be cultivated. This should be oriented towards the research process. In addition to this, students must also be prepared to prove themselves in the 'virtual world'.
> (2000: 13)

The convergence of f2f and distance modes is already evident in Britain, though perhaps has been slower to develop here than elsewhere because of the predominant position occupied by the Open University (UK) since the early 1970s, which has had the effect, until recently, of insulating the mainstream sector from the effects of change. In UK universities, f2f education has been provided for selected school leavers in full-time (often residential) settings over a period of years, while distance programmes have been provided with mature students in mind, almost always those who are part-time and have to fit their studies in and around the competing demands of work and family. With the adoption of the new technologies this has begun to change, and in the UK, the shift became increasingly institutionalized as the student body has expanded and diversified, and as the costs of higher education have been progressively shifted from general taxation to family debt.

The new communications technologies increasingly offer functionalities that make possible teaching that is much more interactive than the conventional correspondence text. Students can talk to each other through conferencing software, can access texts and resources on the web and can do their academic work while firmly rooted in their own work and domestic economy. The 'distance' student can just as easily be the 'full-time' student who lives within walking distance of the campus but who prefers the intimacy of the screen to the alienating experience of being taught in the lecture hall, as it can be the student caught in the isolation of a rural community or a physical disability.

As universities have wrestled with the need to accommodate more and more students with relatively fewer lecturers and diminishing resources, so the Internet appears to provide a solution. And throughout there has been a globalization item on the agenda. Funding structures in most of the Western nations put a premium on high fee-paying overseas students that makes them favoured customers. As overseas students and their governments have found the cost of providing a UK, North American or Australasian education increasingly difficult to fund, so distance programmes appear to offer at least a neat solution that can be packaged in the discourse of modernization.

As distance programmes expanded, so they became a larger part of the institutional profile and more influential in budget, resource and other decisions. And key resource-hungry elements of the institutions, especially computing services and libraries, have been quick to see digital solutions as a means of increasing their leverage on resource allocations and increasing their power relative to academic departments. In this too, the distance institutions have provided an organizational design prototype that was built on the assumption of centralized resource allocations, albeit (somewhat confusingly) often presented within a discourse of 'devolved budgets'.

Peters' argument is that, in the contemporary context, the differences between distance and f2f teaching are rapidly diminishing, and that the decisions that are made about curriculum, pedagogy and assessment are essentially the same for both, once the technology becomes the medium for converging the educational experience.

This provides the opportunity for the development of the new form of 'open' university, oriented to a set of educational values that has tended to become subsumed in the rush to manage the demands of government that higher education expand its numbers but without extra funding. Rather than develop the kind of research-led teaching that Peters envisages, we have instead driven along paths that separate teaching from research, to the detriment of both. Despite the Humboltian tradition, which Michael Peters (Chapter 4 of this book) identifies as critical in the university tradition, Otto Peters now sees a picture in Germany that is depressingly familiar to academics in the Anglo-countries:

> In German universities, teaching continues to have a lower priority than research. Lectures, classes, seminars and periods of practical training are usually overcrowded. There is a general lack of support services for students. The jungle of courses, degrees and examination requirements ... means that students are faced with almost insurmountable problems.
>
> (2000: 10)

Similarly, in the UK it could be argued that the dual accountability structures that apply to research and to teaching, create a similar politics, particularly as assessment of research carries with it large grants and subsidies, while the assessment of teaching does not. More than this, the move to course unit/course credit curriculum structures creates a 'jungle' very similar to the one that Otto Peters describes in the German universities. In most UK universities, though, the heavy reliance on text books that characterizes much teaching in North America has been resisted, courses have become modular and unit based, leading to a micro-scale, pervasive and constant assessment that has a similar effect. With the Bologna agreement over the horizon (which will provide students with the ability to transfer between European universities), it is unlikely that the institutional grip of this structure will loosen.

Virtual learning environments and possibility

The University of Illinois seminars offer one institutional perspective on educational change in their emphasis on the need to focus discussions around online learning on pedagogy (teaching and learning) and the quality of student experiences. Otto Peters, writing from a European perspective has pointed to the impact of digital technologies on notions of 'flexible delivery' for all students, not just those studying at distance. He has offered an agenda for lifelong student learning which chimes with many of the points Melanie Walker makes in the previous chapter in her concerns for the social relations for learning, as much as for cognitive processes. And in the UK e-learning has been advocated by policy makers, embraced by some and greeted with scepticism by others but there is no gainsaying the impact of technological developments for education as virtual learning environments proliferate. Wherein then lies hope and possibility, not least where e-learning is often presented as a way for us to scale down (manage) our teaching commitments and free up more time for research? We can of course choose to contain the potential of new technologies for transforming learning opportunities, or we can choose change, and sometimes we may well do both at different times and under particular circumstances.

Elsewhere (see Walker 2002), I have written at length about my own development as a distance (virtual) educator having to confront the significant pedagogic switch required by virtual curriculum design and development and teaching. It was, in brief, as I and my colleagues found, harder than we had anticipated to break out of our existing pedagogical routines as we confronted new challenges from a different mode of performing what we know to the way we taught, and to the way we thought about teaching. But we also learnt a lot from one another and in different and often unexpected ways these changes in the way that we worked played back into the courses that we taught and particularly into the way we were as university teachers.

The point is that shifts in technologies for teaching and learning (and in their administration) create new (and sometimes unexpected) opportunities to develop new sets of practices and new forms of interaction. They may suggest the need for conformity but they also require us to think about social change. When students studying at a distance, whether physically, virtually, or indeed both, ask of the teachers 'Is there anyone there?' (as we found they did), they are partly asking from a sense of social dislocation, from being caught up in the process of social change and being personally troubled by the experience. What they want is not simply an organizational response but access to the means of understanding their circumstances and capacity to act in new ways.

The dangers lie in taking the visions that lie in technology, as for instance in Andrew Zolli's 'Catalog of Tomorrow' (Zolli 2002), and thinking that all we need to do is to use the new technologies, and that social change will follow. In this area, as elsewhere, we need to work to reconnect research and teaching, to bring together vision and practice in both technology and organization. So long as we can retain spaces in and around universities where we can think critically about what we do, then a viable intellectual community is possible. We may have to concede that these spaces are not what they once where, that they may take different forms and shapes from those we are used to, and that they will probably lie outside the bureaucratic boundaries as to what constitutes research or scholarship. But what we should be doing is locating and inhabiting these spaces and using them to reinvent academic life. Hope lies in our capacity to imagine, and to make a bold, not a timid, educational response.

References

Blumenstyk, G. (1998) Western Governors U. Takes shape as new model for higher education, *The Chronicle of Higher Education*, XLIV, 22 (6 February), A21–24.

Brand, S. (1987). *The Media Lab. Inventing the Future at M.I.T.* New York: Penguin Books.

Carnegie (1995) *Vision 2010 Interim Report to the Carnegie Foundation November 1995* http://www.si.umich.edu/V2010/carnegie.html. Last accessed 3 August 2003.

Evans T. and Nation, D.E. (eds) *Changing University Teaching: Reflections on Creating Educational Technologies.* London: Kogan Page.

Harasim, L., Hiltz, S.R., Teles, L. and Turoff, M. (1995). *Learning Networks: A Field*

Guide to Teaching and Learning Online. Cambridge, MA: The MIT Press.
Manning, S. (1998) *Letter to TID faculty members,* 2 July.
Negroponte, N. (1995). *Being digital.* London: Hodder and Stoughton.
Noble, David F. (1995) *Progress Without People: New Technology, Unemployment, and the Message of Resistance.* Toronto: Between the Lines.
Noble, David F. (1997) *America by Design: Science, Technology, and the Rise of Corporate Capitalism.* Oxford and New York: Oxford University Press.
Noble, David F. (1999). Noble papers on *Digital Diploma Mills* collected: http://communication.ucsd.edu/dl/
http://www.TheAtlantic.com/issues/97jul/computer.htm.
Peters, O. (2000) in T. Evans and D. Nation (eds) *Changing University Teaching: Reflections on Creating Educational Technologies.* London: Kogan Page.
Regalbuto, J.R. (1998) *Opening remarks, TID Faculty seminar retreat 10 Sept* http://www.vpaa.ullinois.edu/reports_retreats/tid/meetings/090898/jrr-intro.html.
University of Illinois (1999) http://www.vpaa.uillinois.edu/reports_retreats/tid/ Regularly updated, this site was last accessed on 3 August 2003.
Walker, R. (2002) Is there anyone there? The embodiments of knowledge in virtual environments, in C. Vrasidas and G. Glass (eds) *Current Perspectives on Applied Information Technologies, Vol 1: Distance Learning.*
Zolli, A. (ed.) (2002) *Catalog of Tomorrow: Trends Shaping your Future.* Indianapolis: Que Publishing.

10

Under New Management? A Critical History of Managerialism in British Universities[1]

Colin Bundy

'Vice-Chancellors get a bad press' (Carter 1990: 55). This is a throw-away line in Ian Carter's mordant and beguiling study of British university fiction. His concern is to analyse that genre's dominant discourse; how that discourse meshed with broadly hostile contemporary political and public attitudes to universities; and ultimately the connections between campus fiction, the ideological assault of the Black Papers on education (in the early 1970s) and the damage done to British higher education in the 1980s by 'relentlessly utilitarian modernisers' and 'a barbarous government' (Carter 1990: 257, 259). Carter is not primarily interested in how the governance and administration of universities changed in the post-war years. His brief treatment of principals and professors (1990: 54–62) deals with the fictional difference between Oxbridge life – with its assumptions of collegiality and comity – and the more hierarchic, more centralized exercise of authority in 'not-Oxbridge universities'.

Here the focus is upon *why* Vice-Chancellors have been lampooned and unloved in campus novels over the decades: or rather, upon the ways in which their unloveliness has altered. Specifically, this chapter outlines ways in which university leadership has changed in the United Kingdom, and elsewhere, over the past 50 years. It sketches the history of how universities have been administered, governed and managed. It locates the rise of 'managerialism' in British universities within an overall set of changes which have been abundantly chronicled; but from the skein of that broader history it teases out the particular thread of administrative and executive functions in higher education. And finally it asks whether the more highly managed university can be reconciled with basic academic values, norms and aspirations.[2]

A novel experience: the advent of new managerialism

Following Ian Carter, let me introduce three Vice-Chancellors. The first was principal of a minor redbrick university in the late 1950s. He was 'a small ventricose man with a polished, rosy bald head' with a laugh like a sound effect in 'films about murder in castles'. 'Have you got anything new to tell us?' he asked a young academic about to give a public lecture: 'I mean, it's a subject that has been fairly worked over, isn't it? I don't know whether it's possible to get a new slant on it these days, but personally I should have thought ... ' He was interrupted by the Head of Department – 'It's hardly a question, sir, of ... '

> A remarkable duet ensued, the Principal and Welch both going on talking without pause, the one raising his voice in pitch, the other in volume, giving between them the impression of some ambitious verse-speaking effect ... Finally the Principal broke free, and, like an orchestra that has launched a soloist on his cadenza, Welch abruptly fell silent. 'Worth restating in every generation or not', the Principal concluded.
>
> (Amis 1961: 255)

The Principal has little more than a walk-on role in *Lucky Jim*. He is a comic figure rather than a malign character, wielding nothing like the power over Jim Dixon's life and career that was exercised by the baleful Professor Welch, head of History. Above all, the Principal is immediately recognizable as an academic; his foibles and focus are similar to those of his colleagues.

In each of these respects, he is quite unlike some Vice-Chancellors who took fictional office in the 1980s. Consider the Vice-Chancellor of an unnamed university, previously 'a comfortable backwater of quiet learning and modest scholarship'. His own career had been in Consolidated Tractor Fuels and his sole academic qualification was a Diploma in Laundry Administration from the Pontypridd College of Commerce. We first hear his voice as he dictates a memo to Heads of Departments:

> It has again been brought to my attention that certain junior lecturers have been failing to clock on for the afternoon shift. Professors will, in future, validate the timesheets of their junior staff as well as counter-signing all claims for overtime payment. Furthermore ... productivity bonuses will now be determined by departmental performance over the calendar year, not the academic year as hitherto. The question of paying teaching staff a small retainer during vacations will be considered at the next meeting of the Senate Subcommittee on Wages and Conditions, together with the vexed question of the chalk allowance.
>
> (Parkin 1986: 13, 10)

He has abolished the departments of Classics, Mathematics and English and has Philosophy in his sights. He favours the example of the professor of Politics who boosts departmental income advising military dictators and the professor of Jurisprudence who serves as legal adviser to the Mafia in Palermo. In this broadbrush satire, the Vice-Chancellor is caricatured as a philistine, crassly utilitarian, and out of depth in a university culture.

However, he was not as vicious nor as successful as a third university head, Sir Stanley Oxborrow, who was running East Midlands University at about the moment the Blair Government was first elected. His closest associates on campus were the senior partners in Winkett and Bacon, management consultants. Let us listen to an exchange between him and one of his departmental chairs. She confronted him directly:

> 'To be frank, I believe that on several key points these decisions are likely to prove counter-productive. I believe that what they will do is decrease our research and teaching standing and therefore lead to a fall in our share of the HEFCE cake.'
>
> 'Now "believe" is an interesting word', ruminated Sir Stanley. 'Interesting and possibly dangerous. You see, what you believe about the future of this university, Professor Mallinder, is quite different from what I believe. Which of us is right? That's the question. I shan't pull rank over you, because it's not my style, but as you know I do have considerable experience of strategic management, not only in universities but in industry and international public relations ... That's why I *believe*,' he paused, in order for the word to carry the right element of force, 'that introducing a more rational system of planning and accountability to our schools and departments will be like a breath of fresh air that will sweep [this university] successfully into the twenty-first century.' 'Yes', he said, answering himself like a boomerang, 'that's the key principle here. We must have a New System for a New Age.'
>
> (Oakley 1999: 68–9)

Sir Stanley is an intelligent, able and ruthless ideologue. He *believes* in what he is doing; he has the courage of his managerial convictions. As he put it, waving aside an appeal to procedural niceties by another Head of Department, normal lines of communication might have to be short-circuited: 'It's my job as Vice-Chancellor to make this university work.' (Oakley 1999: 96).

Fictional though this trio may be, they provide a recognizable outline of how British university leadership has changed over the past forty years – a shift from a self-governing profession to a self-consciously managerial authority. That shift is, of course, only part of a larger picture, but it is the detail that this chapter seeks to illuminate.

The context of that larger picture may be very briefly summarized. It is a set of changes that have characterized higher education throughout the industrialized world, although as Trow (1994: 11) points out, 'British higher education has undergone a more profound [re]orientation than any other system in industrial societies.' Higher education, in turn, reflected an epochal shift: the move from Keynesian economics to neo-liberalism, the rolling back of the welfare state, and shrinking public sector provision in favour of a market-driven private sector. The impact of these global developments on British universities was accompanied by a set of changes within those institutions – changes so familiar to readers of this book that they may conveniently merely be listed here:

- The most obvious change is that the system expanded very rapidly. Between 1982 and 1991 the number of students rose by 91 per cent; in the next decade, they nearly doubled again. As recently as 1988 the participation rate for 18–24-year-olds reached 15 per cent for the first time; official policy now slightly hedges its bets on how and when a 50 per cent rate might be reached.
- Second, public funding per student fell sharply – by about 40 per cent in 20 years. Universities have had to cope with expansion and at the same time to adapt to resource scarcity. The most obvious survival mechanism is that institutions have sought to increase their income from other sources. In 1981 British universities raised about 10 per cent of their funding from private sources; by 1991 this proportion had doubled; and in 2001 for the sector as a whole it stood at over 30 per cent.
- A third change – really a set of linked changes – saw the redefinition of the relationship between universities and the state. Historical forms of autonomy were modified by the rise of the 'regulatory state' and by the discourse of efficiency and economy. Universities have become increasingly accountable to a whole range of parastatal organs. Funding is tied to audit and review; teaching and research are subject to performance indicators and targets.
- Fourth, higher education has become increasingly subject to market forces. The system has been deregulated so as to create overt competition for student places, for resources, and for esteem. Knowledge and instruction are frequently packaged, promoted and sold in accordance with the norms of late consumer capitalism.
- Fifth, the academic profession has been directly and adversely affected. The classic analysis of this is Halsey's (1995) persuasive account of the profession's loss of status and deteriorating terms and conditions of employment.
- Sixth, patterns of learning and teaching have undergone major changes. These are defended by some as appropriate adaptations to the different composition of the student body (more diverse, less prepared for tertiary study). Critics hold that students are ill-served by the academic menu on offer; that modularization is the intellectual equivalent of the take-away meal, and that many vocational degrees are low-fibre, pre-packaged, heat and eat courses.

- Finally, academics and students operate within drastically narrowed expectations of higher education. There is scant public value set on the notion of intellectual enquiry as an inherent good. The White Paper of January 2003 and subsequent policy pronouncements promote a coherent, instrumental and utilitarian view of higher education.

Alongside and intertwined with all these developments has been the growth and elaboration of more *managerial* techniques, styles and assumptions in British higher education. Managerialism is variously defined as an ideological approach, described as a cluster of practices, or characterized in terms of governance and power relations. An early and influential commentary on British university managerialism by Martin Trow (1994) distinguished between two distinct *ideological* forms. A 'soft' concept of managerialism emphasized the improvement of institutional effectiveness and efficiency; and was critical of at least some of the norms and attitudes of British academic life – including complacency, conservatism, aloofness and elitism. A 'hard' version elevated management to a dominant position in higher education, with the intention of reshaping and redirecting academic activities through funding formulae, audit regimes and forms of control similar to those operating in the commercial world.

The literature includes many definitions that proceed by enumerating the definitive *practices* of managerialism. It involves (for instance) 'the overt management of sites, finance, staff, students, teaching and research' (Deem 1998: 48) or 'an obsession with certain quantifiable kinds of efficiency, a tendency to require people to report on their activities more frequently' (Enslin et al. 2003: 6). John Dearlove (1998: 117) and others locate the phenomenon as a new form of institutional *governance* – 'the broad trend of change has been away from collegiality towards a kind of "managerialism" that eats into notions of professionalism and into the rights of academics to manage themselves.'

More recently, there has been a fruitful application to higher education of the concept 'new managerialism', originally derived from research into changes in the National Health System and other public sector domains. ' "New managerialism" represents a way of trying to understand and categorise attempts to impose managerial techniques, more usually associated with medium and large "for profit" businesses, onto public sector and voluntary organisations' (Deem 1998: 49). Rosemary Deem and her colleagues have provided a useful definition of new managerialism in terms of three overlapping elements. It is *a narrative of strategic change* constructed so as to persuade and enrol others in new ways of governance and management. Second, it is *a distinctive organizational form* that creates the mechanisms and processes through which to realize these changes. Third, it is *a practical control technology* through which strategic policies and their implementation are translated into viable techniques and devices (Deem 2001a). In sum, new managerialism is a self-justifying discourse with a ready-made toolkit. It views higher education as a commodity-providing service in which needs and priorities can be measured and monitored.

In what follows, I outline how and why university administration has changed; assess the impact of those changes; and make some tentative proposals about appropriate and feasible forms of management while rejecting the excesses of the new managerialism.

Managing to survive? A brief history of university management

To begin with, it is worth recalling that university management has a relatively short history. As recently as the 1960s, outside America, most universities were small, comparatively homogenous, and by contemporary standards had rudimentary managerial structures.[3] Peter Scott (1995) usefully characterizes the management of British universities over the past 80 years in three phases: donnish, democratic and managerial.

The donnish dominion ran from the 1920s to the 1960s, with academic self-government its main feature. Its heyday was in the two decades after World War 2. Management before 1945 was minimal. After the war, universities developed more elaborate administrations. Finance, estates and personnel became regular activities alongside the admission and examination of students (Scott 1995). In the model of collegial governance, the express function of Principals and Vice-Chancellors was 'not to act in an independent executive capacity, but to convene and chair the collective decision-making body' (Graham 2002: 87) such as the Senate. University administrators first emerged as a coherent professional group in the UK in 1961, with the launch meeting of University Academic Administrative Staff, grandparent of today's Association of University Administrators (Town 1996). Even so, university administration was still low profile, discreet, largely unseen.

During the 1960s and 1970s — accelerated by the student protests of 1968 — there ensued an ephemeral chapter in the history of British university administration: the democratization of academic governance (Scott 1995). Vice-Chancellors were reduced in authority, and required to govern by consensus. Hierarchy was weakened by committees that included rank and file academics and some students. Departmental headship became an elected or rotational post instead of professorial right. This moment was memorably visited in Malcolm Bradbury's *The History Man* (published in 1975) and fleetingly graced by the appearance of Vice-Chancellor Millington Harsent, 'all things to all men ... but in reverse; he was thought by the conservatives to be an extreme radical, by the radicals to be an extreme conservative' (Bradbury 1984: 47). But within the heady brew of democratization, another yeast was at work. The expansion of post-Robbins universities required an upgrading of the managerial capacity. 'A managerial cadre began to emerge, ready to support a more executive leadership, in place of the docile clerks who had instinctively acknowledged the innate authority of academics' (Scott 1995: 64). Academic planning, financial systems, estates management, personnel policies, marketing and external relations were all expanded during the 1970s – a precursor to the decisive shift which took place in the first half of the 1980s.

The crucial years in the emergence of managerialism were 1981–85: from the first Thatcher cuts to the Jarratt Report on efficiency. The Jarratt Report was the first salvo fired in a relentless and often contemptuous ideological critique of universities. It persists today: it charges that universities have an '*endemic* lack of external accountability, economic sustainability, managerial effectiveness and operational efficiency' (Reed 2001: 1).

Larger, more heterogenous universities required active management, even before the cuts. Under the whip of reduced incomes, and hectored by Jarratt, British universities rapidly adopted managerial techniques. They restructured and they planned. They redesignated Heads of Departments as line managers and departments as cost units. This was the backdrop to Frank Parkin's scatological farce, *The Mind and Body Shop* (1986) – and also Malcolm Bradbury's *Cuts*, Andrew Davies's *A Very Peculiar Practice* and David Lodge's *Nice Work*. All these novels were published between 1985 and 1988, all written by university academics. They shared 'a very similar theme: the collapse of not-Oxbridge university life under Visigoth government policy ... [and] a similar tone: baffled rage' (Carter 1990: 254). This was the higher education sector's fictional response to Thatcher and Jarratt.

Across the Atlantic, exactly midway between the Thatcher cuts and the Jarratt Report, in 1983, an American called George Keller wrote the indispensable text for this moment, a book called *Academic Strategy* (1983). It blended educational sociology, case studies of successful innovators, and unqualified enthusiasm for academic managerialism. In the USA, as in the UK, educational costs were rising even while the recession of the 1970s sapped revenues. Keller, like Jarratt, bewailed the lack of management capacity of contemporary university: it lacked the power, inclination or expertise to lead itself positively. 'It tends to posture when it should be planning and deciding priorities.' But help was at hand. 'The age of laissez-faire campus administration is over. The era of academic strategy has begun ... The time has arrived for college and university leaders to pick up management's new tools and use them' (Keller 1983: 26, 38).

What were the managerial tools, and where did this persuasive set of ideas come from? Essentially American and European universities in the 1980s drew directly on some of the most influential management theories of the 1960s and 1970s. There were other influences: universities were developing new academic disciplines in organization studies, industrial psychology and operations theory. But for the most part, they drew upon ideas and practices that had established themselves in large corporations and (in America) in government. In the 1960s PPB – planning, programming and budget – set in train an explosion of interest in strategic planning as the methodology of competitiveness. Alfred Chandler decreed as early as 1962 that 'structure follows strategy'. In the recession seventies, Management by Objectives was perhaps the most influential single theme, and this decade also saw the move to flatter structures, championed by Peter Drucker and Charles Handy. By the 1980s, the basic vocabulary of mission, vision, objectives and strategy had migrated from boardroom to senate chamber.

What were the managerial tools trends adopted by British universities in the 1980s? Especially for those who worked in higher education during these years, the briefest summary will serve as *déjà vu*:[4]

- the ubiquitous technique of management was the strategic plan, an instrument of self-analysis, goal-setting, and basis for resource allocation;
- the establishment of new organs of decision-making, prototypically a new committee that brought together the university executive, key administrators and senior academics;
- a shift towards fewer levels of decision-making, streamlined committee systems, flatter administrative structures; inextricably linked with this was a centripetal tendency towards stronger leadership powers at the centre;
- an adoption of decentralized budgeting variously styled as lump-sum, cost-centre or responsibility centre budgeting;
- closer collaboration with industry and commerce: more contract research, product development, and science parks;
- technology as more integral tool of management, with the related development of Management Information Systems;
- a commitment to explicit training for administrators and managers.

This set of innovations did not arrive suddenly in the Thatcherite 1980s. Some British universities and polytechnics adopted some of these approaches in the 1960s and 1970s. As Scott puts it, 'the emergence of the "managerial" university was not a dramatic break with the past, a brusque repudiation of collegiality and academic self-government' (1995: 64–5). The more heavily managed university was nascent, taking shape before the 1981 cuts: it had stronger executive leadership; its professional administrators were running larger and more complex units; and its forms of academic self-government were diluted or overridden by centripetal decision-making. The significance of the 1980s was that such practices became generalized across the sector as the relationship between higher education and the state was redefined. New rules for reporting, new layers of 'accountability', and new forms of external assessment were accompanied by funding formulas based on compliance and performance. And correspondingly, the internal workings of institutions embedded these pressures in their own bureaucratic structures and practices.

In the 1990s, the external requirements *and* internal adjustments towards managerial universities increased. The 'new public management' of the late 1980s and early 1990s was primarily associated with the health and welfare sectors, but its motifs permeated universities too, particularly after the 1992 abolition of the binary system. What happened in universities was one instance of a more insistent extension to the public sector of key precepts of private sector management theory (Hoggett 1996): deregulation in favour of market forces, inter-institutional competition, pay for performance, and a major shift towards contract appointments. There is a savage little irony in all this. Several management theorists have pointed out that many commercial and industrial organizations shifted in the 1990s to more holistic and less formulaic modes of management. But British universities (remarks David Preston) 'have largely ignored such criticism and doubt ... [and] have taken on the strategic approach with the uncritical fervour and enthusiasm often associated with new disciples' (2001: 354–5).

Assessing the impact: pros and cons

To recapitulate: university management has its own distinctive history, one that has gathered momentum dramatically since the mid-1970s. Three main reasons have been identified for the increased volume, reach and experimentation of university management. Universities became larger and more complex institutions, required to perform novel and multiple roles. Shrinking public revenue for universities impelled their leaders into action on a spectrum from crisis management through painful adaptation to successful new organizational structures and patterns of activity. The relationship between universities and the state altered fundamentally, yielding a contradictory blend of more explicit forms of state oversight and review, on the one hand, and deregulation in favour of more robust market forces, on the other.

The main outcomes were a steady growth in the number of specialized, professional administrators at universities; the adoption of a self-consciously corporate style of university executive management; and a diminished role for academic professionals in the governance of their institutions. Some commentators take a positive view of these changes. Gibbons proposes that:

> This managerial revolution has not only produced a much tighter organisational framework but created at the centre of the university, in its administration, a managerial energy that competes with as well as complements the academic energy of its constituent departments and research teams ... they have re-defined the university in organisational rather than normative terms.
>
> (Gibbons 1998: 19)

Michael Shattock agreed, arguing that the more competitive climate of Organization for Cooperation and Development (OECD) higher education 'demands fast response times, quick decisions and improved implementation skills ... universities will have to become more entrepreneurial to survive'. The sector required 'an injection of corporate flair and corporate imagination' in the shape of administrators who no longer look inwards to institutions but outwards to society as a whole, who have the confidence to enter new alliances, and the flexibility to adapt to new ways of working (1997: 30, 33). Burton Clark's detailed advocacy of the entrepreneurial university was argued via five case studies from four European countries. Clark's key elements of success (a strengthened steering core; the growth of new units; a diversified funding base; a stimulated academic heartland; and the integration of an entrepreneurial culture across the institution) (1998: 5–8) are cross-cut with managerial issues. These 'include the search for new, more effective and efficient ways of doing things ... the setting up of new organisational forms ... [and] emphasis on the heightened importance of managers' (Deem 2001b: 12).

Such enthusiasm for 'the managerial revolution' is countered by a number of critics.[5] Their objections can only be summarized here. One line of criticism, pioneered by Halsey, is concerned with the proletarianization of the academic profession. 'Their prestige, salaries, autonomy and resources have been much humbled.' (Halsey 1995: 135–46, 146). More recently, but in similar vein, Mike Reed asks whether the new managerialism inevitably results 'in the further dilution and weakening of academic professionalism ... enhanced casualisation of academic work and the fragementation of the academic profession' (2001: 2).

Second, in addition to deteriorating terms of employment and income, others stress the erosion of academic self-governance. For Scott the main feature of the managerial university 'has been a reordering of authority within the university, with the organs of academic self-government losing effective (as opposed to formal) power and senior managers gaining influence' (1995: 66). Deem surveys this approach and concludes: 'Thus control and regulation of academic labour seem to have replaced collegiality, trust and professional discretion' (1998b: 52).

A third, related, set of criticisms bear upon the incompatibility of managerialism and core academic values and the deleterious effect upon institutional relations. 'There is no question' writes Oliver Fulton 'that many traditional values and practices (democracy, community, individual autonomy, the right and obligation to both teach and research) are threatened by current trends' (2001: 2). The consequent flagging morale amongst academics has been identified in a number of different settings. Meek and Wood (1998), reporting on a major study of management practices in Australian universities, found increased conflict and alienation amongst rank and file staff with executive leadership increasingly distant from what was described as the collegial needs and philosophical outlooks of most academic staff. The past President of Stanford University warns that academics in the USA have experienced severe crises of morale and status; that they are alienated from their institutions and estranged from administrators: 'A kind of pessimism has set in', faculty do not feel 'accepted, appreciated and protected' (Kennedy 1998: 273, 285–6).

Finally, there are critics entirely hostile to managerial precepts and practices, scornful of its vocabulary and values, resentful of its results. The embrace of managerialism in British universities, it has been noted, was in many quarters fervent and even exaggerated, and has provoked its fair share of derision. It is the longest-running joke in Laurie Taylor's tailgunner column in the *Times Higher Educational Supplement*. In Poppleton and beyond, the new managerialism is guyed for its indiscriminate enthusiasm for corporate practices and a copy-cat vocabulary of missions, visions, brands, niches, cost-centres and zero-based budgets. An essentially similar conclusion is reached by the head of an Oxford college:

> the offices of Vice-chancellors ... are clogged with press statements and fliers proclaiming ... how effective their institutions are in inculcating 'enterprise skills' ... how successful their co-operation with industry ... But there is a marked reluctance to articulate a motivating purpose, to address questions about the *raison d'être* of higher education.
> (Smith and Webster 1997: 4)

Proponents and critics, then, occupy little common ground. As Gordon Graham has remarked, their divergent approaches tend to leave little scope for more balanced appraisals. He argues instead for an approach 'that will allow us *both* to take full account of altered circumstances *and* to continue those purposes which alone can make sense of the university as a distinctively valuable idea' (2002: 96). This is essentially the approach in the following section.

Contradicting the habits, inhabiting the contradictions

An ineluctable conclusion of this historical survey is that more extensive management in the universities of industrialized societies is here to stay. This is ensured partly by mounting external demands on universities, but also by the limited capacity of the traditional university to respond: 'collegial relations and academic governance rendered difficult the making of hard, divisive, choices' (Dearlove 1998: 115) in the era of cuts and quality assurance. Contemporary universities require structures and procedures that their predecessors did not. Collegial self-management by academics – to whatever extent it ever existed[6] – is an historic form and not a current option.

However, to acknowledge the reality of more extensive management does not also require uncritical acceptance of the trappings of corporate management on campuses. To accept that universities should be run along more business-like lines 'does nothing to support the much more ambitious contention that universities are themselves businesses' (Graham 2002: 96). Living with the new managerialism should not equate to living subserviently under its sway. The central challenge, to administrators as much as to academics, is to contest the excesses of managerialism, conserve the successes of management, and reconstruct the purpose, worth and value of the university.

More concretely, what space exists for academics and administrators to refashion forms of governance that support rather than inhibit the kinds of research and teaching that universities do supremely well? The available solution (it seems to me) is dialectical. It confronts the reality of more highly managed universities, but interrogates and resists the logic of managerialism. If we are critical of the (mis)fit between managerialism and academy, we must identify and then work within its contradictions.

Such a solution proceeds – must proceed – in the first instance by mounting an intellectual critique; by contesting the sales pitch of the ideologues and hucksters of managerialism. 'Culture and discourse are always open to contestation', argues Eve Bertelsen in making the Gramscian case:

> whatever is articulated can, in turn, be dis-articulated and re-articulated. If advocates of the market can transform university discourse by yoking its terms to the imperatives of business, it follows that this process can be *reversed*. While organised resistance (through social and political movements with well-defined objectives) may seem out of reach within the current climate of market hegemony, intervention is still possible at the institutional level. We can use such autonomy and influence that still remains to us (albeit as a 'stakeholder' constituency) to regroup and mount a debate which may interrupt this self-satisfied campaign of persuasion and open up other options.
>
> (1998: 155)

For example, even while higher education becomes narrower and more instrumental, there is a pervasive rhetorical commitment to its 'relevance' and to the importance of partnerships. Relevance and partnership, surely, can be put to progressive ends. 'We should emphasize the potential of partnerships with communities and social movements – regionally as well as nationally and internationally – for developing new, symbiotic alliances, new curricular approaches and new forms of pedagogy. Edward Thompson's advocacy in the 1960s of a dynamic dialogue between "education and experience" remains as relevant today as it was at the time' (Taylor et al. 2002: 153).

In the same way, the tendency to devolution of power is much more ambiguous than some managers suppose. Decentralization and devolved responsibility, as virtues in themselves, come from the management gurus. But they are consistent with an older view of academic governance, and should be regarded not merely as a mechanism for improving efficiency, but as establishing the minimal requirements of an acceptable system of decision-making. The past president of Cornell is no radical, but he writes with a calm certainty about the need for academics to take decisions on academic matters that is only seldom heard in British universities. 'Campus governance is by its nature collective ... all decisions should be made at the lowest appropriate level of responsibility – the department, say, rather than the college – so improving participation and understanding, and encouraging added responsiveness and accountability' (Rhodes 2001: 221).

Second, we can surely learn from experience. Kenneth Edwards, previously Vice-Chancellor of Leicester University, defined a central challenge of change management as setting up structures which 'combine the capacity for rapid response to external changes with a high level of involvement and commitment' by academics. 'A centralized and highly "managerial" system can achieve speed but not involvement, while a highly "democratic" system cannot possibly be quick.' He has described how the tough task of restructuring a threatened Arts Faculty was carried out through a combination of central steering and devolution of decision-making, by involving the members of that faculty in the key decisions, but ultimately executing these at the centre (Edwards 1994: 145–7). The same generic solution was achieved at Laurentian University, in Ontario, Canada. It has been observed above that traditional governance relations render difficult the making of tough choices, especially choices involving contraction, closure, retrenchment and redundancy. The leadership at Laurentian insisted that the process of programme review should be driven by academic considerations, and initiated a process at once consultative, conscientious and conclusive – a model of its kind (Cappon and Falter 1996).

Another pair of case studies comes from South Africa – a higher education system coping simultaneously with the transition from apartheid and with the rapid introduction of managerial practices. Cloete and Kulati (2003) report a recent major study of higher education governance in that country[7] that distinguishes between *management-focused institutions* and *democratic, well-managed institutions*.[8] The former exemplify new managerialism; the latter (there were two in the study), they suggest, 'have achieved an impressive record in governance through combining the strengths of participatory governance with the advantages of well-developed, formal systems of delegation of authority and responsibility' (2003: 6). The authors characterize the approach of these two institutions as 'strategic managerialism', combining elements of leadership with features of co-operative governance or 'the management of the tension between leading and consulting' (2003: 8, 10). They quote Paul Ramsden: 'deep at the heart of effective leadership is an understanding of how academics work' (1998: 13) and give theoretical expression to the process in the Leicester case study cited above: 'In order to push the transformation agenda through the institution, decision making is centralised, decentralised and re-centralised' (Cloete and Kulati 2003: 13).

Ramsden's observation on 'how academics work' is not as straightforward as it seems. Rifts increasingly exist not only between academics and administrators, but within the academic community itself. The advancing specialization of fields, a funding environment that promotes competition between disciplines, and more pressured work environments have accelerated the loss of shared identity and vision amongst academics, even in the same institution. This further complicates the relationship between management and the academic project. Michael Worton (Vice Provost at UCL) and Geoff Whitty (Director of the Institute of Education) pondered on this when they were interviewed in September 2000.[9] Worton posed the issue as an unacknowledged correspondence between the managerial drive towards an institutional vision and collegial identity:

> One does need to re-establish some sense of shared purpose. One can use terms like 'corporate will' which will alienate an awful lot of people, but that rhetoric is actually saying the same thing as collegiality. We do need to see ourselves as belonging to an institution which has a purpose rather than a series of individuals within departments on their own ... We need corporately to recognize that change is necessary and desirable.

Ron Barnett has also tried to tease out the apparent contradiction between management and collegiality. In *Higher Education: A Critical Business* he threw down a gauntlet to managers:

> If a management team can reduce community and critical thought, it can also expand those features of university life through the promotion of cross-disciplinary communication ... The new managerialism has only just begun. It has in front of it an even greater challenge of helping the university become the academic community it always claimed it was ... The managerial role ... has to be reconceptualised as opening up the possibility of academic community.
>
> (1997: 59)

More tentatively, in his most recent book, Barnett revisits the issue. He wonders whether there is a possibility of expanded academic freedom in the interstices of managerialism: 'There may be more space to recruit non-traditional students, to start up businesses ... to travel abroad, to engage via the internet with world-wide communities and, generally, to take on multiple agendas and identities.' Like Worton, he warns of the fraying of coherence and commitment in the academic community and recognises that 'some academics will dismiss as mere "managerialism" any such attempt to remind academics of their collective accountability to each other' (2003: 46, 162).

The goal – it follows – is to find ways of bridging the divide between academics and administrators, of coupling effective and decisive management with the disciplinary expertise, professional pride and intellectual passion of academics. David Damrosch wryly noted that one of the few benefits of the resource crisis at Columbia University was that administrators and faculty began talking to each other about systemic issues (1995: 203–4). The case studies cited above provide sketchy templates for fusing managerial imperatives with academic priorities, for creating a shared organizational space, structure and culture. The editors of a special issue of *Higher Education Policy* found some solace in a 'Winter of Discontent' from the case of the University of California. At that institution, as described by

Martin Trow, an overriding *esprit de corps* enabled academics and administrators to pursue jointly excellence and autonomy. From this vantage, they surmised, it was not 'managerialism' that dwelt at the core of contemporary problems so much as 'an absence of shared vision between academics and administrators, and an absence of institutional governance and management seen as giving active support to education and research rather than as autonomous processes' (de Boer et al. 1998: 110).

A shared vision of universities – this shapes my final point. It is not much advance to reconstitute an academic community if that community lacks credibility, influence and engagement with the broader society. There is scant gain from rapprochement between administrators and academics unless this can change not merely the internal functioning of their institutions but their social standing and purpose. The reining in of new managerialism is of limited value if the horse has bolted – if universities do not make a concerted attempt to reassert their worth, and to win back a measure of recognition and esteem by society at large. It will be difficult to win the argument for the importance of social knowledge on a single campus so long as the system at large pays cynical service to the prior claims of market know-how.

For 30 years British universities have been subject to acute external pressures – to ideological critique, to regulation and quality assessment, and to the market. In response they have sought to be relevant; they have pursued partnerships with other social agents; and they have aligned curricula and research agenda to local or national socio-economic needs. The price paid for this is that the critical, reflexive, and independent function of higher education has too often been reduced to an opportunist and instrumental parody. In repudiating the image of ivory tower, some universities have opted instead for the function of service station – checking plugs and points, topping up fuel levels, and inflating the tyres of the engine of economic competitiveness.

This chapter clings to an alternative position: one recognizing that universities are deeply implicated in the modern state; but holding that they should be conscious of and make choices about the terms of that involvement. If universities are called on to be the brains and the skilled hands of their immediate community they can also be the conscience of society. Academics may be involved in 'knowledge production' – with its echoes of the conveyor belt – but their toolkit also includes imagination, scepticism and open-ended enquiry. Thus equipped, research can and should be disinterested. Teaching can and should be a moral vocation. Universities can and must link education and democracy. They must, because only they can.

Notes

[1] A preliminary version of this text was delivered to the 13th International Meeting of University Administrators, University of Edinburgh, 1999. A reworked text was delivered as the keynote address at a conference on 'The Degradation of Higher Education' in January 2003.

[2] This essay falls somewhere between participant observation and action research. My perspective is that of a lapsed historian: one who fell amongst administrators a decade ago and has encountered managerial modes in South African and British universities. Experience as poacher turned gamekeeper must have shaped my analysis, but I hope it does not lend itself to special pleading.

[3] The benchmark for modest management at a major university was probably set by the University of Queensland. It did not appoint a Vice-Chancellor until 1938, 20 years after its foundation; and its first V-C served without any remuneration for the next 22 years before he retired at the age of 87! (Wilson 1997: 213).

[4] When I delivered a version of this history to the International Meeting of University Administrators, a registrar at a leading British university told me that it was like drowning: 'the whole of my professional life flashed before my eyes'.

[5] Useful introductions to the critical literature are provided by Deem (2001a, 2001b).

[6] A number of commentators point out that collegial self-government is 'a mythological view of institutional history' (Watson 2000: 7) drastically understating the trade-off between bureaucracy and collegium (Henkel 2000: pp.52–3) or 'compromise between corporate bureaucracy and professional association' (Deem 2001a: 6) that prevailed in universities after 1945.

[7] Martin Hall, A. Symes and T. Luescher, *Governance in South African Higher Education* (Pretoria, Council on Higher Education, 2002).

[8] I am grateful to Nico Cloete for a mimeo copy of Cloete and Kulati (2003) prior to its publication. I have not been able to see Cloete, N., Bunting, L. and Bunting, I. (2002) *Transformation Indicators Applied to Two South African Institutions*, Pretoria: Centre for Higher Education Transformation, which provides in-depth case studies of the two institutions referred to above.

[9] The transcript of the interview will be published in Volume 8, No 4 (October 2003) of *Teaching in Higher Education*. I am grateful to Jon Nixon, editor of the journal, for access to the typescript prior to publication.

References

Amis, M. ([1954] 1961) *Lucky Jim*. Harmondsworth: Penguin.
Barnett, R. (1997) *Higher Education: A Critical Business*. Buckingham: Open University Press.
Barnett, R. (2003) *Beyond All Reason: Living with Ideology in the University*. Buckingham: Open University Press.
Bertelsen, E. (1998) The Real Transformation: The marketisation of higher education, *Social Dynamics*, 24(2): 130–58.
Bradbury, M. (1975) *The History Man*. London: Secker and Warburg.
Bradbury, M. (1984) *The History Man*. London: Arrow Books.
Bradbury, M. (1987) *Cuts*. London: Hutchinson.

Cappon, P. and Falter, H. (1996) Making Difficult Choices: The academic review process. Paper presented at 10th International Meeting of University Administrators, Cape Town, January.

Carter, I. (1990) *Ancient Cultures of Conceit*. London: Routledge.

Clark, B.R. (1998) *Creating Entrepreneurial Universities: Organisational Pathways of Transformation*. Oxford: Pergamon for International Association of Universities.

Cloete, N. and Kulati, T. (2003) Managerialism within a framework of co-operative governance? Mimeo of chapter to be published in A. Amaral, O. Fulton and L.V. Meek (eds) *International Perspectives on Managerialism*.

Damrosch, D. (1995) *We Scholars: Changing the Culture of the University*. Cambridge, MA: Harvard University Press.

Davies, A. (1987) *A Very Peculiar Practice*. London: Methuen.

Dearlove, J. (1998) Fundamental changes in institutional governance structures: the United Kingdom, *Higher Education Policy*, 11: 111–20.

de Boer, H., Goedegebuure, Meek, L. (1998) In the Winter of Discontent, Business – as usual, *Higher Education Policy*, 11: 103–110.

Deem, R. (1998) 'New Managerialism' and Higher Education: the management of performances and cultures in Universities in the United Kingdom, *International Studies in Sociology of Education*, 8(1): 47–70.

Deem, R. (2001a) 'New Managerialism' and the Management of UK Universities. End of award report of the findings of an ESRC funded project, October 1998–November 2000.

Deem, R. (2001b) Globalisation, New Managerialism, Academic Capitalism and Entrepreneurialism in Universities: is the local dimension still important? *Comparative Education*, 37(1): 7–20.

Edwards, K. (1994) Focussing the University: The Changing Role of the Vice-Chancellor, in S. Weil (ed.) *Introducing Change from the Top*. London: Kogan Page.

Enslin, P., Pendlesbury, S. and Tjiattas, M. (2003) Knaves, Knights and Fools in the Academy: Bureacratic control, social justice and academic work. Mimeo of article to be published in *Journal of Education* (University of Natal) in October 2003.

Fulton, O. (2001) Managerialism and the academic. Paper presented to UUK/SRHE seminar, 20 June.

Gibbons, M. (1998) *Higher Education in the 21st Century*. Washington: World Bank.

Graham, G. (2002) *Universities: The Recovery of an Idea*. Thorverton: Imprint Academic.

Halsey, A. H. ([1992] 1995) *Decline of Donnish Dominion: The British Academic Professions in the Twentieth Century*. Oxford: Clarendon.

Henkel, M. (2000) *Academic Identities and Policy Change in Higher Education*. London: Jessica Kingsley.

Hoggett, P. (1996) New modes of control in the public service, *Public Administration*, 74: 9–32.

Keller, G. (1983) *Academic Strategy: The Managerial Revolution in American Higher Education*. Baltimore: Johns Hopkins University Press.

Kennedy, D. (1998) *Academic Duty*. Cambridge, MA: Harvard University Press.

Lodge, D. (1988) *Nice Work*. London: Secker and Warburg.

Meek, L.V. and Wood, F.Q. (1998) Higher education governance and management: Australia, *Higher Education Policy*, 11 (1998): 165–81.

Oakley, A. (1999) *Overheads*. London: Flamingo.

Parkin, F. (1986) *The Mind and Body Shop*. London: Fontana.
Preston, D.S. (2001) Managerialism and the Post-enlightenment Crisis of the British University, *Educational Philosophy and Theory*, 33(3 & 4): 343–63.
Ramsden, P. (1998) *Learning to Lead in Higher Education*. London: Routledge.
Reed, M. (2001) New Managerialism: Theoretical Debates and Issues. Abstract of paper at UUK/SRHE seminar, 20 June.
Rhodes, F. (2001) *The Creation of the Future: The Role of the American University*. Ithaca: Cornell University Press.
Scott, P. (1995) *The Meanings of Mass Higher Education*. Buckingham: Open University Press.
Shattock, M. (1997) The managerial implications of the new priorities, *Higher Education Management*, 9(2): 27–34.
Smith, A. and Webster, F. (1997) Changing ideas of the university, in A. Smith and F. Webster (eds) *The Postmodern University?* Buckingham: Open University Press.
Taylor, R., Barr, J. and Steele, T. (2002) *For a Radical Higher Education: After Postmodernism*. Buckingham: Open University Press.
Town, J. (1996) Old heads on young shoulders: Management development for UK university administrators. Paper presented to 10th International Meeting of University Administrators, Cape Town.
Trow, M. (1994) Managerialism and the Academic Profession: The Case of England, *Higher Education Policy*, 7(2): 11–18.
Watson, D. (2000) *Managing Strategy*. Buckingham: Open University Press.
Whitty, G. and Worton, M., interviewed by Barton, L. and Rowland, S. (2003) Mimeo of paper to be published in *Teaching in Higher Education*, 8(4).
Wilson, B.G. (1997) Australia, in M.F. Green (ed.) *Transforming Higher Education: Views from Leaders around the World*. Phoenix: Oryx Press.

11

Beyond the Impossibly Good Place: Research and Scholarship

Melanie Walker

It is no chance matter we are discussing, but how one should live. (Plato, *The Republic*)

Research purposes

This chapter sets out to examine what it means to understand our research and scholarship as ethical and 'thoughtful practice'. Thoughtfulness is taken to involve the capacity to be mindful of the public good, transcending individual, institutional or sectoral interests in forming and making judgements regarding right action (Nixon et al. 2003). Who then decides which are the important questions for which we need to produce and collect evidence? Whose questions get asked and answered? Whose problems are investigated? What counts as evidence and whose evidence (or voice) counts? Evidence-based policy and practice or empirical scientific research offer no inherent guarantee that such research will benefit communities, or inflect towards thoughtful deliberation. Indeed, they may as easily turn away by privileging outcomes and ends at the expense of processes and purposes.

Here are two examples of what might be considered as 'thoughtless' or more generously 'not thoughtful enough' research. First, the practices of pharmaceutical companies in funding research into drugs and then ensuring that scientific papers promote the efficacy of those same drugs. For this they require the collusion of those members of the scientific community willing to become 'well paid spokesperson's' for these companies, rather than the public good (see Barnett 2003: 150). A second example is that of academia's links to the oil industry which include sponsored university chairs, interventions in the geology curriculum through oil company sponsorship, and commercial sponsorship of university research in which what is investigated and published is tightly controlled (see Crace 2003: 9). Thus, comments Matthias Beck, professor of risk management at Glasgow Caledonian University:

> 'I am consistently surprised that colleagues don't take a more critical attitude towards the questionable public relations policies of the oil industry'. He points out that in the case of the Exxon Valdez oil disaster there was considerable difficulty in finding impartial scientific experts 'as the university scientists with suitable scientific expertise were compromised through working in collaboration with the oil industry'.
>
> (quoted in Crace 2003: 9)

At stake is an ethical project which takes as central to social inquiry our individual and collective responsibilities for the human condition, and which asks from diverse disciplinary and national locations: 'How do we live well?' 'How do we foster human flourishing through our scholarly work?' I am reminded of Carr's (1998) injunction that what to teach and how to teach, and for our purposes here equally what to research and how to research it, are themselves always a particular expression of a political question about whether existing patterns of cultural, economic and political life ought to be reproduced or transformed. The point is that our normative commitments and beliefs about higher education will shape our approaches to research. Apple (2001) also usefully points to the particular kinds of morality which underpin competing versions of education, and hence of our scholarship in universities. On the one hand, a 'thick morality' is grounded in notions of the common good as the ethical basis for policy and practice, while a 'thin morality' is grounded in competitive individualism and hierarchical divisions. Put another way, would be to ask whether the purposes of higher education hold ethical values to be central as much as the generation of knowledge, *both* ethics *and* gaining knowledge. Will our scholarly commitments support pernicious ideologies, or virtuous *idealogies? (Barnett 2003).*

As the philosopher Martha Nussbaum (1990: 211) writes in her discussion of the fictional text, *The Princess Casamassima*, 'If in the process of concerning ourselves with hunger, we allow life to be emptied of that which holds people to the world, that which inspires love of life and humanity itself, then we will have, in the end, at best well fed pigs'. So are we only for well-fed pigs, or also for an ethical project of critical learning in which we ask what developing our scholarship is for? Bourdieu (1999) argues that 'criticism and watchfulness' are required in our scholarship, but these must be both inward and outward looking: towards a critical and purposeful engagement with both our own research practice and with society. Thus Bourdieu might enjoin us to prise open the current hegemony of contemporary higher education policy in which scholarship is inflected by market values, corporate cultures, ontological individualism, knowledge as a commodity, and entirely empty notions of 'excellence'.

This chapter specifically focuses on just two research projects. No claim is made regarding their disciplinary representativeness or their moral perfection. Rather the idea is to think about our research practices in the spirit of what Arendt (1978: 152) eloquently describes as 'the wind of thinking' which makes us 'fully awake and alive' so that 'you will see that you have nothing in your grasp but perplexities, and the best we can do with them is share them with each other'. My intention thus is to offer tentative examples of how an ethical professionalism might take shape in relation to practices of scholarship, while also pointing more broadly to some of the difficult issues that surround our research practices. I attempt to avoid easy answers – for there are none under contemporary conditions of higher education – but more modestly to point to (some) hope, and to open up a debate now too often muted by the bottom-line money discourse, about the ends and purposes of university research. The idea of 'beyond the impossibly good place' is intended to gesture towards enabling dialogue and research practices towards and beyond where we currently find ourselves. In this I signal how we might keep together both our aspirations towards Utopian (hopeful) notions of the 'impossibly good place' and a pragmatic orientation towards producing counter-cultural pathways and a landscape which is 'good enough' by developing our inquiries under conditions which are mostly less than hopeful.

The scholarship of teaching

I turn now to a scholarship of teaching research project in which I was closely involved over two years in 1998–2000 (see Walker 2001). In this collaborative action research project into university teaching, I worked with five colleagues from departments of computer science, electrical engineering, hispanic studies, german and management at the University of Glasgow. Crucially, in action research we connect research to practical attempts to develop our teaching in a process of 'reflective equilibrium' in which research informs practice, and practice talks back to research, rather than doing research at a distance from the everyday social world (see Chapter 2 in Walker 2001). Our starting point for this work together was how we conceptualized the idea of a critical professionalism (Barnett 1997), and arising from this how we might do criticality both in our teaching and in our dialogic professional learning with and from each other. Our project comprised an interwoven iterative layering of the higher education policy environment and our particular institutional context, student learning in particular subjects, and a reflexive professional dialogue arising from our action research case studies.

We shared the view that university teaching is a scholarly activity and worth effort and attention. As Stenhouse (1979) would argue, developing our teaching through research suggests the need for educational research which produces actionable evidence, relevant to the problem of how to make our practical actions and interactions with students more consistent with the values and principles that define for each of us a worthwhile educational process, worthwhile ways of knowing and worthwhile knowledge. For Stenhouse, our own professional skill and understanding is made the subject of doubt and perplexity. Any knowledge generated by such research into practice could only ever be provisional and open to review under new conditions of practice. As Alison Phipps, a participant in the Glasgow project and a lecturer in German, said:

> What I was really getting out of teaching my course before I started action research was a sense of something that was working, there was a buzz in there ... and I wanted to understand what that might be and what the ingredients of that might be. Yet as soon as find the ingredients I think, OK, this was it, this set of questions, or this way of working or this particular set of student groups. And then I put the ideas into practice again this year but it didn't quite work out in the same way. I was constantly having to think on the spot and work out why the same formula, even with some of the same students, wasn't working a year later.
>
> (quoted in Walker 2001: 192)

The problems chosen for investigation, Stenhouse argues, are educational problems as these arise in our professional practice; from our own action research we sought to generate and refine our explanations of worthwhile educational action in specific contexts of action. Such a view of our academic professionalism acknowledges and celebrates the complexity of professional judgements in which outcomes may, but cannot always be determined in advance, and where reflection and improvement is integral to professional work in higher education. Uncertainty is then a part of the job, not a troublesome process to be tamed by performance indicators.

Crucially, our Glasgow action research studies also involved other epistemological communities – students, and their perspectives, experiences and concerns. Student voices counted in the creation and legitimization of knowledge about education and learning. Thus, for us, action research was also consistent with the kind of pedagogical principles that we articulated - where students are agents in the construction of knowledge about curriculum, about teaching and about learning. Everyone then has a stake in developing pedagogical knowledge. This is not to say that involving students is uncomplicated; it may work patchily in practice. When power 'speaks' in particular ways in higher education pedagogy, it is not surprising that students are unsure. But there are also significant possibilities for student learning and participation:

> I think what this sort of research sets off, is a chain reaction, not just in ourselves and in each other, but also in the students that we've been involving ... I thought at first, here is another opportunity for me to go and milk the students for all the data I can get, and write another text ... And yet what seems to have happened for me is that, suddenly,

> I've seen that these focus groups, these opportunities for the students that we have given them because we want to reflect on our practice, actually gives them an opportunity to reflect on their practice. They get very excited by discovering that other people feel the same way about learning as they do and other people feel that what they are experiencing with us in certain ways is different and unusual and is part of what they think they're at university for. What we're doing is releasing it through the method of looking at our practice.
>
> (Alison Phipps, quoted in Walker 2001: 33)

While action learning was central to our professional development, as significant was sharing that learning as it unfolded for each of us. There were important epistemological aspects to such collaboration. If hegemony works to perpetuate the status quo and maintain control, then keeping open different ways of seeing and voicing different experiences is significant, while expunging disagreements and eliminating frictions may well simply mask the power relations which are present in any interactive encounter. In our project it was often the rasp of conflict that opened space for the most interesting discussions and *dis*-agreements about student learning. At issue is that working with many different voices and different perspectives in a framework of mutual support and knowledge, generates more responsible and inclusive knowledge. This is very unlike dominant modes of knowledge production in the academy, which are competitive and adversarial (even where working in teams is part of the process).

Three points can be emphasized about our collaborative learning. First, through our joint work we began to understand each other's work and to share expertise. Second, the nature of the collaborative development (dialogue, knowledge exchange, experiential learning, reciprocity, mutuality, and so on) provided opportunities to elaborate our practical theories of teaching and learning, to examine these theories in use and so both generate change ('improvement' in classrooms and context) and the dynamic energy to sustain this change. Third, professional dialogue was enhanced, and the analytical insights generated contributed to improving classroom practices and created spaces for new conversations to emerge. Such conversations in our case involved a critical dialogue about practice in different disciplines, and at the same time a challenge to conventional disciplinary boundaries by conversations across these disciplinary boundaries, and the learning that this then generated for us. We spoke about how practice could be improved and about how we might disseminate our ideas more widely by writing case study accounts. We discussed education not just in terms of classrooms, but as part of a wider institutional and policy environment and discourse.

In undertaking action research, as educators we are also changed as the process unfolds; we do not stand outside or above the process of educational change. Quintin Cutts described his experience of changing through undertaking action research in this way:

> If I do traditional computer science research, the fact that I'm doing it is not really particularly important in my reporting of it. I mean, it's the mechanisms that have happened in the machine and what goes on, and I report on that and I relate it to other work. But in action research, I am part of the research and I'm prepared to be reflexive upon myself and I may change. I mean the whole research project involves me in a way that it doesn't always [do]. It's actually that I'm in it. It's not just that my beliefs go into it, or my viewpoint on the world; it's about us writing about us doing our own teaching.
>
> (quoted in Walker 2001: 26)

Thus threaded through our book of case studies is the story of our own shifting self-identities as we struggled to practise a new professionalism that sought to develop dialogic forms of agreement-making with each other and with students regarding the ends and purposes of learning in the university. An interwoven 'patchwork' narrative both of professional and student learning was then at the heart of our action research process and cases. In different ways, each of the five lecturers in the Glasgow project presented a reflexive view on their own professional work in departments and with each other, in overlapping processes of knowledge about the subject and pedagogy, self knowledge and our action research.

What then did we understand as effective teaching or improvement, in other words how did we judge the 'success' of our research into teaching and learning? Mike Gonzalez, lecturer in Hispanic Studies, reflected almost a year into our collaboration:

> I think part of what brings us here in the first place is to ask a question which could be framed in exactly the same way in two different contexts. One is what is 'effective' teaching, might be answered by saying it more efficiently produces the functional ends to which the institution is dedicated and therefore renders it more efficient, more effective, more cost beneficial. The other might be an altogether less tangible purpose which is to more effectively encourage a critical response to the world by individuals and groups of people, whose outcome is not easily quantifiable or measurable or functional, except in a broader sense of making people richer, fuller in their engagement with the world ... The real benefit, the most profound benefit, for the students is discovering how to discover the world, how to ask and answer questions about the world and how to do it with other people in a context which they define. They create their own educational milieu. I think that's in a sense what we're doing.
>
> (quoted in Walker 2001: 19)

On the other hand, ours were not stories of unambiguous success, constrained as they were by the intersections of subject knowledge, teacher and student interactions, departmental and institutional cultures, the intensification of academic work, and the current hegemony of the economy over education. For example, as Judy Wilkinson explained in her case study of teaching mathematics to engineering students, what she now takes to be success has shifted and changed. In concluding her case study she asked: 'Is the course successful?' She goes on to say that in a conventional sense the course had been successful. The degree results were good with an average 86 per cent pass rate over the last three years. The students seemed 'happier' about learning mathematics than previously. But, she then continues, 'Before I joined the Barcelona group and started reading Barnett and Freire, I would have been happy with the results. I may have recommended minor changes. Most of the tutors and lecturers were in broad agreement with the aims and methods and, on the whole, it was a good course'. However, as an academic, she says, she designs learning environments and, as an engineer, she believes that there should be a social dimension in all her courses:

> How we teach reflects our respect for the students, our commitment to the academic community and our responsibility for the world. Thus respect for the students demands that we acknowledge their previous experiences and work with them to design a course which fulfils their expectations. Our commitment to our community entails inculcating in the students an enjoyment of 'the pursuit of difficulty' (Ryan 1999) so that they reach the highest intellectual level of which they are capable. Responsibility to the world means developing, with students, critical and reflective tools so that they can discuss and act, with authority, on the dominant political issues which affect their lives. My concerns are now whether all academic courses should satisfy these criteria. Are they relevant in a mathematics course for engineers? Can we design a course, which encompasses these wider aspirations, as well as teaching students specific skills?
>
> (Wilkinson 2001: 167)

Quintin shared many of her concerns as he wrestled with the dilemmas of how best to teach his large first year computer science class. The outcomes were uneven, although there were interesting moments of equity as he struggled to establish a different kind of relationship with his students, one which at least some of them recognized and welcomed. Chris Warhurst, teaching in a department of management, pointed to complex outcomes from his attempt to integrate critical thinking into his class, where his goal was not the limited kind of 'skills' training increasingly prevalent today, but for students to develop a capacity to critique the knowledge they were encountering and become themselves producers of critical knowledge. Not all students welcomed this, while some were confused by how the power worked between lecturer and students in this class. Alison's frustrations turned on what she saw as the cramped 'banking' learning experiences many of her students encountered elsewhere. Similarly, some of Mike's students voiced a robustly critical view of the limits of many other aspects of their university education.

Moreover, we need to be careful not to conceptualize the boundaries of university teaching and hence the focus of action research case studies too narrowly or too tightly, and in doing so we need better to understand the constraints as much as the spaces within which we work in higher education. We worked within a tradition of critical social research which assumes that 'a critical process informs knowledge' and that does not take 'social structure, social process or accepted history for granted' (Harvey 1990: 6). Instead critical social research asks what surface appearances conceal as much as what they reveal, and how social (educational) systems work to control human subjects. In the Glasgow project we were not naively unaware of the constraints within which we worked and the need both to survive in departments, and to broaden our influence in the University. At one point, for example, Chris raised his concern: 'The problem with [micro level change] is it's about being critical within the world rather than of the world; you would have to make a huge leap of faith to suggest that people can tinker with the system through education' (quoted in Walker 2001: 14). We were only too aware of the institutional and higher education conditions under which we worked. We were both implicated in these conditions, even as we sought to change them. As Mike Gonzalez explained:

> In professional terms our role has shifted to become one of consistently and successfully fulfilling targets and objectives that arise not from an ethical set of imperatives but instrumental needs and ends. Insofar as we are organic to the institution we are obliged to fulfil institutional targets and objectives – and increasingly external tests and assessment designed to measure that. Insofar as we are educators, we have ethical obligations which generate different logics which are not measured or assessed, and indeed are probably impossible to quantify in that way. The big question is whether they can be reconciled.
> (quoted in Walker 2001: 9)

Contextual conditions of possibility shape pedagogical action in significant ways because pedagogy is always a relay for relations of power and privilege at particular historical moments (see Bernstein 2000). In the same way our research practices do not stand apart from relations of power and influence, and these will be inflected by prevailing historical conditions of possibility. It would seem hard to deny that the conditions under which we now undertake research in universities in the UK, and are acknowledged in career terms or not, look somewhat different from those still obtaining even 15 years ago. I would therefore not want to overstate teaching or research success and underemphasize structural constraints, especially in a policy climate in which official attempts in the UK to improve university teaching erase ambiguities (see Abbas and McLean 2003). But we might also ask if there are other equally significant 'grand' kinds of questions: How do we live well? How might research into learning and development enable full human flourishing? Perhaps all we can do is ask 'What can I do from where I am', recognizing that research as development may well yield only small, incremental local changes. Nonetheless, critical forms of action research at least aspire to expand the horizon of influence and action. There is a responsibility to try and draw things to the attention of a bigger audience, to create a bigger space, to draw more people into alternative spaces, because if you don't, said Mike 'you rest, you leave it there, then in a sense, the octopus will come back and swallow it all'. Yet what might also emerge over time, are critical pathways which place educational practice, professional judgement and thoughtful research at their centre.

Producing 'liberating knowledge'

My second somewhat briefer example takes research by Jean Barr (1999) in which she revisits three of her own inquiries into women's education using feminist ideas. The first project was an evaluation of a pre-school community education project in Glasgow, as part of a national study of alternative forms of pre-school provision in 1979–81. Her second research project was a study conducted in 1989–90 for a Masters dissertation in which she explored the influence of different forms of feminism on New Opportunities for Women courses in the North of England. Her third was a funded research project from 1991–93 on Women's Perceptions of Science in the adult education curriculum. Her research practices demonstrate her own enduring concern with the 'democratic control and development of knowledge' as 'an ideal of citizenship' (1999: 191), and hence with education, research and social practices where power and culture intersect with real material effects for people's lives.

Adopting an autobiographical approach, which acknowledges the richness of our 'storied lives', she nonetheless recognizes that personal experience as a source of knowledge is not some kind of 'trump card of authenticity' (1999: 4). Indeed, Barr is careful to point out that our understandings are open to reworking and to critique, and that other voices, including theoretical resources, are key to being personal *and* critical. In other words, she has in mind not some form of narcissistic self review but a public dialogue. Moreover, the self also changes and develops over time – the reflexive self assembled by Barr in this book is not quite the same as the selves that undertook each of the research projects. Her critical scrutiny includes her own practices and judgements developed in and from the space between thought and action; it is not aimed primarily or only at others. Thus her process of review and reappraisal of what her research 'masks as well as reveals, for its blindspots as well as its illuminations' (1999: 4) demonstrates practically her belief that we need to cultivate greater self understanding, even though such self-knowledge is itself always provisional and open to further reworking.

As importantly as her self critical scrutiny is the way in which she locates her research in particular social contexts and historical moments. Threaded through these accounts is the story of the culturally and historically specific forms which feminism took in the UK in the 1970s, the 1980s and into the 1990s. In each case she provides extracts from the original research reports and then critiques the silences and gaps. In the case of the pre-school research project her Marxist-feminist theoretical categories are now seen to have excluded whatever 'escaped' these categories, for example women's caring work and the 'small transgressions' and resistances by working class women. In her second project, still 'seduced by theory with a capital T' (1999: 156), she veered uncomfortably close to a 'banking' view of feminist education in which tutors deposit expert theoretical knowledge in the heads of their students. In the third study, however, a more reflexive personal voice 'was allowed in' and there was not the same attempt as in her previous two research projects to fit what women said into pre-determined categories of the researchers. Eschewing then a narrow view of reflexivity, she locates this work within a wider social and historical context of knowledge production, shaped by the prevailing discourses, power relations, and material conditions.

There is much to be gained epistemologically, methodologically and, indeed, pedagogically from this book for those of us committed both to an ideal of thoughtful research and the 'scholastic attitude', and to research as a common resource. As Barr points out, the democratic knowledge-making project, resonant with complexity and values, is currently under siege from a technicist (thoughtless) discourse and practices which position student and pupil 'consumers' as the recipients of knowledge for purely instrumental ends. Education (including schooling, higher and adult) is increasingly being seen as a private asset rather than a public good so that we risk erasure of the underlying educational purposes that give educational and institutional practices a particular kind of meaning for learners and teachers. Barr explicitly raises the importance of articulating 'urgent problem with people other than academics' (1999: 163). She seeks to heal the breach between 'words' (ideas, discourses, academic knowledge) and 'things' (material conditions, everyday experiences). As she explains, 'knowledge contained in books is limited if it is not connected to people's aspirations for knowledge about how to live in the world' (1999: 163). Barr urges those privileged to have time for research and theorising 'to leave the internal debates of the academy' (1999: 163). In her view, being overly deferential to academic knowledge 'all too often goes hand in hand with a failure to produce really useful knowledge, that is, knowledge which enables an understanding of human experience, enhances self-respect and helps people to deal critically and creatively with the world in order to change it' (1999: 163). It means enabling 'subjugated knowledges' to be heard and listened to in enlarged and inclusive conversations.

Barr's text demonstrates the difficulties and ambiguities of this commitment both to scholarship and the inclusion of many voices. She cites Lorraine Code who points out the complexity of struggles to hear and be heard. Barr herself has produced a fine and compelling text of her own reassembling of the self and of 'responsible knowledge', and she has taken care to review the experiences and voices of women in her earlier research. But while she aligns herself with those who believe that we can develop better self-understanding of our social world through more 'democratic knowledge-making practices and structures' (1999: 9), her own text, deftly and elegantly woven though it is, is also resonant with difficult theoretical ideas. Yet this same calm analytical narrative is indispensable to her text and to her methodology. Eder (1999) asks the hard question: 'Why is it so difficult to change the world? The answer would be: because societies don't like to learn. They would rather stick to what they know and to the rules that stabilise what they know' (quoted in Muller 2000: 137). The point is that a metanarrative of critical theorizing is central to a 'thoughtful' research practice, to the possibility of generating emancipatory insights and to developing critical resources for participatory approaches and a common resource. Participation in research and public deliberation as a goal or ideal and participation and deliberation as an assumption of equality are, then, not the same thing. As Muller (2000: 141) reminds us: ' "equality" and "empowerment" as desired social ends, will be fatally stymied if we do not have ways of understanding how our very social arrangements...collude with the status quo in ways that are not immediately evident to common sense'. The point is the non-transparency of everyday life. The challenge is how to deal dialectically and relationally with systemic issues from the vantage point of the self-understanding of actors; or, put another way, how to explain how our positionality and 'habitus' shapes our dispositions to act in one way rather than another (Bourdieu 2003).

Concluding reflections

The scholarship of teaching project and Barr's research described in this chapter raise some broad areas for discussion and no doubt, disagreement, around the doing of research: what knowledge is being generated; producing provisional not absolute knowledge; how and with whom we collaborate; which epistemological communities are admitted into the research process and dissemination; how we reflexively interrogate our own values and assumptions; how we judge success or effectiveness or influence; how the policy environment shapes our work; and, who benefits from our research?

Three tentative, reflexive comments about research and scholarly practices might now be advanced. *The first is that as academic researchers we have a professional commitment to view the world analytically; such a critical function is essential to research.* At the very least, then, our disposition through our research to be rigorous, reflexive and to hold our own taken for granted assumptions up for critique is in itself to expose domination and exploitation to public debate. It is to traverse the 'rough ground' (Wittgenstein, quoted in Geertz 2000: xii). *Second, this analytical detachment need not stand in opposition to our particular moral commitment and values.* Our commitments offer starting points (as distinct from conclusions) for our investigations. Moreover, as researchers we might model habits of thoughtfulness which inflect towards dialogue, deliberation and democracy, producing knowledge through our critical inquiry such that political action might take account of all the effects of domination. As Villa (2001: 56) suggests in his explorations of what 'Socratic citizenship' might look like, the more people (individuals) who develop a genuine politics of conscience and who are 'alive to the false virtue that underwrites political evil, the more they will be willing to say no to that evil'. *Third, in so far as our research seeks to engage the public (or publics), it is arguably also a form of ethical agency.* By placing our research in the public domain, we help to create actual public spaces in which imaginative, critical and shared undertakings are enabled. Debate and deliberation are then a form of political action. But more than this, through our writing we might also create a quasi-political imagined realm, suggests Arendt (1958), a kind of 'public space' which readers might enter and which requires in Arendt's understanding of public space, that each of us take into account the perspectives of other participants. (see also Barr and Griffiths, Chapter 5 of this book). Even while we must nonetheless undertake the critical task of interpretation for ourselves, it is now an interpretation informed by multiple views under conditions of ethical, collective and deliberative communication. In other words, conditions vital to revisioning a deliberative democracy and repairing our battered public institutions, even while we cannot guarantee that the outcome will be a recovery of the public realm.

What might be the more general points that could be made about our work as researchers in higher education? Current conditions seem to undermine our ethical dispositions at almost very turn as we confront awkward and sometimes impossible dilemmas and decisions about bidding for projects, perhaps under pressures 'to bring in the money', perhaps to keep contract researchers in post, perhaps at times against our own ethical judgements, often not quite in line with our preferred research interests, or perhaps because success in external funding determines our career prospects. At times our own agency might seem so constrained in the face of increasing selectivity in research funds from the RAE in the UK, described by Lisa Lucas in Chapter 2, that few options for continuing research activity exist, not least in areas like Education which offer little in the way of high pay offs in knowledge transfer or technology innovation.

All this then seriously complicates how we engage in research and scholarship which sets out to support 'virtuous ideals' in our universities, rather than undermining them. Such ideals are well described by Barnett (2003: 178) as 'generosity, openness, self-critique, reasonableness, tolerance and imagination'. Barnett's virtues (or principles) direct us to an ethical concern for others so that we 'reject activities, institutions and practices that gratuitously or systematically deceive, thereby destroying or fragmenting trust and social bonds and so indirectly injuring the connections between lives' (O'Neill 1996: 180). His virtues in relation to our research practices and production of knowledge then inflect to the building of 'reasonable' institutions and the realization of the university's contribution to democratic life. Bourdieu argues optimistically that there is the possibility of 'collective intervention' in relation to developing critical research, as he explains:

> The whole edifice of critical thought is thus in need of critical reconstruction. This work of reconstruction cannot be done, as some thought in the past, by a single great intellectual, a master-thinker endowed with the sole resources of his singular thought, or by the authorized spokesperson for a group or an institution presumed to speak in the name of those without voice, union, party and so on. This is where the collective intellectual [academic] can play its irreplaceable role, by helping to create the social conditions for the collective production of realist utopias.
>
> (quoted in Said 2002: 36)

What is demanded of us, as Said so eloquently says, is 'the courage to say that *that* is what is before us' (2002: 39), to retain some reasonable possibility of researching in the interstices of power, speaking back to the hegemonic bottom-line accounting view of a neo-liberal moral order through our own critical and dialogic webs of meaning, the scepticism of our scrutiny, our personal integrity, and the play of our imaginations. The hard task and the choices that confront us means finding ways, big and small, to produce Said's 'countermemory', one 'that will not allow conscience to look away or fall asleep' (2002: 38) as we address such questions. At issue, is a counter [research] practice, says Said, that grasps 'the difficulty of what cannot be grasped' and then goes forth to try anyway, hoping for the best while preparing for the worst' (Bourdieu 2003).

Acknowledgements

A version of this paper was first presented at the ESCalate conference on Teaching and Learning in Higher Education, Institute of Education, 25 April 2003.

References

Abbas, A. and McLean, M. (2003) Communicative competence and the improvement of university teaching: insights from the field, *British Journal of Sociology of Education*, 24(1):69–82.
Apple, M. (2001) Comparing neo-liberal projects and inequality in education, *Comparative Education*, 37(4):409–23.
Arendt, H. (1958) *The Human Condition*. Chicago: Chicago University Press.
Arendt, H. (1978) *The Life of the Mind*. New York: Harcourt Brace.

Barnett, R. (1997) *Higher Education: A Critical Business*. Buckingham: SRHE/Open University Press.
Barnett, R. (2003) *Beyond All Reason: Living with Ideology in the University*. Buckingham: SRHE/Open University Press.
Barr, J. (1999) *Liberating Knowledge: Research, Feminism and Adult Education*. NIACE: Leicester.
Bernstein, B. (2000) *Pedagogy, Symbolic Control and Identity*. London: Routledge.
Bourdieu. P. (2003) Against objectivism: the reality of social fiction, in P. Sikes, J. Nixon and W. Carr (eds) *Knowledge, Inquiry and Values: The Moral Foundations of Educational Research*. Buckingham: Open University Press.
Carr, W. (1998) The curriculum in and for a democratic society, *Curriculum Studies*, 6(3):323–40.
Crace, J. (2003) Oil on water, *Guardian Education*, 25 February 2003, 9.
Eder, K. (1999) Societies learn and yet the world is hard to change, *European Journal of Social Theory*, 2:199–215.
Geertz, C. (2000) *Available Light*. Princeton: Princeton University Press.
Harvey, L. (1990) *Critical Social Research*. London: Unwin Hyman.
Muller, J. (2000) *Reclaiming Knowledge: Social Theory, Curriculum and Education Policy*. London: Falmer Press.
Nixon, J., Walker, M. and Clough, P. (2003) Research as thoughtful practice, in P. Sikes, J. Nixon and W. Carr (eds) *Knowledge, Inquiry and Values: The Moral Foundations of Educational Research*. Buckingham: Open University Press.
Nussbaum, M. (1990) *Love's Knowledge : Essays on Philosophy and Literature*. Oxford: Oxford University Press.
Nussbaum, M. (2000) *Women and Human Development*. Cambridge, MA: Cambridge University Press.
O' Neill, O. (1996) *Towards Justice and Virtue*. Cambridge: Cambridge University Press.
Ryan, A. (1999) *Liberal Anxieties and Liberal Education*. London: Profile Books.
Said, E. (2002) The public role of writers and intellectuals, in H. Small (ed.) *The Public Intellectual*. Oxford: Blackwell.
Stenhouse, L. (1979) Research as a Basis for Teaching. Inaugural lecture at the University of East Anglia, Norwich. Subsequently published in Stenhouse, L. (1983) *Authority, Emancipation and Education*. London: Heinemann Educational.
Villa, D. (2001) *Socratic Citizenship*. Princeton: Princeton University Press.
Walker, M. (ed.) (2001) *Reconstructing Professionalism in University Teaching: Teachers and Learners in Action*. Buckingham: SRHE/Open University Press.
Wilkinson, J. (2001) Designing a new course, in M. Walker (ed.) *Reconstructing Professionalism in University Teaching: Teachers and Learners in Action*. Buckingham: SRHE/Open University Press.

Epilogue

Reclaiming Universities from a Runaway World

Ronald Barnett

Introduction

The idea of 'reclaiming' universities surely implies a loss of some kind; something has been lost that deserves to be – or even needs to be – reclaimed. There at once arises questions over who is doing the reclaiming; who, in other words, feels the loss? But there are also issues that can sensibly be raised about the actual loss in question. In particular, we may distinguish:

i) a loss of idea (a sense that the idea of the university has dissolved);
ii) a loss of practices that could have been said to be constitutive of the university (the 'academic community' as it was once felt to exist is no longer evident);
iii) a loss of the social space that universities once occupied (the university no longer enjoys the academic autonomy it once possessed).

We may name these three senses of loss respectively a loss of narrative, of identity and of position – and the chapters in this volume engage with one or more of these losses – but it is at once clear that these losses intermingle with each other.

A sense of loss over the idea of the university (i) is in part the fall-out of losses attached to the fluidity that attaches to the changing relationships between the university and the wider society (iii). In particular, concerns about the purposes of the university arise from the closing off of the space that the university historically enjoyed and in which it could see itself as 'the critical conscience of society'. Those changing relationships between the university and the wider society also bring in turn alterations in the practices found within the university (ii). Indeed, the very idea of 'within the university', of there being a kind of enclosed space that is the university's, is now suspect as the boundaries between universities and the wider society are breached. In the context of such 'transgressivity' (Nowotny et al. 2002), it is no longer clear that we can sensibly talk of boundaries between the universities and the wider society. The two swim in and out of each other.

Against such a background of loss – indeed, losses – can the idea of reclamation make any sense? Prima facie, it may be felt to herald simply the pleas of the dispossessed. The world has changed: let's move on. To call for universities to be 'reclaimed' from 'a runaway world' is, it may be considered, to call for a return to a kind of university that cannot now be recovered; and perhaps never existed in the first place. But even if that was possible, the reinstitution of a form of an earlier form of the university in what is now 'a runaway world' must be a doomed project. After all, 'a runaway world' is a world in which all bets are off, in which – QED – the old world order has no standing. This is a world that has lost its anchor in the past (cf. Giddens 2002). Old institutions, much as old ideas, or ways of going on, are *ipso facto* redundant. The whole idea of reclaiming universities from this new world must make no sense.

In what follows, I want to try to show why such a reading – which does have some plausibility on its side – is premature and in doing so, I shall draw lightly on the preceding chapters. It is my contention that we can legitimately and sensibly talk of reclaiming our universities, even amid a runaway world. More than that, we can talk of reclaiming our universities in each of the three senses I have just distinguished – of idea, of practices and of social space. Nor is this to argue that we can recover an older form of university or even to resort to ideas of tradition and continuity. The world has moved on and our universities have to be rethought. But it is just possible that some earlier concepts that helped mark out the identity and location of universities may still do some work for us, even in new times.

Reclaiming an idea of the university

In the twenty-first century, it is surely impossible to hold to a single idea of the university, at least so far as its surface features are concerned. A book that took the title 'The Idea of the University' and which attempted to sustain a single idea of the university as a legislative device ('all "universities" have to take this form') could hardly be credible. On the one hand, in the context of mass higher education, there are going to be a wide range of institutions bearing the title 'university' that possess considerable differences. Indeed, in the UK at least, it is part of government policy that universities should be as diverse and that that diversity should grow. This policy intention is, of course, giving rise to a nice policy question: just where, if at all, lie the limits of 'the university'? Are there any criteria that should attach to the name 'university' or, in a marketized system of higher education, should not any institution that wishes carry the name for itself? Putting a limit on the scope of institutional interpretations of 'the university' may undercut precisely the wished for innovation and entrepreneurialism that it is intended to promote.

On the other hand, difficulties attach to trying to determine a single idea of the university because, being eight hundred years in being, the institutional embodiment of the name 'university' is a set of strata of ideas, sentiments, beliefs, practices and institutional relationships that have accrued over that length of time. Drawing on Bill Readings (1997), Michael Peters reminds us that the past 200 years have witnessed several grand ideas of the university, reposing the university in the (Kantian) idea of reason; understanding the university as a vehicle of cultural production, whether as in fulfilment of a national culture or of a more organic kind as represented in a language; and in the modern – if rather empty – bureaucratic notion of 'excellence'. In other words, in wanting to reclaim 'the idea of the university', it is by no means clear which idea we are supposed to be reclaiming.

Michael Peters' response to this situation, in which there are multiple narratives even of the liberal university, is to urge that 'we might substitute for a single unifying idea the constellation or field of overlapping and mutually self-reinforcing ideas of the liberal university, based on family resemblances'. The Kantian idea of Reason can be preserved in ideas of self-criticism, self-reflection and self-governance; and the idea of Culture can be reconstructed in ethically based learning processes, cultural self-understandings and multiculturalism on the one hand, and in the educational potential of the new techno-cultures on the other hand.

One possible difficulty with this agenda is that it by no means exhausts the possibilities of even a liberal sense of the idea of the university. Other contemporary notions include fashioning the university as 'a critic and conscience of society' (The *Dearing Report* (NCIHE 1997)), following New Zealand state policy, as a vehicle for the promotion of citizenship (Delanty 2001) and as a means of sustaining the traditions of disciplines (Graham, 2002). In short, reclaiming the narrative of 'the idea of the university' is in difficulty because of the fecundity of the plausible interpretations of the idea as we move into the twenty-first century. The reflection that such a multiplicity of interpretations is inevitable in a pluralist society leaves us with the conundrum: are their family resemblances such that the members of this particular family have *anything* in common with each other?

After all, there are going to be many interpretations of what is to count as liberal education: perhaps a liberal education is now to be precisely one that emerges from an unfettered market situation? Or is it to be one that stamps in a presumed canon of Western civilization, as a mark of what we, in the liberal West, stand for? *Both* interpretations of liberalism are, as Steven Selden describes it in this volume, part of the 'neo-conservative assault on the undergraduate curriculum'. Presumably, those kinds of extension of the liberal idea of the university are not going to be felt to be legitimate by some; there can be no reclamation in going down those routes. So which ideas are legitimate and which are not? Which ones are going to be allowed to join the 'family' of acceptable interpretations and which are to be repudiated? Which ideas of the university are going to enable us to 'reclaim' universities in a runaway world?

'A runaway world', I am suggesting, is evident in three dimensions of the contemporary university: its narrative or self-story; its practices; and its social space; and, here, for the moment, we are focusing just on the first of these dimensions, the way in which we might understand the purposes of the university. This is by no means, we might note, a purely academic inquiry. Becoming clear about the purposes of institutions that bear the title 'university' has practical implications as governments around the world juggle with their higher education systems and determine which institutions might be deserving of the title of the university, the criteria that should attach to the title and, indeed, whether the title needs to be protected at all. There is much to play for, therefore, in pursuing the matter in hand.

'Reclamation' is a nicely ambiguous term: it can point us in somewhat backward or downward directions, either suggesting that we might seek to regain that which has been lost; *or* suggesting movement onwards and outwards, as we seek to reclaim for new purposes that which is currently not available (as, for instance, land is 'reclaimed' and put to new uses). Yet, even here, in this more positive notion of reclamation lies a sense of possible destruction of an ecology as the natural environment is reduced and put to productive use. So justification is going to be a tricky business; and, as we have seen, assertions of holding true to liberal causes are far from straightforward.

Against this complex of backgrounds – of complexity in policy, in discourses of liberal education and in the very idea of reclamation itself – a runaway world threatens the end of the idea of higher education, *even as a narrative*. That is to say, it is beginning to look as if we cannot, except in cloaking ourselves with hubris, even adopt the story of the idea of higher education, however we might dress it up in terms of family resemblances or other such gambits. This outcome should hardly be surprising: if we really are in a runaway world, then the very idea that there can be secure large ideas or principles must be in doubt; for otherwise, we could hardly be said to be in a runaway world.

Such a pessimistic viewpoint does not have to win the day, however. There are two further argumentative moves available to us. First, we might try to see whether it makes sense to consider the narrative of the idea of the university as a meta-narrative. That is to say, we might imagine our way towards an argumentative space in which talk of the idea of the university can be pursued. It would be a space in which debate about the university itself made some kind of sense, whatever the weight given to particular ideas of the university. Such a debate could make sense in two ways. On the one hand, we could be in an institution in which such a discourse was perceived as valuable and even as necessary to the sustaining of the practices of the institution itself. Such an institution we could call 'a university'. (This is, I take it, Alistair MacIntyre's position.)

On the other hand, we might be able to identify the possibility of a space in which a discourse about the idea of the university could be maintained in virtue of an overriding idea or set of ideas that particular takes on the university might share to a greater or lesser extent. For what it is worth, my sense is that just such a meta-narrative might possibly be found in the concept of ethically based freedom. Such a concept, of a freedom that is anchored in some sense of allegiance to another (whether communities, society, disciplines or even institutions such as universities), could furnish a meta-narrative under which many different kinds of ideas of the university could find shelter and support.

Such a meta-narrative could harbour all manner of legitimate ideas of the university. Under such a meta-narrative of an ethically founded freedom, for example, even the idea of the university as a therapeutic institution could find a place for, ultimately, the therapeutic university is one, surely, that enables individuals to live at peace with themselves in a runaway world. Such a university could work its therapeutic achievements both directly with individuals (in its 'teaching') and indirectly, in making available new frameworks of understanding in comprehensible ways ('research'). And all this could be brought off even as the same university was also helping to fuel the runaway world, through both its knowledge production and knowledge transfer acitivities.

Reclaiming the practices of a university

If it is difficult, and perhaps even impossible, formally to legitimize the university through the identification of abstract principles, perhaps another tack lies in practices as such. The claim here would be that it is through our practices that we live out an idea of the university. Through our practices, too, we give meaning and identity to the university as an institution, and not abstractly, but as this particular university as against that particular university. This, I take it, is Jon Nixon's view, in urging us towards a sense of the university as an institution in which human virtues are sustained as dispositions intrinsic to the internal goods of the university. This is not to presume that there will always be a consensus on significant matters; on the contrary, there will be different perspectives and discontinuities. The university, therefore, has especially to be an institution characterized by 'pedagogies of recognition', in which difference is acknowledged. Coherence, accordingly, arises out of our 'moral purposefulness': in 'learning', I acknowledge 'the capacity of others to learn and to go on learning'. Such mutual learning points us towards a situation of 'perfect friendship', which is founded on 'the reciprocity afforded by our shared aspiration to help one another'.

The human agency necessary for such learning processes cannot be expected just mysteriously to emerge but requires support from the surrounding institutional structure. But, then, just what kind of organizational structures are likely to foster 'perfect friendship'? (this being just one of three questions that Jon Nixon raises). A number of related problems present themselves immediately, both practical and conceptual in nature: Is there space for 'perfect friendship' in a complex organization such as a university, with its hierarchies of power and its pressing need for propitious decision-making? What might 'perfect friendship' mean in a pedagogical situation, with its necessary imbalance of expertise and understanding? What relationship might there be between 'perfect friendship' and the processes of knowledge generation, whether in empirical inquiries or in the more scholarly disciplines?

The very asking of questions such as these are indicative, perhaps, that the idea of 'perfect friendship' can serve – at best – as a regulatory concept, against which we can examine the character of human relationships in a university but bearing always in mind that it is a utopian idea that cannot fully be brought off (cf. Halpin 2003). Indeed, it may be felt that, so far as the pedagogic relationship is concerned, it may be inappropriate even as a utopian ideal for it points possibly to a relationship of reciprocity that should not even be an ideal in such a setting. On the other hand, it may be that we can invoke a conception of proper professional mutuality, devoid of authoritarianism on the one hand and an undue eros on the other hand.

The idea of a proper professional mutuality is easily enough invoked but its working through on campus is fraught, not only with practical difficulty but also with conceptual difficulty. What might the idea of a proper professional mutuality mean in the context of an external audit of the university, that is imposed upon the university? What might it mean in the context of the pedagogical relationship? What might it mean in the context of a continuing tightening of the resource environment within which a particular university is operating? Each of these questions poses particular difficulties.

On the first, let us assume, by way of an example, a context of an external audit of the research profile of a university. This is the ground essayed by Lisa Lucas in her chapter: there, we see graphically not only the symbolic violence but also the material violence to academic identities that such audits can produce. In such a situation, we may add, certain kinds of research activity are often privileged; it is not just the 'quality' of the work or its scope but the very kind of research that it is. Even among those who are 'research active' – as distinct from those classified as non-research active – fine but important discursive distinctions may develop as to particularly prized forms of 'research'.

What is surely required, in these circumstances, analogous to the 'pedagogy of recognition' that Melanie Walker urges in the teaching situation, is what we might term a 'management of recognition', in which those in management positions creatively find ways of valuing different forms of academic identity and of human being among those in their midst. 'A proper professional mutuality' thus becomes here a condition of academic life in which individuals understand that, whatever the external environment in which the university finds itself and whatever the difficult managerial decisions that are made in projecting the university in that milieu, different forms of academic identity are not only valued but also understood to be mutually complementary. In turn, those whose identities are affirmed in this way may be expected to feel a higher level of commitment to the internal academic community. Indeed, here we have a nice instance as to how the very idea of 'academic community' can be brought off and become more than mere rhetoric.

Of course, as Judyth Sachs implies in her chapter, such a professional mutuality cannot be accomplished easily amid the managerial and accountability regimes to which academic practices are now subject. The same person, indeed, may be called into academic practices fuelled by considerations of both effective management and accountability while, at the same time, attempting to prize out new forms of academic mutuality in the process. In other words, professional mutuality is not simply *there*, even latently, but has to be painstakingly negotiated day by day and even hour by hour.

Our second instance, that of the pedagogical situation, also raises difficulties for any notion of mutuality on campus. How can the idea of mutuality be understood in a university where the two parties in the pedagogical relationship stand in an unequal relationship to each other? We may wish to invoke ideas such as 'a pedagogy of becoming' or (as Melanie Walker suggests) 'a pedagogy of recognition', but implicit in both such ideas is precisely a recognition of an unequal relationship. In the first of these, the tutor is invited so to structure a learning environment that the student can come into herself. In the second, the tutor is enjoined to recognize the student as a person. Yet both notions take their point of departure from a sense that the prior and the first responsibility falls upon the tutor who is both in authority and possesses an authority (whether won through research, through expertise in teaching or in 'academic practice' more generally).

Qualifications to these general reflections can certainly be entertained. For instance, postgraduate work redresses the imbalance in the relationship; at PhD level, the student will acquire an expertise that the tutor will not possess. 'Mature students', too, will have all manner of knowledge, competences, and professional understandings that their tutors will never master. In interdisciplinary work, too, even at undergraduate level, students will be delving into matters and emerging with ideas of their own. Especially in the sciences, at third year honours level, students may be working on projects linked to their tutors' research interests. In professional education, too, students will be engaged with professional problems – and not only in 'clinical practice' – and will produce design solutions of real creativity. In all these examples, tutors can and will learn from their students. More generally, too, it is a commonplace that teaching acts themselves are an excellent way of learning; this is for a number of reasons, not least of which is that questions and points raised naively by students prompt a self-questioning and new lines of thought and inquiry.

In the pedagogical relationship, then, learning is reciprocal; both students and tutor can be learning. But this consideration as to the mutuality of learning hardly dents our earlier reflections as to the imbalance in the pedagogical situation. The learning of the student, after all, is a necessary condition of the pedagogical relationship being effective; the learning of the tutor is a highly desirable but hardly a logically necessary condition of such effectiveness. The tutor has pedagogical responsibilities towards the student that the student does not have towards the tutor. There remains an imbalance in expertise, authority and even, we should say, power between the parties in the pedagogical situation.

And yet, there surely remains a genuine mutuality in the pedagogical situation in universities. Students, after all, are adults who are studying voluntarily. They are their own centres of being. They have their own responsibilities towards their own authenticity. There is, therefore, a mutuality of authenticity-in-the-making, a making that is never finished. In practice, it is true, students are not always accorded the space and the dignity in which they can be truly authentic. Students can be said to be part of the academic community insofar as they are willing to accept their responsibilities towards producing and sustaining their own authenticity. Perhaps, indeed, this is one of the key pedagogical tasks, to enable students to understand the challenges, and demands, of becoming and sustaining an authenticity of self. Tutor and students are united, therefore, in a joint enterprise of mutual authenticity-making.

Let us now turn to our third and final setting to see how concepts such as 'perfect friendship' and 'professional mutuality' might fare, that of decision-making and management in the contemporary university. Characteristically, almost anywhere in the world, that environment is highly complex, involving multiple income streams, increasing competition (both from within the academic 'community' and beyond), knowledge transfer, new pedagogies, setting up of parallel companies or semi-independent ventures and changing markets (for both knowledge and pedagogical services). How can concepts such as perfect friendship and professional mutuality gain a purchase in such an operating environment? Does not the press of decision-making, of tight deadlines, of a sense that the world is not going to wait, mean that 'managers have to manage' and that the university – this particular university – needs to move on briskly, as it positions and repositions itself in the academic marketplace?

The sentiments are understandable and, in a sense, rational. But, here, all we are doing is attempting to see whether, in principle, such an orientation – we might even term it a 'performative orientation' – fills out the possibilities for the conceptual landscape of university life. The matter can be raised directly in the form of a question: amid 'academic capitalism' (Slaughter and Leslie 1997) and in the context of 'the entrepreneurial university' (Clark 1998), does it make sense to invoke an idea of academic community? To put the matter in this way could imply just that which needs to be in question: was any idea of academic community ever realized? But we can side-step that heretical musing for what is at issue, to repeat, is the plausibility of the idea of academic community here-and-now. In fact, it is apparent that the balance sheet is nicely weighted. While some space may have diminished as universities become institutions in the marketplace and are also subject to insistent national evaluations, some space may also be opening as universities are challenged to work out their own mission and positioning in the new academic milieu.

'Perfect friendship' and 'professional mutuality' may yet, therefore, be concepts that have mileage in them. They would, in the first place, be ideals against which actual practices could be judged. They would form part of the critical discourse through which the university wished still to know and understand itself. But, more than that, they would be glimpsed, at least, in everyday encounters and exchanges, in the corridor and in the committee room, in the ways in which individuals recognized each other. They would be apparent in the ways in which teams and committees went about their tasks. This is not to say that any particular encounter or exchange would or even *could* be an instance of *perfect* friendship or *utter* mutuality. Indeed, the concepts may be fictive, but they would be hopeful fictions; encounters could take place *as if* they could be instances of perfect friendship or utter mutuality; and the 'as-ifness' could go far, perhaps, in encouraging forward the ethos of mutuality that the concepts themselves yearn for.

Instead of 'perfect friendship', perhaps the idea of '*professional friendship*' might take root. In the idea of professional friendship lies mutual recognition within a professional and even an organizational milieu. Multi-faculty universities are largescale enterprises, against any standard, and their success in uncertain times calls for the university to take on characteristics of organizations. Being 'professional' in such a setting in turn calls for adroitness and subtlety in the handling of multiple agendas. And, in turn, and further still, friendship has to be nuanced, played out as it must be amid roles, agendas, and multiple identities as universities call for ever wider sets of relationships among their staffs if their continuing repositioning is to be 'successful'. Professional friendship, therefore, is precisely that friendship in which actors acknowledge each other's value as persons and contribution to the good of the community that is the university, even as they play their part in the university's continuing self-reconstruction.

Reclaiming spaces in the university

Jon Nixon surely offers us a plausible gambit in urging that we need to specify the structural conditions of genuinely reciprocal relationships on campus. What, in general terms, are the structures that are likely to prompt such forms of human agency? What kinds of infrastructure are likely to bring on dispositions of mutual recognition? A temptation might be to launch off into an effort to bring about a form of a Habermassian 'ideal speech situation' on campus, in which all parties to a conversation abide by reciprocal norms of interactional reason (such as sincerity, appropriateness and truthfulness). But such an approach is surely too formalistic; it by no means captures the character of situations in which those who stand in positions of unequal power (whether as teachers, researchers or managers) reach out to the other as human beings.

A different tack suggests itself, therefore. Rather than looking to structures that are going to prompt a disposition towards mutual recognition, perhaps we should look instead to agency as such. What, after all, is preventing such an orientation? One answer could be precisely structure itself! The contemporary university, after all, is beset with evaluation processes – internally driven just as much as externally so – with a declared mission (that doubtless includes entrepreneurial activity), with a pace of work and with a sense of its own positioning that forecloses on reciprocal relationships; on relationships of recognition and affirmation. Or, at least, it may appear that these structures – 'structure' understood generally – impose themselves in this way. The space for the academic community to be an academic community is shrinking; or it may be seen as if it is. What is at issue, therefore, is not so much lack of structure but the presence of far too much structure.

This view, that the space available for reciprocity on campus has shrunk so far that the idea of an academic community must be felt to be jejune and a relic of the past, has prima facie plausibility. But that is all that it is. In fact, the university probably has more space now than it has ever had. At least, in an entrepreneurial age, in an age in which it is enjoined to secure clients for its knowledge services, this counter view also must be said to have plausibility. This, certainly, seems to be the view of Colin Bundy, that there is space yet for an enlightened institutional leadership to seize and be creative in the new spaces that have become available to the university.

The response that there is no such space has to be contested; it may turn out to be an apologia precisely of those in positions of power, of apparent control or simply of relatively low risk and limited professional identities. To admit to space being available would raise awkward questions as to personal responsibility not only in engaging in that space but, by implication, in engaging genuinely and authentically with others. One's own agenda may be called into question; ideologies – both external and internal to the university – may be shown to be just that.

I return to my earlier question: what is preventing reciprocity from breaking out on campus? Structures may be aiding the current situation; they may be acting so as to discourage reciprocity; and they may be serving to encourage inauthenticity, in both teaching and research (as many of the chapters in this book remind us). More structure, therefore, may not be the answer. There are at least three considerations here. First, as implied, structure as such may tend to obtrude into the human relationships of a community. Second, a concern with structure may divert attention away from more fundamental matters of ethos, of the ethical positioning of a university and of the forms of human being that are encouraged. Third, structures may be logically out-of-tune with human being as such: structures foster means-end orientations whereas what is perhaps vanishing from campuses is precisely an acknowledgement of the other in its own right.

The question surely emerges, therefore: as well as 'the entrepreneurial university' or 'the university in the knowledge economy', might we admit the term 'the ethical university' into the lexicon of the academy's self-understanding? An ethical university, I take it, would move on two levels. It would be an institution in which interactions, whether formal or informal, whether in an explicit context of management or of academic practice, were characterized by a sense of otherness. Terms such as 'respect', 'recognition' and 'affirmation' would help to provide a vocabulary that did justice to the character of relationships on campus. Differences – in gender, power, interest, epistemological location, societal agendas, and even value orientations – would still be present; but differences would be acknowledged and respected.

Such an ethical university would be one that worked at the concept of space, both practically and theoretically. It would not only work on the character of its internal relations (of the kind to which Colin Bundy underscores) but also be sensitive to the kinds of possibility to which Jean Barr and Morwenna Griffiths alert us in which the university can imaginatively construct new public spaces in its interrelationships with communities around it. Space does not exist *in abstracto* but is realized through its being created *as space*. What, too, those chapters indicate, in their different ways, is that the university has spaces to create yet more space and in doing so, can create spaces for new forms of understanding both within and beyond the university. New 'bodies politic' can emerge, which play upon the fuzziness of the boundary between inner (within the university) and outer (inter-relationships between the university and the wider world) and which, indeed, enhance that fuzziness.

The university remains a privileged institution. Even as it fears that the space available to it is shrinking, that space may be growing. That is to say, the opportunities to create space are growing and widening. As those two chapters, together with those of Melanie Walker indicate, space can be developed in teaching, research and in the way the university engages within itself as a community. The new computer-based technologies can assist, offering again facilities for imaginatively engaging, for forming communities across boundaries through e-mail and web-based discussions (university/public; disciplines; academics/managers; students/staff), yet they merely complement an expansion of other media (interactive radio and television; open conferences; discussions in newspapers; seminars between professionals and academics; quality magazines; and so on and so forth).

Such a set of reflections invites further reflections. First, this kind of ethical university not only carries forward the metaphor of 'body politic' but also resonates with the metaphor of 'the body of the discipline'. Disciplines are here given new energies as they are embodied in conversations and engagements that straddle discursive and communicative boundaries.

Second, this ethical university actually is intent on the fashioning of communities both within and beyond itself, communities that themselves are far from unities and that call forth a recognition of difference. It is a university that is helping to take forward into the twenty-first century our ideas of democracy. Third, in forming new kinds of community, both across and beyond the academy, this university is sponsoring new forms of knowledge. Indeed, it would be better to say that this university is sponsoring new forms of knowing, for this knowing – multimedia, bound up with social and personal projects, interactive, situated in differing milieu – takes form through the knowing activities of new communities. This is a university that takes both its knowledge functions and its civic responsibility to society seriously. Talk of Mode 1 and Mode 2 knowledges (Gibbons et al. 1994; Nowotny et al. 2002) becomes hopelessly inadequate to capture this epistemic variety and creativity.

Conclusion: towards the authentic university

It just may be possible, after all, to reclaim the university in a runaway world. Reclamation, as we have seen, can be possible in three dimensions, of the university's self-story, of its practices and of space – or rather spaces – in which the university can be itself. What is emerging here, perhaps, is a glimpse of an 'authentic university'. Authenticity becomes possible precisely where authenticity is threatened. The authenticity is won in a milieu of inauthenticity, and only so. But, as we have surely witnessed in the preceding chapters, that authenticity has to be fashioned, chiselled out and crafted. It is not there, waiting to be taken. The gaining of the authenticity, too, as implied, is a set of creative acts, in which new pedagogies, new academic practices, and new research approaches are painstakingly and even painfully developed.

There are two apparent paradoxes here: the authentic university is to be 'reclaimed' only through relentless effort, creativity, and innovation; *and* such a programme could be said to be the discourse of the new neo-liberalism of entrepreneurialism and even managerialism, in relation to which the contributors in this volume have – by and large – sought to distance themselves. Both paradoxes are more apparent than real.

First, the apparent paradox of 'reclamation' coexisting with innovation, of going back and going forward, all at once dissolves when it is understood that that is how things are. We draw on a traditional value background of the university as independent, as a forum for truth-oriented inquiries, and as a community-in-itself and for-itself, but we do so, understanding that such a value background can only live in a runaway world by being radically and continually reinterpreted. The value background becomes a resource for hope and energy for the transfiguration of the university in an ever-challenging world. The university gains its independence not merely financially – through a marketized academic capitalism – but discursively, as it seeks both to build bridges with wider communities and to play its part in widening knowledge, understanding and human life itself. In the process, new discursive communities and new knowledges may be formed. We go forward by going backwards and we go backwards for resources for the future.

The second paradox also dissolves. Innovation, enterprise, entrepreneurialism, participation in the knowledge economies: all of these self-understandings of the contemporary university are simply present, more or less. And they threaten the prospect of 'the authentic university' taking off for they are emblems of our age, denying first-hand self-understandings by the university of and for itself. The space for authenticity, therefore, appears to be diminishing to the point of its vanishing altogether. But authenticity is won, if at all, through its being wrought, with care, amidst countervailing forces. Authenticity gains its spurs, its own authenticity, in the midst of inauthenticity. Without the potent challenge of inauthenticity bearing in on the university, its being authentic would be a pyrrhic victory.

The contributions to this volume have indicated that space is still available for the university to win back its own authenticity, in the curriculum, in research, in its own internal arrangements, and in the fashioning of communities, both within itself and with the wider society. None of this can be achieved, either quickly or finally. The authentic university in the twenty-first century is one in which efforts go on daily to rediscover sources of authenticity – of dialogue, of truthfulness, of professionalism, of wise judgement, of communication, of mutual learning – even as large ideologies of the modern university take hold. There are certainly challenges to those in leadership positions who care for such a sense of the authentic university but, just as significantly, there are challenges, too, on every member of staff. The authentic university can only be brought off through individuals within it acting authentically and being authentic. The authentic university, in other words, places significant responsibilities on each individual within it.

References

Clark, B.R. (1998) *Creating Entrepreneurial Universities.* Oxford: Pergamon.
Delanty, G. (2001) *Challenging Knowledge: The University in the Knowledge Society.* Buckingham: Open University Press.
Gibbons, M. et al. (1994) *The New Production of Knowledge.* London: Sage.
Giddens, T. (2002) *Runaway World: How Globalisation is Reshaping Our Lives.* London: Profile.
Graham, G. (2002) *Universities: The Recovery of an Idea.* Thorverton: Imprint Academic.
Halpin, D. (2003) *Hope and Education: The Role of the Utopian Imagination.* London: Routledge Falmer.
MacIntyre, A. (1982) *After Virtue: A Study in Moral Theory.* London: Duckworth.
NCIHE (1997) *Higher Education in the Learning Society.* (Report of the National

Committee of Inquiry into Higher Education – the *Dearing Report*.) London: HMSO.
Nowotny, H., Scott, P. and Gibbons, M. (2002) *Rethinking Science*. Cambridge: Polity.
Readings, B. (1997) *The University in Ruins*, 2nd imprint. Cambridge, MA: Harvard University Press.
Slaughter, S. and Leslie, L. (1997) *Academic Capitalism: Politics, Policies and the Entrepreneurial University*. Baltimore: Johns Hopkins University Press.

Index

Abel, D. 64
Academic Board(s), Australia 100–13
academic capital 39–40
    vs research (scientific) capital 39, 45, 46
academic field 39–40
academic standards *vs* political ideology *see* neo-conservatism
academic *vs* managerial values 169, 172–3
accountability 102–3
action research 180–3, 185
activist academic professionalism 111–12
administrative *vs* research work 45–8
agents/agency 37, 40, 123
American Association of University Professors (AAUP) 63–4
American Council of Trustees and Alumni (ACTA) 60–4
Amis, K. 161
Apple, M. 5, 52, 179
Arendt, H. 88, 89–90, 116, 120, 131–2, 140–1, 142, 143, 145, 180, 189
Aristotle 123, 124–5
    'new Aristotelianism' 115–17, 118, 119–20, 126
Aronowitz, S. and Giroux, H. 6
audit 102–3, 104
Australia
    Divisional Pro Vice Chancellor (PVC) 16, 17, 18, 20, 26–7, 28, 30–1

federalism 15, 24–5
funding 15, 24–5, 27–8, 30
Head of Schools (HoS) 16, 17–18, 20, 26–7, 28, 29, 30
managerialism 15–33
middle-level (line) managers 27, 28, 29–30
quality improvement project 100–13
RAE 36
restructuring 24–7
University of Sydney 102, 104–5, 106–9
Vice Chancellors (VCs) 16–17, 25–6, 30–1
Australian Universities Quality Agency (AUQA) 100, 103, 104–5
authenticity 122–3, 202, 206–7
autonomy and restructuring 25–6

Ball, S. 2, 25
Barnett, R. 173, 178, 179, 180, 189–90
Barr, J. 186–8
Battersby, C. 94
Beck, M. 179
Beck, U. and Beck-Gernsheim, E. 3, 4, 114
beginning, pedagogies of 131–45
Bennett, W.J. 57, 59–60
Berger, J. 117, 119
Bernstein, B. 131, 185
Bertelsen, E. 171

210 Index

'bivalent theorizing' 114–15, 123–4
Blair, T. 76–7
Bloom, A. 57
body, notions of 93–4
body politic 93–5
Bok, D. 52–3
Boston Globe 63, 64
Bourdieu, P. 16, 19, 20–1, 22–3, 27, 31–2, 36–40, 45, 48, 49, 179, 188, 190
Bradbury, M. 165
Brown University, US 58
Buckley, W.F. 53–4
budgets *see* funding
Bush, T. 43

Calhoun, C. et al. 37
Canada 94–5
capabilities, fostering 133–7, 143, 145
capital
  academic 39–40
  cultural 38
  culture and curriculum 53–4
  economic 38
  forms of 38–9
  research (scientific) 39, 45, 46, 47–8
  symbolic 36–7, 38, 39–40, 43, 46
Caplan, P. 103
'care for the world' 116
Carr, W. and Hartnett, A. 5
Carter, I. 160, 161, 166
Cheney, L.V. 60–1, 63
Choosing the Right College, US 59–60
citizenship
  and dissidence 116
  participation 112
  'Socratic citizenship' 189
'civic mindedness' 89
Clark, B. 169
Cloete, N. and Kulati, T. 172
Cockburn, C. 88, 95
codifiable knowledge 77
Cojean, A. 90
collaborative discussion 134–5
collaborative learning 182, 183
collegiality 109–10, 111

'restricted collegiality' 43
The Common Sense Guide to American Colleges 57–9, 60
communications and computing technologies (CCTs) 147–8, 154–7
  Internet 74, 94–5
  University of Illinois 148–54
  virtual learning environments (VLEs) 157–8
competitive workaholism 91
conditions of learning 123–5
conflict 88, 89, 138–9
  see also dissidence/resistance
conservatism *see* neo-conservatism; neo-liberalism
contesting educational purposes 4–6
Covington, S. 54, 55, 56
Crace, J. 178–9
crisis
  concept of 67–8
  of the idea of university 69–73
cultural capital 38
culture
  capital and curriculum 53–4
  'knowledge cultures' 79
  notions of 70, 80
  vs 'excellence' 71
curriculum, neo-conservatist influences, US 51–65
Cutts, Q. 144, 182–3, 184

Damrosch, D. 173
de Boer, H. et al. 174
Dearing Report, UK 73, 197
Dearlove, J. 164, 170
Deem, J. 164, 169
Defending Civilization, US 62–3, 64
deliberation 119, 120, 121, 122–3
deliberative democracy 111–12
deliberative dialogue, enabling 137–40
democratic knowledge-making 187, 188
democratic participation 6
depth dimension 122–3
detraditionalization 3
Dickens, C. 1–2
differentiation

'differentiated solidarity' 89
principles: 'relegating' academic staff 44–8
RAE 43–4
'dis-illusionment' 115
dissidence/resistance 57–8, 60–1, 116, 143
see also conflict
distance *vs* face-to-face models 155, 156
Divisional Pro Vice Chancellor (PVC), Australia 16, 17, 18, 20, 26–7, 28, 30–1
Dunne, J. 125

economic capital 38
economy of time 45, 46
Eder, K. 188
Edwards, K. 172
Edwards, M. 105
'effective' teaching 183
Egen, R. 54, 56, 57, 59
emotion and reason 122
enabling deliberative dialogue 137–40
Enslin, P. et al. 164
ethics
'ethical university' 205–6
suppression of 19–20, 32–3
see also morality; virtue(s)
Evans and Nation, D.E. 147
'excellence' 70–1, 72
vs culture 71
exclusion of minorities 86–7

face-to-face *vs* distance models 155, 156
federalism, Australia 15, 24–5
feminist perspectives 87, 88, 92–6, 186–8
fields/forces 22–3, 27, 28, 36–8
academic 39–40
and forms of capital 38–9
and habitus 20–4, 38
Finn, C. 57
Flowers, R. 64
fostering capabilities 133–7, 143, 145
Foucault, M. 20, 79–80
Foundation for Individual Rights in Education (FIRE) 63, 64

Fraser, N. 87, 120, 140
free speech 63–4
friendship
notions of 124–5
'perfect friendship' 123–5, 199–200, 202, 203
Fulton, O. 169
funding
Australia 15, 24–5, 27–8, 30
by conservative organizations, US 53–4, 55–6, 57, 58, 59, 60, 61
cuts 25, 166
and distance learning 156
OECD countries 68–9
research 36

'games' 20–1, 23–4, 28, 37, 38
and 'illusio' 37, 40
RAE 41–4, 48–9
Geertz, C. 132, 188
Georgetown University, US 62
German Studies 133–5
Germany 156
Gibbons, M. 168
Giddens, A. 125, 196
Global Alliance Limited (GAL) 74–5
globalization 3, 4, 69–70, 71, 73, 163–4
see also knowledge economy
Gonzalez, M. 135–6, 139–40, 142–3, 183, 185, 186
governmentality(ies)/governance 20, 23, 24
restructuring, Australia 24–7
see also managerialism
Graham, G. 165, 170
Gramsci, A. 52, 65
grand narratives 72–3
grants *see* funding
Gray, R. 94–5
Greene, M. 92
Grenfell, M. and James, D. 37
Grimshaw, J. 92, 93

Habermas, J. 86–7, 90
habitus 21, 22, 27, 28, 36–7
academic 39

crisis 31–3
and field 20–4, 38
primary 21, 27, 28
secondary 22, 27, 28
Halsey, A.H. 35, 163, 169
Haraway, D. 93–4
Harley, S. and Lowe, P. 35, 43, 48
Harvey, L. 185
Head of Schools (HoS), Australia 16, 17–18, 20, 26–7, 28, 29, 30
Hispanic Studies 135–6
history of university management, UK 165–8
Hofstadter, R. 6
Honneth, A. 120, 121
hooks, b. 140
Horner, C. 57
Humboldtian idea of culture 70
Hutter H. 123, 125

idea of university
crisis of 69–73
reclaiming 196–9
sense of loss 195–6
'illusio' 37, 40
individualization 3
courses of study 58–9
inequalities 86–7
Institute for Educational Affairs (IEA), US 56
intentionality 118, 119
Intercollegiate Studies Institute (ISI), US 54–6, 59, 60, 61
international links, research 46, 47
Internet 74, 94–5
see also communications and computing technologies (CCTs)

Jarrat Report, UK 166
Judeo-Christian moral standards 54

Kantian idea of reason 70, 197
Keller, G. 166
Kennedy, D. 169
Kenway, J. 4
knowledge

codifiable 77
conveyed as poetry 95–6
dissemination across boundaries 94–5
producing 'liberated knowledge' 186–8
public 85
reflective self-knowledge 141
tacit 77
'knowledge cultures' 79
knowledge economy 73–8

Lakoff, G. and Johnson, M. 92–3
language 131
see also metaphor
leadership, displacement by managerialism 26–7
learning identities 140–2
liberal arts 58–9, 60
liberalism 90
see also neo-liberalism
line-management see middle-level (line) managers
loss, sense of 195–6
Lyotard, J.F. 25, 67, 72, 73

MacIntyre, A. 86, 117–18
'McUniversity' 4
Madison Center, US 56–7
Madison Center for Educational Affairs (MCEA), US 57–60
managerialism 68, 202–3
Australia 15–33
displacement of leadership 26–7
negative effects 35–6
RAE 43
UK 160–75
US 166
see also governmentality(ies)/governance
Marginson, S. and Considine, M. 15, 27
market discourse 52–3
Martin, J.L. and Neale, A.D. 61, 62–3, 64
Massey, D. 91
massification 25, 71
Maxwell, N. 96
meta-narrative, university as 198–9

metaphor 92–8
  see also language
middle-level (line) managers, Australia 27, 28, 29–30
mission statements 71
morality
  Judeo-Christian standards 54
  moral purposefulness 117–20
  moral relativism 63
  'thick' and 'thin' 5, 179
  see also ethics; virtue(s)
Muller, J. 188
multiculturalism 55

National Alumni Forum (NAF), US 60–4
'negative wisdom' 114, 115, 116, 119
neo-conservatism 51–65
neo-liberalism 4, 52–3, 68, 72–3
'new Aristotelianism' 115–17, 118, 119–20, 126
new 'governmentalities' 20, 23
new growth theory 76
new managerialism *see* managerialism
new media *see* communications and computing technologies (CCTs)
'newness', preserving 142–3
Nixon, J. 131
  et al. 102, 178
Noble, D. 153–4
Nussaum, M. 1–2, 5, 6, 88, 115–16, 122, 133, 140, 179

Oakley, A. 162
Olin Foundation, US 54, 55, 56, 57, 58, 59, 60
O'Neill, O. 1, 4, 189
Organisation for Economic Co-operation and Development (OECD) 68–9, 168–9
overseas students 156

Pahl, R. 124
Parker, M. and Jary, D. 4, 35, 43
Parkin, F. 161
participation 6, 112, 121
patriotism 57, 63

pedagogical relationship 201–2
pedagogies
  of beginning 131–45
  of recognition 120–2, 200–1
'perfect friendship' 123–5, 199–200, 202, 203
performativity 2, 25
Peters, O. 77, 154–5, 156–7, 197
Phipps, A. 133–5, 137, 141, 181–2, 184
plurality
  and conflict 88
  and natality 142
  and participation 121
  and solidarity 89
poetry 95–6
political correctness, resistance to 57–8, 60–1
political ideology *vs* academic standards *see* neo-conservatism
post-historical university 71, 73–5
postmodernism 25, 65, 72
Power, M. 102
power relations 26, 39, 185
practices of university, reclaiming 199–203
preserving 'newness' 142–3
private and public spaces 90–1, 119–20
privatization 68
'proceduralism' 26
producing 'liberated knowledge' 186–8
professional learning 144–5
professional mutuality 200–1, 202, 203
professionalism, activist academic 111–12
public discussion 88–90
public knowledge 85
public space(s) 85, 189
  and private spaces 90–1, 119–20
  and their uses 86–7, 89
  ways of understanding 90–6
Pyott, P. 57–9

quality assessment *see* Research Assessment Exercise (RAE)
quality improvement project, Australia 100–13

racial admissions set-asides, US 58
Ramsden, P. 172
Rath, J. 95–6
Ravitch, D. 51–2
Rawls, J. 54, 90, 120
Readings, B. 69–70, 71–2, 78, 197
reason
  and emotion 122
  Kantian idea of 70, 197
  notion of 87
reciprocity 119, 203–5
recognition, pedagogies of 120–2, 200–1
Reed, M. 166, 169
reflexive sociology methodology 19–20, 32–3
research
  funding 36
  regulation and relegation 35–49
  and scholarship 178–90
  (scientific) capital 39, 45, 46, 47–8
Research Assessment Exercise (RAE) 36, 41–4, 48–9
resistance/dissidence 57–8, 60–1, 116, 143
'restricted collegiality' 43
restructuring, Australia 24–7
Rhodes, F. 171–2
Richardson, T. 138, 143
risk assessment 102–3, 104–5
Rowland, S. 102
'runaway world', perspectives 3, 198

Said, E. 132, 190
St. John's College of Annapolis and Santa Fe, US 58, 60
Saito, M. 143
Schmidt, P. 54
scholarship of teaching 180–6
Schrag, C. 51, 65
scientific (research) capital 39, 45, 46, 47–8
Scott, P. 165–6, 167, 169
self review 104–5
self-directed learning 136
The Shakespeare File, US 51, 61–2, 64
Shattock, M. 168–9

Shore, C. and Wright, S. 102
Skeggs, B. 132
Slaughter, S. and Leslie, L. 15, 44, 48, 202
Smith, A. and Webster, F. 170
social class 132
social justice 6
social world (structure) *see* fields/forces
sociological approach 19–20, 32–3, 36–40
Socrates 114, 115–17, 119
'Socratic citizenship' 189
Stefanic, J. and Delgado, R. 52, 55
Stenhouse, L. 180–1
Stimpson, S. 64, 65
student participation in action research 181–2
Stukel, J.J. 149–50
symbolic capital 36–7, 38, 39–40, 43, 46

tacit knowledge 77
Taylor, C. 120
Taylor, R. et al. 171
teaching
  scholarship of 180–6
  vs research work 45–8
techno-bureaucratic idea of excellence 70–1
techno-cultures 80
technology *see* communications and computing technologies (CCTs)
Telling the Truth, US 60–1
therapeutic university 199
'thick' and 'thin' morality 5, 179
Thurow, L. 75
Touraine, A. 67, 121
town planning 138
'training the imagination to go visiting' 140–2
Trow, M. 162–3, 164, 173–4

undergraduate curriculum, neo-conservatist influences, US 51–65
United Kingdom (UK)
  CCT 155, 156
  Dearing Report 73, 197

DTI Report: *Our Competitive Future* 76–7
funding 69, 166
impact of globalization 163–4
Jarrat Report 166
managerialism 160–75
RAE 36, 44, 48
University of Glasgow 180–6
Vice Chancellors (VCs) 160, 161
United States (US)
　Brown University 58
　Choosing the Right College 59–60
　The Common Sense Guide to American Colleges 57–9, 60
　Defending Civilization 62–3, 64
　funding 53–4, 55–6, 57, 58, 59, 60, 61
　Georgetown University 62
　Institute for Educational Affairs (IEA) 56
　Intercollegiate Studies Institute (ISI) 54–6, 59, 60, 61
　Madison Center 56–60
　managerialism 166
　National Alumni Forum (NAF) 60–4
　neo-conservatism 51–65
　racial admissions set-asides 58
　St. John's College of Annapolis and Santa Fe 58, 60
　The Shakespeare File 51, 61–2, 64
　Telling the Truth 60–1
　The University in Ruins 69–70
　University of Chicago 57–8
　University of Illinois 148–54
　Vassar College 58–9
　Yale University 55–6
The University in Ruins, US 69–70
'unity of human life' 117–19
University of Chicago, US 57–8
university departments 91

University of Glasgow, UK 180–6
University of Illinois, US 148–54
University of Sydney, Australia 102, 104–5, 106–9

value conflicts 138–9
Vassar College, US 58–9
Vice Chancellors Committee, Australia 31
Vice Chancellors (VCs)
　Australia 16–17, 25–6, 30–1
　UK 160, 161
Villa, D. 114, 115, 189
virtual learning environments (VLEs) 157–8
virtue(s) 115, 117–19, 123
　friends of 124
　'virtuous ideals' 189–90
　see also ethics; morality
vocationalism 68
voice 137, 142–3

Walker, M. 114, 123, 134, 135, 136, 138, 143, 144, 157–8, 180, 181–2, 183, 185
Warhurst, C. 184, 185
Wesker, A. 131
Western Civilization, study of 55–6, 57
Wilkinson, I. 102
Wilkinson, J. 144, 184
Williams, R. 6
Wilson, J.K. 56, 62
Wolfe, G. 60
workload policy, Australia 15–33
World Bank 76
Worton, M. 173

Yale University, US 55–6
Yardley, J. 51, 61–2
Young, I. 5, 87, 89, 121–2, 137
Yuval-Davis, N. 141